Anonymus

Accounts and works of railways in Ireland

First report from 1868

Anonymus

Accounts and works of railways in Ireland
First report from 1868

ISBN/EAN: 9783742822468

Manufactured in Europe, USA, Canada, Australia, Japa

Cover: Foto ©knipser5 / pixelio.de

Manufactured and distributed by brebook publishing software
(www.brebook.com)

Anonymus

Accounts and works of railways in Ireland

RAILWAYS (IRELAND) COMMISSION.

REPORT

OF

THE COMMISSIONERS APPOINTED TO INSPECT THE ACCOUNTS AND EXAMINE THE WORKS

OF

RAILWAYS IN IRELAND,

MADE TO

THE LORDS COMMISSIONERS OF HER MAJESTY'S TREASURY.

Presented to both Houses of Parliament by Command of Her Majesty.

LONDON:
PRINTED BY GEORGE EDWARD EYRE AND WILLIAM SPOTTISWOODE,
PRINTERS TO THE QUEEN'S MOST EXCELLENT MAJESTY.
FOR HER MAJESTY'S STATIONERY OFFICE.

1868.

CONTENTS.

TREASURY MINUTE dated the 15th of October 1867, appointing the Commission.

REPORT.

	Page
Course of Proceedings - - - - -	5
RAILWAYS.	
Railways, Class I., authorised but not commenced (Table A.) - - - - -	8
Railways, Class II., commenced but not completed (Table B.) - - - - -	9
Railways, Class III., completed and carrying traffic (Table C.) - - - -	10
Railways completed and carrying traffic, revenue computed on the three years' average (Table D.) - -	11
Railways completed and carrying traffic, revenue not computed on the three years' average (Table E.) - -	12
Railways commenced but not completed. The works of which are so far advanced that it is assumed they will be finished (Table F.) -	13
Summary of all the Railways in Ireland, with their mileage, authorised capital, financial position, and corrected annual revenue (Table G.) -	13
Railways completed or expected to be completed, with an estimate of net divisible profits (Table H.) - - - -	14
Rolling Stock. Table in Appendix noticed -	14
Directors and Staff employed by Railway Companies carrying traffic. Table in Appendix noticed - - - - -	14
Other Tables in Appendix noticed - -	14
Traffic arrangements - - - -	14
Loans to Irish Railway Companies from Public Commissioners - - - - -	14
Railway deposits in the Court of Chancery in Ireland - - - - -	15
Act of Parliament of 1844 - - -	15
Position of Railways with respect to purchase under the Act 1844 (Table I.) - -	15
CANALS AND RIVER NAVIGATIONS -	15
Length of Canals (Table K.) - - -	16
Canals and River Navigations belonging to Companies, Financial position and corrected annual Revenue (Table L.) - - -	17
Assistance to Canals in Ireland - - -	17
Prospects of Railways in Ireland - -	18
Progress of traffic earnings from 1864–65 to 1866–67 (Table M.) - - -	18

APPENDIX.

PART I.—*Tables compiled by the Commission.*

	Page
Table (AA.) length and capital of Railways, Class I., authorised but not commenced -	21
Table (BB.) capital and financial position, with total estimated cost of completing the works of Railways, Class II., commenced but not completed - - -	22
Table (CC.) length and capital expenditure, as per Company's accounts in each year of the three years' period embraced in the Treasury Minute, of Railways, Class III., completed and carrying traffic - -	23
Table (DD.) financial position at the date of the last published accounts prior to the 15th of October 1867, of Railways, Class III., completed and carrying traffic -	24
Table (EE.) Railways, Class III., completed and carrying traffic. Progress of traffic during three years, excluding rents and miscellaneous receipts - - - -	27
Table (FF.) showing position of Railways in Ireland with respect to their liability to be purchased under the Act of 1844 (7 & 8 Vict. c. 85.) - - -	28
Table (GG.) Number of the Directors and of the different classes of officers employed on the several Railways completed and carrying traffic - - - -	30
Table (HH.) Number of locomotive engines and tenders, and of carriages and wagon stock belonging to the several Railway Companies in Ireland - - - -	32

PART II.—*Documents and Returns.*

	Page
1. Copy of Treasury Minute dated the 14th of October 1867, addressed to Railway Companies in Ireland under Stat. 30 & 31 Vict. c. 104 - - - - -	33
2. Copy of letter from the Secretary of the Treasury to the Secretary of the Commissioners extending the inquiries of the Commission to Canal Companies - - -	33
3. Copy of Letter from the Secretary of the Treasury to the Commissioners, dated the 4th of April 1868, directing particulars to be furnished in the Report with respect to agreement for limiting the charges for traffic -	33
4. Return of the particulars of all agreements that Irish Railway Companies have entered into among themselves or with Canal Companies, with respect to limiting the charges for traffic, the accommodation to the public, or the assistance to be given to Railway Extensions or new Railways, in cases where there was a competition between routes of communication for the traffic of any district or place - - -	33
5. Return of Advances made by the Public Works Loan Commissioners to Railway Companies in Ireland, showing as to each the name of the Railway, total advances, date of security, period for which the loan was made, rate of interest, principal repaid, principal unpaid, interest in arrear, and costs paid to the solicitor of the Commissioners up to the 31st of January 1868 - -	36
6. Return of all advances made by the Commissioners of Public Works to Railways in Ireland, specifying the name of the Company, the amount advanced and the year in which advanced, the period for which such loan was made, the rate of interest charged, the amount of principal now paid off, the amount remaining due, the amount of interest now due, and the cost paid in each case to the solicitor of the Board of Works by the Company applying for such loans, with totals in the case of each Railway, and also gross totals - -	40
7. Return showing the amount of Railway deposits standing in the name of the Accountant-General of the Court of Chancery, Ireland, on the 1st of October 1867 - - - - - -	40

Part III.—*Description of Railways.*

Showing the length of the undertakings and their branches, the Acts of Parliament under which it was constructed, the capital authorised and raised, the dates of opening for traffic of the several railways, the net revenue for the three years comprised in the Treasury Minute, the dividends on ordinary and preference shares, the interest on the different classes of borrowed money, the floating assets and liabilities, and the area and population of the district of country which may be considered as accommodated by each Railway.

Railways, Class I.—*Lines authorised but not commenced.*

No. in Appendix and on Map		Page
1.	Bray and Enniskerry	43
2.	Central Ireland	43
3.	Clonmel, Lismore, and Dungarvan	44
4.	Dublin Metropolitan	45
5.	Dublin, Rathmines, Rathgar, Roundtown, Rathfarnham, and Rathcoole	46
6.	Dundalk and Greenore (Co. Louth)	47
7.	Limerick and North Kerry	48
8.	Navan and Kingscourt	49
9.	Sligo and Ballaghaderreen	50
10.	Waterford, Lismore, and Fermoy	51
11.	Waterford and Passage	52
12.	Waterford and Wexford	53

Railways, Class II.—*Lines commenced but not completed.*

No.		Page
13.	Athenry and Ennis	55
14.	Banbridge Extension	56
15.	Belfast Central	57
16.	Downpatrick, Dundrum, and Newcastle (County Down)	58
17.	Dublin and Antrim Junction	59
18.	Dublin Trunk Connecting	60
19.	Kilrush and Kilkee	61
20.	Letterkenny	62
21.	Midland Counties and Shannon Junction	63
22.	Newry and Greenore	64
23.	Parsonstown and Portumna Bridge	65
24.	Southern	66
25.	Waterford, New Ross, and Wexford	67

Railways, Class III.—*Lines completed and carrying Traffic.*

No.		Page
	Explanation of principle on which area and population of district accommodated by each completed railway is estimated	70
26.	Belfast and County Down	70
27.	Belfast, Holywood, and Bangor	73
28.	Belfast and Northern Counties	74
29.	*Carrickfergus and Larne*	77
30.	*Londonderry and Coleraine*	78
31.	Cork and Bandon	80
32.	*Cork and Kinsale*	83
33.	Cork, Blackrock, and Passage	83
34.	Cork and Macroom Direct	84
35.	Dublin and Belfast Junction	85
36.	*Banbridge Junction*	87
37.	Dublin and Drogheda	89
38.	Dublin and Meath	93
39.	Dublin, Wicklow, and Wexford	94
40.	*Dublin and Kingstown*	98
41.	Great Southern and Western	100
42.	*Cork and Limerick Direct*	105
43.	Irish North Western	108
44.	*Enniskillen, Bundoran, and Sligo*	111
45.	*Finn Valley*	112
46.	*Londonderry and Enniskillen*	114
47.	Londonderry and Lough Swilly	116
48.	Midland Great Western	118
49.	*Athenry and Tuam*	123
50.	*Great Northern and Western*	124
51.	Newry and Armagh	125
52.	Newry, Warrenpoint, and Rostrevor	128
53.	Ulster	130
54.	*Banbridge, Lisburn, and Belfast*	133
55.	*Portadown, Dungannon, and Omagh*	134
56.	Waterford and Kilkenny	136
57.	*Kilkenny Junction*	138
58.	Waterford and Limerick	140
59.	*Limerick and Castleconnell*	143
60.	*Limerick and Ennis*	145
61.	*Limerick and Foynes*	146
62.	*Rathkeale and Newcastle*	148
63.	Waterford and Tramore	150
64.	West Cork	151

Part IV.—*Canals and River Navigations.*

I.—*In the Possession of Companies or leased to Companies by Private Owners.*

No.		Page
65.	Barrow Navigation	154
66.	Upper Boyne Navigation	155
67.	Grand Canal	156
68.	Lagan Navigation	159
69.	Newry Navigation	161
70.	River Suir Navigation	162
71.	Royal Canal (Midland Great Western Railway Company)	163
72.	Foyle Navigation (Strabane to River Foyle)	165

II.—*Under Local Trustees.*

No.		Page
73.	Ballinamore and Ballyconnell Navigation	166
74.	Lower Bann Navigation	167
75.	Upper Bann Navigation	169
76.	Lough Corrib Navigation	170

III.—*Under Public Works Commissioners.*

No.		Page
77.	Lower Boyne Navigation	172
78.	Maigue Navigation	173
79.	Shannon Navigation	174
80.	Tyrone Navigation	176
81.	Ulster Canal	177

Map to accompany Report - - - - *to follow page* 178

Treasury Minute appointing Commission.

Dated October 16, 1867.

My Lords have under consideration the several Reports of the Royal Commission on Railways (19th December 1865), so far as they relate to railways in Ireland, and my Lords read the Act 30 and 31 Vict. c. 104.

It is stated in the Act that the Commissioners of Her Majesty's Treasury may call for an account of all monies received and paid by any railway company in Ireland during a period of three years previous to the date of the last half-yearly account; and also an account of the assets and liabilities at such time or times during such period as the said Commissioners shall specify; and further, that it shall be lawful for them to appoint any proper person or persons for all or any of the purposes following, that is to say:—

To inspect the accounts and books of any railway company in Ireland during such period of three years;

To examine the railway stations, works, &c., of any railway company in Ireland, with power to call for documents, and examine on oath.

My Lords do not deem it necessary at present to enter upon the large and important questions raised in the Reports under consideration, namely, whether it is expedient that measures should be taken for the purchase by Government of the Irish lines of railway, with a view to either leasing them or working them.

Previous to the consideration of so important a question, such an inquiry as that which is provided for in the Act of last Session as regards the present financial position of each company, of the state of the rolling stock, and the condition of the permanent way is obviously essential.

My Lords have already, by their Minute of October 14, directed every railway company in Ireland to furnish to this Board such accounts as are mentioned in the Act, and they are of opinion that such an investigation as is above referred to can be most usefully conducted by a Commission, under the authority of the said Act, consisting of gentlemen having financial, mercantile, and railway experience, with the assistance of a Secretary.

It is to be understood that it will be the duty of the Commission to obtain full information as to the position, prospects, and value of such railways.

Their Lordships will cause the accounts of the several railway companies, as soon as rendered, to be supplied to the Commissioners, and it will be incumbent upon them to examine and verify such accounts, with a view to ascertain the income and expenditure of each railway company in each year, and its assets and liabilities at the end of each year.

For ascertaining the assets, an inspection should be made of the line, buildings, and works, to compute the time requisite to put them in such good order and repair as will enable them to earn the estimated income, with only the estimated annual outlay for repairs and restoration. The rolling stock should also be valued.

The income of each year should be analysed to ascertain how much arose from gross profits, and how much from capital, loans, or other sources.

The expenditure of each year should also be analysed to ascertain how much ought properly to be charged to capital, and how much, being for ordinary wear and tear, and repairs and restorations likely to recur from time to time, should be deducted from gross profits in estimating the net divisible profits contemplated as the basis of purchase under the Act of 1844.

In conclusion the Commissioners will understand that the inquiry is to include all the Irish railways, whether completed or not, and to be directed to all the facts which the Commissioners may consider that a prudent person or company would require to be made acquainted with as a preliminary step towards entertaining the question of purchase as a commercial speculation.

My Lords are pleased to appoint the following gentlemen to be the Commissioners:—

Sir Alex. Y. Spearman, Bart.
John Mulholland, Esq.
John Fowler, Esq., C.E.
Seymour Clarke, Esq.
and Christopher Johnston, Esq.;
and W. Neilson Hancock, Esq., LL.D., Secretary.

Transmit a copy of this Minute to each of the Commissioners and to their Secretary, and to the Irish Government, together with copy of the Minute of October 14 on the same subject. Let a copy of this Minute be also sent to each Railway Company in Ireland.

RAILWAYS (IRELAND) COMMISSION.

REPORT.

My Lords,

On receiving the instructions conveyed to us in the Treasury Minute dated the 15th of October 1867, we proceeded to take the measures which after careful consideration we deemed to be best for collecting the requisite information to enable us to report on the railways of Ireland, especially having reference to the last comprehensive paragraph of the Minute, viz.: *Supra, p. 1.*

"In conclusion the Commissioners will understand that the inquiry is to include all the Irish railways, whether completed or not, and to be directed to all the facts which the Commissioners may consider that a prudent person or company would require to be made acquainted with as a preliminary step towards entertaining the question of purchase as a commercial speculation."

Under a subsequent Treasury Letter, dated the 1st of November 1867, such of the canal companies as were willing to submit their affairs to the Commissioners were included in the inquiry. *Appendix, Part II., p. 62.*

A careful study of the Treasury Minute, combined with our general knowledge of British and Irish railways, and the varied manner in which their accounts were kept, soon led to the conclusion that it would not be possible to carry out our instructions in a manner useful to the Treasury or satisfactory to ourselves unless an independent inspection were made of the condition of the permanent way, works, stations, and rolling stock as well as of the accounts and financial position of every railway, so as "to obtain "full information as to their position, prospects, and value;" and also, so far as applicable, a similar inspection of every canal.

It was evidently impossible that we could have personally completed such an examination in any reasonable period, even if we had been prepared to devote our entire time to the work (and this from the constitution of the Commission would have been impracticable); it therefore became necessary to organize a thorough examination into the state of the railways, the canals, and the accounts, by a staff of experienced Engineers and Accountants individually known to ourselves.

Our first step was to prepare forms of returns to be sent to each Company, so as to obtain (in addition to the information required of them by the Treasury Minute of the 14th of October 1867) such particulars of their respective properties and accounts as were in our opinion an essential preliminary to our examination. *Appendix, Part II., p. 62.*

These returns were unavoidably elaborate, and their preparation involved considerable labour to the companies, (especially to those smaller companies whose accounts were not kept in a way to enable them easily to extract such details,) but in all cases, both in the filling up of the returns, and in our personal examination of works and accounts, we have uniformly received from Directors and Officers the most cheerful assistance.

When we state that considerable portions of the rails, sleepers, fastenings, and ballast of every mile of railway in Ireland, every station and repairing shop (with their tools), nearly every locomotive engine, and a large proportion of the carriage and wagon stock, were critically examined by the Engineers, and the accounts and books for the last three years by the Accountants, it will be readily understood, that in saying that we have been met in an excellent spirit by the companies, much more is implied than a mere formal compliment.

Although such an inspection of the lines of railway, examination of accounts, and analysis of expenditure and income as we have indicated, were contemplated in the Treasury Minute, and were obviously essential to the proper performance of the duties intrusted to us, we believe that neither the Treasury, ourselves, nor the companies were prepared for the amount of detailed labour which has been required for their complete realisation.

A considerable delay has taken place in the completion of the returns of some of the companies, and we may also say that our own work and the time occupied in preparing this report have been considerably increased, by the want of a correct and uniform system of accounts and of a recognized mode of dealing with capital and revenue expenditure, renewal funds, and suspense and stores accounts.

The many disadvantages of this variety of practice have been strikingly forced upon our attention during these investigations, as it was not only difficult to ascertain the profits actually earned by any individual company, but any comparison was impossible without a laborious analysis.

After sending out to each railway company a set of tabular forms, to be filled up from their own books, we proceeded to Dublin and Belfast, and invited the attendance of the Directors and chief Officers of the several railway and canal companies, in order to explain to them the particulars of the inquiry intrusted to us, to ask their co-operation, and to discuss with them the papers we had sent, so that we might avoid giving unnecessary trouble, in cases where their books rendered it more easy for them to furnish the information under a slight modification of our forms.

These interviews were very useful, and they enabled us to commence operations in the most satisfactory manner.

The work of detailed inspection divided itself, naturally, into three heads—

1st. Permanent way, structural works, stations, and the sidings of all railways completed and working; the condition of railways commenced and not completed; canals and works connected with them.

2nd. Rolling and working stock, including locomotive engines, carriages, wagons, steam boats, barges, machinery, and tools in the workshops.

3rd. Examination of accounts during the past three years, including such an analysis as to ascertain with accuracy, the receipts and expenditure, the financial position, and true net divisible profits.

1.—*Permanent Way.*

For the purposes of the inspection of the railways, Ireland was divided into five divisions, and two inspecting Engineers were appointed to each.

Forms were supplied to each Engineer to enable him to note down in an exact manner the condition of all the works of the railway, including the state of the rails, sleepers, materials in store, slopes, ballast, road approaches, bridges, tunnels, signals, drainage, gas and water supply, sheds, tools, and workshops.

The examination of the permanent way, (rails, sleepers, and fastenings, &c.) for a portion of each mile of line, and of the actual condition of all other works, necessarily involved great labour, but it did not appear to us that a less thorough examination would suffice.

The inspecting Engineers have obtained for us returns of the nature of the permanent way, the steepest gradients, and the quickest curves of each railway, with plans of stations and sidings.

The object of collecting this great mass of information was to enable us, after personal inspection and careful analysis, to arrive at a fair and just conclusion as to the condition of each railway, having reference to the nature and extent of its traffic, and all the circumstances affecting it, and to determine the value of the difference (if any) between its actual condition and a proper state of efficiency.

2.—*Rolling Stock.*

Full returns were obtained from the railway companies of the number and description of their engines and other rolling stock, the cost of repairs, renewals, and running charges, and the mileage run by locomotive engines, during the three years named in the Treasury Minute.

Inspecting Engineers of special experience were selected to make examination of the rolling stock, tools, and machinery. For this purpose the Railway System of Ireland was divided into three parts, and two or three inspecting Engineers appointed to each part.

In this branch of the inquiry two things were requisite. One to make a valuation of the rolling stock, the other to ascertain whether it had been kept up in a proper state of repair, so as to enable us to determine the value of the difference (if any) between the condition of the stock and such proper state of efficiency.

To accomplish these objects it was decided that a detailed examination of every locomotive engine should be made, and an equally detailed examination of about 50 per cent. of the total number of carriages and wagons; and, in the case of locomotive engines, the quality of the coal, coke, and water (influencing the duration of boilers, tubes, and fire-boxes,) were carefully noted for our consideration and any other special circumstances affecting the rolling stock.

3.—*Inspection and Examination of Accounts.*

A staff of Accountants was appointed to make a thorough investigation of the books and accounts of every company for the three years embraced in the Treasury Minute.

1st. For all railway and canal companies having their head offices in Dublin and the south of Ireland.

2nd. For all companies having their head offices in the north of Ireland.

3rd. A central department in London for such of the companies as have their head offices in London; for the general superintendence of the other divisions, and for working out under our immediate directions the final results, from the information obtained.

The published accounts for the past three years, furnished by the several companies under the Treasury Minute of the 14th of October 1867, were subjected to a thorough examination, and we were thereby enabled to direct attention to those points requiring special consideration. Appendix, Part II., p. 32.

For the purpose of securing uniformity in the results a set of forms (27 in number) were drawn out so as to obtain the following information,—

1st. The different descriptions and amount of share and loan capital authorized, raised, and remaining unissued.

2nd. The capital expenditure under various heads at the commencement of the period of three years, or (in the case of new lines completed within that period,) at the commencement of their carrying traffic, and the additions made to each head during the half year.

3rd. The revenue receipts and expenditure for each of the six half years embraced in the three years' period, shewing the net balance for that period after payment of all expenditure, other than interest and dividends.

4th. The balance sheets of floating liabilities and floating assets, at the date of each half-yearly balance during the three years' period.

5th. The particulars of leases or working agreements between railway companies, and of all other agreements, and any information of a general character bearing on the inquiry.

The companies have, almost without exception, filled up with great care the forms which were supplied to them, and have in every way facilitated the work of the Accountants.

After the information, as above described, had been obtained and carefully checked and analyzed, the results of our examination of the permanent way and works, rolling stock, and accounts, were applied, and statements therefrom were prepared, shewing the present financial position of each of the companies, and their true net annual revenue.

We felt it to be our duty personally to travel over and examine every part of the railway system of Ireland, to confer with our inspecting Engineers and Accountants on the spot, and to give special instructions to them as new questions arose, and also to inspect carefully every work of importance or anything requiring our personal attention.

In doing this, we have received every facility from the several companies, and the utmost candour was evinced by all the Officers with whom we were placed in communication.

We have prepared a new map of Ireland founded on the Ordnance Survey, to accompany this report, shewing railways and canals, whether constructed or authorized, and for facility of reference we have had engraved upon it an alphabetical list, with their several lengths. To follow p. 174.

We give in the Appendix to this Report a description of each railway, shewing the length of the undertaking and its branches, the Acts of Parliament under which they were sanctioned, the capital authorized and raised, the dates of opening for traffic of the Appendix, Part II., p. 18.

several railways, the dividends on ordinary and preference shares, the interest on the different classes of borrowed money, the floating assets and liabilities, and the area and population of the district of country which may be considered as accommodated by each railway.

Appendix, p. 42. For the purpose of more conveniently describing the railways of Ireland, and giving the result of our inquiries respecting them, we have divided them into three general heads or classes, and in doing so we have treated railway companies whose powers have been allowed to expire as if not in existence:—

			Miles.
Ibid., p. 48. Class I. Railways authorized but not commenced.	(Table A.)	-	339¼
Ibid., p. 44. Class II. Railways commenced but not completed.	(Table B.)	-	252
Ibid., p. 69. Class III. Railways completed and carrying traffic.	(Table C.)	-	1,908¼
	Total	-	2,499½

TABLE A.

No. in Appendix and on Map. Main Lines.	Branches and Extensions.	RAILWAYS, CLASS I.—AUTHORIZED BUT NOT COMMENCED.	Length of Line authorized. Miles.	Total Miles.
		1st.—Lines not commenced.		
1.		Bray and Enniskerry - - - - - - -	8½	
2.		Central Ireland (Maryborough to Mullingar) - - - -	36	
3.		Clonmel, Lismore, and Dungarvan - - - - - -	38	
4.		Dublin Metropolitan (in the City of Dublin) - - - -	6½	
5.		Dublin, Rathmines, Rathgar, Roundtown, Rathfarnham, and Rathcoole (Dublin to Pennsylvania Bridge) - - - - - -	9¼	
6.		Dundalk and Greenore (Co. Louth) - - - - -	13	
7.		Limerick and North Kerry (Newcastle to Listowel) - - -	22	
8.		Navan and Kingscourt - - - - - - -	20	
9.		Sligo and Ballaghaderreen (Kilfree Junction to Ballaghaderreen) - -	9¼	
10.		Waterford, Lismore, and Fermoy (Waterford to Dungarvan, and Lismore to Fermoy) - - - - - - -	49½	
11.		Waterford and Passage (Ballytruckle Junction to River Suir, at Passage) -	9¼	
12.		Waterford and Wexford (Ballyhack to Wexford and Greenore, Co. Wexford)	33¾	
		Length of lines not commenced -		254¾
		2nd.—Branches and Extensions not commenced belonging to lines (included in Class II.) commenced but not completed.		
	21 a.	Moylick Extension of the Midland Counties and Shannon Junction Railway (Banagher to Meelick) - - - - -	5½	
	24 a.	Collieries Branches of the Southern (Graystown Junction to the Collieries) - - - - - - - -	9¼	
	23 a.	Waterford Extension (Ballywilliam to Waterford) } of Waterford, New	10	
	25 b.	Ballyhoge Branch (Ballywilliam to Ballyhoge) } Ross, and Wexford	14¼	
		Length of branches and extensions connected with railways in Class II., but not commenced - - - - -		19½
		3rd.—Branches and Extensions not commenced, belonging to lines (included in Class III.) completed and carrying traffic.		
	39 c.	Kingstown connecting branch of the Dublin, Wicklow, and Wexford -	8	
	41 a.	Sligo Extension of the Enniskillen, Bundoran, and Sligo - -	32	
	40 b.	Dublin Extension } of the Great Northern and Western	9¼	
	40 c.	Westport Quay Extension }	1	
		Length of branches and extensions connected with railways in Class III., but not commenced - - - - -		65
		Total mileage authorized but not commenced -		339¼

Table AA., Appendix, p. 81. The total share and loan capital authorized for the railways in the first division of the above table (254¾ miles) is 3,245,900*l*.

The capital for the uncommenced branches and extensions of lines in the second and third divisions of the above table, forms part of and is included in the capital of the main lines, Tables B. and C. (Classes II. and III.), of which they severally are branches.

From local and other information we have obtained there appears to be little probability of the above railways (Table A.), or at least the greater part of them, being carried out under their existing powers, and although their completion would be a public convenience, it is very doubtful whether they would be profitable to their shareholders, and in the present collapsed state of railway enterprise, it is not probable that capital could be obtained for their construction.

TABLE B.

No. in Appendix and on Map: Main Lines.	No. in Appendix and on Map: Extensions and Branches.	RAILWAYS, CLASS II.—COMMENCED BUT NOT COMPLETED.	Length of Line authorised and in part commenced: Miles.	Length of Line authorised and in part commenced: Total Miles.	Estimated Cost of completing the Railways, and providing Rolling Stock.
		1st.—Lines where after some expenditure has been made the Works are at a standstill.			
14		Banbridge Extension (Banbridge to Ballyroney)	9½		
17		Dublin and Antrim Junction (Knockmore Junction to Antrim)	18½		
19		Kilrush and Kilkee	8		
20		Letterkenny (Letterkenny to Farland)	16¼		
21		Midland Counties and Shannon Junction (Clara to Banagher)	17¾		
24		Southern (Thurles Junction to Clonmel)	24		
	54 a.	Skibbereen Extension of the West Cork	16		
				111	
		2nd.—Lines which may be expected to be completed by the Companies to which they belong.			
12		Athenry and Ennis	35½		
13		Belfast Central (in the town of Belfast)	3		
15		Downpatrick, Dundrum, and Newcastle (Co. Down), (Downpatrick to Newcastle)	11		£ 753,946
23		Parsonstown and Portumna Bridge	12½		
	39 a.	Foxford Branch of the Great Northern and Western	11		
	40 a.	Shannon Extension of the Limerick and Castleconnell			
				74¾	
		3rd.—Line closed for three years which would require to be put in order before being re-opened.			
25		Waterford, New Ross, and Wexford (Bagenalstown to Ballywilliam)		20¼	
		4th.—Line incomplete at the period named in the Treasury Minute, but since opened for traffic.			
	57 a.	Maryborough Extension of the Kilkenny Junction (Abbeyleix to Maryborough).		9¼	
		Total mileage in Divisions 1, 2, 3, and 4		215¼	
		5th.—Lines where only a small amount of Work compared with the entire Undertaking has been executed.			
16		Dublin Trunk Connecting (in the City of Dublin)	7¼		
22		Newry and Greenore (Co. Louth)	14		
	59 d.	Wexford Extension of the Dublin, Wicklow, and Wexford	15		
				36¼	
		Total mileage commenced but not completed		251½	

We have not been able to collect evidence which would enable us to report with accuracy upon the value of the land which has been acquired or of the works which have been constructed in connexion with the lines forming the first four divisions of the above table, but we have prepared an estimate of the amount which would have to be expended to complete the works and provide rolling stock, and have given it in the last column of Table B.

We have included the line from Bagenalstown to Ballywilliam in this class, because since the bankruptcy of the Bagenalstown and Wexford Railway Company, it has been closed for three years, and it would have again to be put into proper order before it could be safely used.

We have not made an estimate of the cost of completing the lines in the last division of the table, inasmuch as, only a very small amount of work having been executed, they are almost in the same position as lines authorised but not commenced.

TABLE C.

No. in Appendix and on Map.	RAILWAYS, CLASS III.—COMPLETED AND CARRYING TRAFFIC.	Mileage		
		Single.	Double.	Total.
26	Belfast and County Down	44¼	—	44¼
27	Belfast, Holywood, and Bangor	12¼	—	12¼
28	Belfast and Northern Counties	82½	6½	89
29	*Carrickfergus and Larne*	15	—	15
30	*Londonderry and Coleraine*	35¼	—	35¼
31	Cork and Bandon	20	—	20
32	*Cork and Kinsale*	10¾	—	10¾
33	Cork, Blackrock, and Passage	6½	—	6½
34	Cork and Macroom Direct	23½	—	23½
35	Dublin and Belfast Junction	—	55¼	55¼
36	*Banbridge Junction*	6½	—	6½
37	Dundalk and Drogheda	13	61¼	74¼
38	Dublin and Meath	35¼	—	35¼
39	Dublin, Wicklow, and Wexford	86½	12	98½
40	*Dublin and Kingstown*	[illegible]	6	[illegible]
41	Great Southern and Western	238¾	180¼	419
42	*Cork and Limerick Direct*	17¼	—	17¼
43	Irish North Western	98½	—	98½
44	*Enniskillen, Bundoran, and Sligo*	35½	—	35½
45	*Finn Valley*	13¼	—	13¼
46	*Londonderry and Enniskillen*	50¼	9¼	60
47	Londonderry and Lough Swilly	14	—	14
48	Midland Great Western	131	115¼	246¼
49	*Athenry and Tuam*	15¼	—	15¼
50	*Great Northern and Western*	82¾	—	82¾
51	Newry and Armagh	21	—	21
52	Newry and Warrenpoint, including connecting Line	6¼	—	6¼
53	Ulster	16	48¼	64¼
54	*Banbridge, Lisburn, and Belfast*	15	—	15
55	*Portadown, Dungannon, and Omagh*	41	—	41
56	Waterford and Kilkenny	29	—	29
57	*Kilkenny Junction*	19	—	19
58	Waterford and Limerick	53¾	23½	77¼
59	*Limerick, Castleconnell, and Killaloe Extension*	13	—	13
60	*Limerick and Ennis*	24	—	24
61	*Limerick and Foynes*	25¼	¼	25½
62	*Rathkeale and Newcastle*	10	—	10
63	Waterford and Tramore	7¼	—	7¼
64	West Cork	17¾	—	17¾
	Total	1,408	500¾	1,908¾

Lines leased or worked by other companies are inserted in italics, immediately below the name of the company by which they are worked.

The 39 railways under this head constitute by far the most important class. They possess a total length of 1,908¾ miles, completed at a cost of 27,537,286*l.*, being on the average 14,428*l.* per mile.

In calculating the value of these railways, in their present condition, we found that our mode of proceeding was very clearly indicated by the Treasury Minute of the 15th of October 1867, and by the terms of the Act of Parliament of 1844. The Treasury Minute particularly instructed us to analyse the expenditure of each of the three years, and "to ascertain how much ought to be charged to capital, and how much "being for ordinary wear and tear and repairs and restorations likely to occur from time "to time, should be deducted from gross profits in estimating the net divisible profits "contemplated as the basis of purchase under the Act of 1844."

After obtaining from the Companies their returns of working expenses, we examined their books with great minuteness to ascertain if revenue and capital charges had been properly dealt with, so as to enable us if necessary to make corrections in the returns.

It was obvious, however, that in addition to correct or corrected accounts of money received and expended it was essential to determine,—

1st, Whether the way, works, and rolling stock were in a fair average condition, or whether their state showed a surplus or deficient value above or below that average condition; and inasmuch as the condition of efficiency of nearly every railway in regard to its rails, sleepers, and rolling stock varied according to their careful maintenance or otherwise, to the period during which they had been used, and to the amount of traffic carried, it was indispensable that we should consider the details resulting from the examination of every railway, and deal with them according to the circumstances of each separate case;

2nd. Whether the expenditure against revenue upon the railway and works, and on the rolling stock, had been sufficient to maintain them in a permanent state of efficiency.

The corrections which we have made in order to arrive at the true net annual revenue are founded upon an estimate of the working expenses which, when the line, works, and rolling stock shall have been placed in a state of proper efficiency, we consider sufficient to maintain them in that state for all time. Any expenditure necessary to bring the railways up to that state of proper efficiency we have assumed to be spread over three years, and interest thereon at 4 per cent. per annum has been included in the corrections made in the net annual revenue.

Speaking generally of Irish railways, we may say that the rolling stock on the average has been well maintained and is now in a fair state of efficiency, but that the permanent way is on the average somewhat below that condition.

Referring to the terms of the Treasury Minute we have found it necessary to subdivide the railways in this class (Table C.) into two heads:—

1st. Those which have been carrying traffic sufficiently long to enable the three years' average to be applied. (Table D.)

2nd. Those railways which, by reason of the short time they have been opened, and the consequent non-development of their traffic, or from some special circumstances could not be fairly dealt with on such average. (Table E.)

The following table (D.) of the companies comprised under the first head shows their share capital, the money they have borrowed, and their aggregate net corrected annual revenue.

Table D.

Railways completed and carrying traffic. Revenue computed on the three years' average.

No. in Appendix Map.	Name of Railway.	Mileage.	Financial Position at Date of last published Accounts, as ascertained by the Commission. Ordinary and Preference Share Capital. £	s.	d.	Borrowed Money, including Floating Liabilities, less Floating Assets. £	s.	d.	Total Share Capital and Borrowed Money. £	s.	d.	Net corrected Annual Revenue on Average of Three Years. £	s.	d.
26	Belfast and County Down	44	430,687	10	0	182,852	7	6	611,539	17	6			
28	Belfast and Northern Counties	80	767,808	10	0	374,987	7	9	1,142,188	17	9			
30	*Londonderry and Coleraine*	36¼	522,381	0	0	248,080	18	10	570,465	18	10			
31	*Cork and Bandon	20	352,853	16	7	87,480	5	3	440,314	1	10			
32	*Cork and Kinsale*	10½	27,179	15	0	69,792	13	2	96,972	10	8			
33	*Cork, Blackrock, and Passage	6¼	118,840	0	0	35,052	1	6	154,392	1	6			
34	*Dublin and Belfast Junction	55	873,500	0	0	226,632	3	7	1,100,132	3	7			
35	*Banbridge Junction*	6½	20,928	0	0	17,434	16	11	37,362	16	11			
37	Dublin and Drogheda	74½	894,800	0	0	310,009	17	1	1,204,809	17	1			
38	Dublin and Meath	33¾	316,613	0	0	165,912	6	3	482,542	6	2			
39	Dublin, Wicklow and Wexford	98	1,215,030	0	0	392,173	2	11	1,607,203	2	11			
40	*Dublin and Kingstown*	6	350,000	0	0	62,054	9	6	412,054	9	6			
41	Great Southern and Western	418	5,437,079	13	0	645,035	0	9	6,082,114	13	9			
43	Irish North-Western	98	706,672	19	1	305,168	1	2	1,011,841	0	3	777,942	8	1
44	*Finn Valley*	13½	49,825	19	8	27,038	6	6	76,863	19	9			
45	*Londonderry and Enniskillen*	60	455,000	0	0	209,318	13	9	664,318	13	9			
48	Midland Great Western	246¼	3,327,747	5	4	1,314,130	1	6	4,641,877	6	10			
49	*Athenry and Tuam*	15¼	61,018	0	0	29,399	8	6	90,417	8	6			
52	Newry and Warrenpoint, including connecting Line	6¼	119,910	0	0	43,672	19	7	163,582	19	7			
53	Ulster	54	1,089,855	0	0	314,691	17	11	1,403,546	17	11			
55	*Portadown, Dungannon, and Omagh*	41	365,614	18	0	125,734	4	4	491,349	2	4			
56	*Waterford and Kilkenny	29	146,880	0	0	604,557	5	9	751,447	5	9			
58	Waterford and Limerick	77¼	939,003	10	0	390,659	8	8	1,329,214	13	6			
60	**Limerick and Ennis*	24	95,000	3	0	98,648	1	8	193,536	4	8			
63	Waterford and Tramore	7¼	58,000	0	0	19,535	14	9	77,535	14	9			
		1,384¼	17,709,[illegible]	14	8	6,311,064	17	0	23,975,108	11	5			

Lines leased or worked by other companies are marked in italics.

* These railways will be entirely purchaseable under the Act of 1844 on the 1st of January 18[illegible].

The following Table gives the railways comprised in the second head, with the amount of capital raised by the companies and the money they have borrowed.

TABLE E.

RAILWAYS COMPLETED AND CARRYING TRAFFIC. REVENUE NOT COMPUTED ON THE THREE YEARS' AVERAGE.

No. in Appendix and on Map.	NAME OF RAILWAY.	Mileage.	Financial Position in Line of last published Accounts, as ascertained by the Commission: Share Capital.			Borrowed Money, including Floating Liabilities less Floating Assets.			Total Share Capital and Borrowed Money.			Estimated Net Annual Revenue.
			£	s.	d.	£	s.	d.	£	s.	d.	
37	Belfast, Holywood, and Bangor	12¼	235,085	10	0	99,870	6	4	334,955	16	4	
38	*Carrickfergus and Larne*	13½	82,[illegible]	0	0	42,358	8	9	124,857	8	9	
64	Cork and Macroom Direct	25	69,065	5	0	82,671	6	3	151,777	18	3	
43	*Cork and Limerick Direct*	17	53,157	0	0	65,796	16	11	119,[illegible]	16	11	
44	*Enniskillen, Bundoran, and Sligo*	35½	145,714	6	4	282,811	4	7	428,525	9	6	
47	Londonderry and Lough Swilly	14	24,459	10	0	78,103	1	9	107,[illegible]	11	9	
50	*Great Northern and Western*	82	477,190	18	6	151,000	16	6	628,200	14	0	
51	Newry and Armagh	21	148,061	11	0	852,[illegible]	3	1	[illegible]	14	1	£ 74,[illegible]
54	*Banbridge, Lisburn, and Belfast*	15	122,795	0	0	74,646	10	11	197,418	10	11	
57	Kilkenny Junction	19	93,433	0	0	150,060	8	5	277,[illegible]	5	7	
59	*Limerick, Castleconnell, and Killaloe*	16	61,492	0	0	28,[illegible]	3	6	90,271	3	6	
61	*Limerick and Foynes*	26½	133,[illegible]	0	0	72,532	15	0	[illegible]	15	0	
62	*Rathkeale and Newcastle*	10	26,[illegible]	15	0	46,183	5	4	72,[illegible]	5	4	
64	West Cork	17½	173,[illegible]	0	9	165,[illegible]	3	10	337,[illegible]	4	7	
		325½	1,774,894	16	7	1,778,794	3	9	3,554,179	2	3	

Note.—Lines leased or worked by other Companies are printed in italics.

The data of average receipts do not exist for a sufficient period in the case of the above railways, to enable us to value them in the same manner as we have valued those in the previous table (Table D). We have, nevertheless, felt it our duty to make an estimate on the best evidence we could obtain, but we are anxious it should be understood that the amount is necessarily only an approximation.

The following Table gives the railways commenced but not completed where the works are so far advanced that it is assumed they will be finished.

TABLE F.

RAILWAYS COMMENCED BUT NOT COMPLETED. THE WORKS OF WHICH ARE SO FAR ADVANCED THAT IT IS ASSUMED THEY WILL BE FINISHED.

No. in Appendix and on Map: Main Lines.	Extensions and Branches.	NAME OF RAILWAY.	Length of Line [illegible]	Capital authorized.	Capital expended.	Capital necessary to complete, [illegible]	Estimated Net Annual Revenue.
					£		
14	—	Banbridge Extension (Banbridge to Ballyroney)	9½	180,000	14,[illegible]		
17	...	Dublin and Antrim Junction (Knockmore Junction to Antrim)	18½	150,000	68,[illegible]		
19	—	Kilrush and Kilkee	8½	90,000	83,[illegible]		
20	—	Letterkenny (Letterkenny to Farland)	19½	170,000	88,[illegible]		
21	—	Midland Counties and Shannon Junction (Clara to Banagher)	17¾	*150,000	71,[illegible]		
24	—	Newry ([illegible] Junction to [illegible])	[illegible]	*[illegible]	114,[illegible]		
—	64 a.	Skibbereen Extension of the West Cork	14	† —	—		
15	—	Athenry and Ennis	36¾	255,000	165,[illegible]	£ 702,344	£ 45,160
18	—	Belfast Central (to the town of Belfast)	7	450,000	253,[illegible]		
16	—	Downpatrick, Dundrum, and Newcastle (Co. Down), (Downpatrick to Newcastle)	11	120,000	1,5[illegible]		
22	—	Parsonstown and Portumna Bridge	12½	85,000	85,[illegible]		
—	59 a.	Foxford Branch of the Great Northern and Western	11½	† —	—		
—	58 a.	Shannon Extension of the Limerick and Castleconnell	[illegible]	† —	—		
25	—	Waterford, New Ross, and Wexford ([illegible] to Ballywilliam)	20	*400,000	—		
—	57 a.	Maryborough Extension of the Kilkenny Junction (Abbeyleix to Maryborough)	9½	† —	—		
		Total Mileage	218½	2,454,000	872,000	†[illegible],544	45,160

* These amounts of authorized capital include the capital for four uncommenced branches ([illegible] miles in all) forming the second division of Class I. (Table A.)

† The capital [illegible] or expended for these branches forms part of and is included in the capital of the several main lines of which they are branches.

The traffic upon railways which have not been completed cannot of course be estimated except by analogy, but we have thought it desirable to include them in our report, so as to give, to the best of our ability, the annual value of the whole of the railways of Ireland, which are now, or in a short time will be, carrying traffic. Those railways in divisions 1, 2, 3, and 4, of Table B. (215½ miles), have been compared with other lines as nearly similar as possible in point of population and other conditions governing traffic, and we have given in one total sum in the above Table F. the best approximation in our power to the "net annual revenue" which these railways may probably produce; but this estimate must only be considered an approximate one.

Table G.

SUMMARY OF ALL THE RAILWAYS IN IRELAND, WITH THEIR MILEAGE, AUTHORISED CAPITAL, FINANCIAL POSITION, AND CORRECTED ANNUAL REVENUE.

Number of Railways.	Classification of Railways.	Miles.	Total Miles.	Capital authorised.	Financial Position at Date of last published Accounts.				Computed Net Corrected Annual Revenue.
					Ordinary and Preference Share Capital raised.	Borrowed Money, including Floating Liabilities less Floating Assets.	Capital necessary to complete, including Rolling Stock.	Total.	
	Completed and carrying traffic.								
[illegible]	1. Revenue computed on the basis of three years' average (Table D.).	1,[illegible]½		23,412,[illegible]	17,[illegible]	6,311,[illegible]	—	23,[illegible],1[illegible]	[illegible],347
14	2. Revenue not computed on the basis of three years' average (Table E.).	[illegible]½		[illegible]	1,77[illegible]	1,77[illegible]	—	3,544,1[illegible]	74,[illegible]
	Commenced and not completed.								
11	1. Expected to be completed (Table F.).								
	Main Lines - -	170		3,554,[illegible]	[illegible]	[illegible]	783,341	1,[illegible]	45,1[illegible]
	Branches of Lines completed	39½		* —	* —	* —			
[illegible]			2,[illegible]	31,[illegible]	[illegible]	[illegible]	[illegible]	[illegible]	[illegible]
[illegible]	2. Not expected to be carried out (Table B.)								
	Main Lines - -	81½		641,[illegible]					
	Branches of Lines completed	15		* —					
	Authorised but not commenced.								
1[illegible]	(Table A.)								
	Main Lines - -	[illegible]½		[illegible]					
	Branches of Lines completed	56		* —					
	Branches of Lines to be completed - - -	44½		* —					
			373½						
[illegible]			2,[illegible]½	33,[illegible]					

* The capital authorised or expended for these branches (being part of one) is included in the capitals of the several main lines of which they are branches.

It will be observed that in the foregoing Tables D, E, and F, we have given separately and in the above general summary (Table G.) collectively the "Estimated net corrected "annual revenue" of the railways, but we have not in any of those tables made an actual deduction of the interest on borrowed money, so as to give the "Net divisible profits."

The difficulty we have found in making such deductions in detail, or in other words applying the principle of the Act of 1844 to the railways under the different classes enumerated, has arisen from the fact that of all the railways in Ireland, five only are entirely purchaseable under the Act of 1844, and the others vary considerably with reference to Table FF. Appendix, p. 26.

the dates at which they will come altogether under the operation of the Act, and therefore this mode of computation would not be fairly applicable in all cases, especially to those Companies who have contracted temporary loans at high rates of interest to enable them to complete their undertakings, but whose lines have not been opened for traffic sufficiently long to develop their resources and consolidate their credit as contemplated by the 21 years' period of the Act of 1844.

It is probable, however, that the aggregate result may not be considerably affected by these circumstances, and that it will be useful to give the total results of all the railways on one uniform basis of calculation, with an estimate of their "net divisible profits" as required by the Treasury Minute.

TABLE H.

RAILWAYS COMPLETED OR EXPECTED TO BE COMPLETED, WITH AN ESTIMATE OF NET DIVISIBLE PROFITS.

Number of Railways.	Classification of Railways.	Mileage.	Ordinary and Preference Share Capital.	[illegible] Treasury Loans.	Estimated Cost of Completion.	Total Capital [illegible]	Estimated Net [illegible] Revenue.	[illegible] (Both the latter [illegible] at 5 per cent.)	Estimated Amount of Net Profits divisible on Share Capital.	[illegible]
			£	£	£	£	£	£	£	£
39	1. Companies whose net revenue is estimated to be in excess of interest charges	1,680	17,137,825	2,658,186	175,[illegible]	22,[illegible]	813,[illegible]	[illegible]	347,[illegible]	--
31	2. Companies whose net revenue is estimated to be insufficient to meet current charges	482	2,[illegible],617	[illegible]	[illegible]	6,326,170	44,177	103,[illegible]	. .	74,314
70	Total	2,164	20,071,642	6,314,617	183,364	29,297,437	857,[illegible]	[illegible],157	347,[illegible]	74,314

Rolling Stock.

A table showing the number of locomotive engines, and the amount of carriage and wagon stock belonging to the several railway companies in Ireland, is given in the Appendix.

Directors and Staff employed by Railway Companies carrying Traffic.

We have compiled from returns received from the railway companies a table showing the number of the directors and of the different classes of officers and men employed on the several railways completed and carrying traffic, which is given in the Appendix.

Other Tables in Appendix.

We also give in the Appendix tables shewing in detail the capital authorized for each railway, the financial position of those completed or commenced, and the progress of the traffic during the three years' period.

Traffic Arrangements.

In accordance with instructions received from the Treasury dated the 4th of April 1868, we annex the particulars of agreements that Irish Railway Companies have entered into among themselves or with Canal Companies "with respect to limiting the charges for "traffic; the accommodation to the public or the assistance to be given to railway "extensions or new railways in cases where there was a competition between routes of "communication for the traffic of any district or place."

Loans to Irish Railway Companies from Public Commissioners.

We have obtained a return from the Public Works Loan Commissioners of the United Kingdom of all advances made by them from the year 1842 to the 3rd of January 1868, showing the name of the railway, total advance, date of loan, period for which it was made, the rate of interest, principal repaid, principal unpaid, interest in arrear, and costs paid to the solicitors of the Commissioners. We annex this return in the Appendix, as also a return of the advances made to railway companies by the Commissioners of Public

Works in Ireland between 1839 and 1847, which return was presented to Parliament in 1867.

The following table gives the result of these two returns: –

	£
Total sum advanced by Public Commissioners to railways in Ireland - - - - - - -	2,777,384
Total sum repaid - - - - - - -	1,488,125
Total sum unpaid - - - - - - -	1,289,259
Total interest in arrear - - - - - - -	12,031

Railway Deposits in the Court of Chancery in Ireland.

We have also obtained a return from the Accountant-General of the Court of Chancery in Ireland of the amount of Railway deposits standing in his name on the 2nd of October 1867, and it appears that, taking Consols and New Three per Cents. at par, the total sum deposited was 93,686*l.* Appendix, Part I., p. 40.

Act of Parliament, 1844.

We conclude this branch of the subject by calling attention to the fact that there are only three railways (having a total length of 62¼ miles), which having been authorized previously to the Act of 1844, cannot now or at a future time be dealt with under the powers conferred by that Act.

We give in the following Table (I.) a summary shewing the position of all the railways with respect to purchase under the Act of 1844, and more detailed particulars in the Appendix. Table IV. Appendix, Part II., p. 88.

TABLE I.

POSITION OF RAILWAYS WITH RESPECT TO PURCHASE UNDER THE ACT 1844.

Number of Railways.	Length.	Total Share Capital and Borrowed Money
Purchaseable on 1st of January 1869:	Miles.	
Five entire lines - - - - - -	184¾	
Sixteen lines partly purchaseable - - - -	749 7/16	
Total purchaseable on 1st of January 1869 - -	894	
Purchaseable after 1st of January 1869:		
Parts of 16 lines above mentioned - - - - -	462	
Five lines wholly or in part purchaseable between 1870-1878	34½	
Parts of same lines subsequently purchaseable - -	19½	
Thirteen lines purchaseable between 1878-1888 - -	311	
Total length ultimately purchaseable - -	1,646	
Parts of three lines not purchaseable as having been authorized prior to 1844 - - - - - -	62¼	
Total - - - - - - -	1,708¼	£27,527,286

CANALS AND RIVER NAVIGATIONS.

Since the extension of the railway system, canals and river navigations have ceased to occupy the important position they previously held as a means of transit throughout Ireland, for goods and passengers. The carriage of passengers on canals may be said to have wholly ceased, and only the heavier and less valuable description of goods are now carried upon them.

The canals of Ireland were no doubt in their day of great public benefit, and probably justified the large sums of public money which were spent upon them, but it will be seen that with the exception of the Barrow Navigation, the Grand Canal, and the Lagan Navigation (the Royal Canal being merged in the Midland Great Western Railway), the dividends paid by those which are in possession of public companies are almost nominal.

We have divided the canals and river navigations of Ireland into the three following heads, and have given in the Appendix a short history of each :— Appendix, Part IV., p. 153.

1st. Those in possession of Public Companies or leased to Companies by Private Owners.

2nd. Those under the management of Local Trustees.

3rd. Those under Public Works Commissioners.

TABLE K.—CANALS AND RIVER NAVIGATIONS.

No. of Appendix and on Map	Canals and River Navigations.	Length in Miles.		
	I.—In the Possession of Companies or Leased to Companies by Private Owners.			
65	Barrow Navigation - - - - - -	—	42¼	
66	Upper Boyne Navigation - - - - - -	—	6	
67	Grand Canal Company - - - - - -	82¼		
	(a.) The Liffey Branch - - - - -	3¼		
	(b.) The Kildare Branch - - - - -	7½		
	(c.) The Blackwood Branch - - - - -	5		
	(d.) The Barrow Line Branch - - - - -	11		
	(e.) The Low Town Lateral Branch - - - -	1½		
	(f.) The Milltown Supply Branch - - - -	6½		
	(g.) The Athy Branch - - - - -	14½		
	(h.) The Mountmellick Branch - - - -	11½		
	(i.) The Edenderry Branch - - - - -	1		
	(k.) The Kilbeggan Branch - - - - -	8¼		
	Total Grand Canal	—	165⅝	
68	Lagan Navigation - - - - - -	—	70¼	
69	Newry Navigation - - - - - -	—	35	
70	River Suir Navigation - - - - - -	—	16½	
71	Royal Canal (Midland Great Western Railway Company - -	90¼		
	(a.) The Broadstone Harbour Branch - - -	¾		
	(b.) The Longford Branch - - - - -	5¼		
	Total Royal Canal	—	96¼	
72	Foyle Navigation (Strabane to River Foyle) - - -	—	4	
	Total Mileage in the Possession of Companies			[illegible]
	II.—Under Local Trustees.			
73	Ballinamore and Ballyconnell Navigation - - - - -	—	37¼	
74	Lower Bann Navigation - - - - - -	—	30¼	
75	Upper Bann Navigation - - - - - -	—	31¼	
76	Lough Corrib Navigation - - - - - -	—	3¼	
	Total Mileage under Local Trustees			[illegible]
	III.—Under Public Works Commissioners.			
77	Lower Boyne Navigation - - - - - -	—	19½	
78	Maigue Navigation - - - - - -	—	8	
79	Shannon Navigation - - - - - -	143		
	(a.) The Boyle Branch - - - - -	9		
	(b.) The Strokestown Branch - - - -	6		
	Total inland part of Shannon - - -	—	158	
80	Tyrone Navigation - - - - - -	—	4½	
81	Ulster Canal - - - - - - -	—	44	
	Total Mileage under Public Works Commissioners -			227¼
	Total Mileage			749¾

Six of these may be considered as large and important navigations, viz. :—

	Miles.
The Grand Canal, with its branches, having a total length of -	165⅝
The Barrow Navigation, which may be considered an extension of the Grand Canal - - - - - -	42¼
The Royal Canal and branches - - - - - -	96¼
The Upper and the Lower Bann Navigations, together - -	71⅝
The Ulster Canal - - - - - - -	44
The Shannon River Navigation, with its branches - - -	158

The other canals and navigations (11 in number) are of a much less important character.

As already stated we took the same steps to ascertain the present value of the canals and river navigations which we had adopted for the railways, viz., by the appointment of inspecting Engineers to examine the state of the waterway, tow-paths, bridges, locks, fencing, warehouses, and other works connected with them, also their steam boats and carrying plant; and by the appointment of Accountants to examine and verify the accounts. We supplied forms in which the information could be tabulated, and (as in the case of the railways) we have ascertained their financial position and estimated their net annual revenue.

The following table shows their share capital, the money they have borrowed, and the net aggregate corrected annual revenue.

TABLE L.

CANALS AND RIVER NAVIGATIONS BELONGING TO COMPANIES. FINANCIAL POSITION AND CORRECTED ANNUAL REVENUE.

No.	NAME OF COMPANY.	Financial Position at Date of last Published Accounts.			Net corrected Annual Revenue on average of Three Years.
		Ordinary and Preference Share Capital.	Balance of Borrowed Money and Floating Liabilities or Floating Assets.	Total Share Capital and Borrowed Money.	
		£ s. d.	£ s. d.	£ s. d.	£ s. d.
65	Barrow Navigation	60,000 0 0	Cr. 3,014 13 9	56,985 6 3	23,748 11 8
67	Grand Canal Company	663,838 14 6	Cr. 23,418 7 10	640,420 6 8	
68	Lagan Navigation	80,149 18 11	Cr. 3,034 14 10	77,115 4 1	
69	Newry Navigation	66,496 7 2	Dr. 49,101 12 7	115,598 19 9	
70	River Suir Navigation	8,960 0 0	—	8,960 0 0	
72	Foyle Navigation	4,188 0 0	Cr. 413 15 11	3,774 4 1	
	Total	£ 883,730 0 7	17,180 1 2	902,918 1 10	
66	Upper Boyne Navigation	Particulars not furnished.			
71	Royal Canal	(Included with Midland Great Western Railway Accounts).			

The canals comprised in Table K. (Classes II. and III.), now in the possession of Local Trustees or of the Public Works Commissioners, do not strictly come within the scope of our report, but we have thought that our history of canals and river navigations would be incomplete without adding some account of them. They were all executed by means of public and local taxation, and are now under the charge of Local Trustees or the Commissioners of Public Works, of which the particulars will be found in the Appendix. Appendix, Part IV. p. 164.

The canals and river navigations now in the possession of public companies are all more or less in competition with railways, and undoubtedly any change in the system of working the railways might affect the interests of these canals, but to what extent must of course depend on the nature of the change itself.

Assistance to Canals in Ireland.

The assistance given to canals belonging to companies in Ireland in the last and commencement of the present century was chiefly in the form of loans of public money or by grants from special or general taxes; but we have been unable to obtain from the records of inland navigation in Ireland a complete account of the public loans which were made for such purpose. Appendix, Part IV. p. 171.

The assistance to the navigations under local trustees was by grants of public money and advances secured on local taxation. To those under the Commissioners of Public Works it was given in the case of the Ulster Canal by loans, of the Shannon Navigation by grants and advances secured on local assessment, and of the other navigations by grants from special or general taxes.

Having thus reported, in what we believe to be the spirit of the instructions given by the Treasury, on the condition and value of the railways and canals of Ireland, there remains to be considered only the question of the "prospects" of the railways.

Prospects of Railways in Ireland.

It is provided in the Act of 1844 that, if any railway be purchased under the powers of that Act at 25 years' purchase upon its net divisible profits, if such profits be less than at the rate of 10 per cent. per annum on their subscribed and paid up capital stock, and if the company shall be of opinion that the rate of 25 years' purchase is an inadequate rate of purchase, it shall have a right to require that it shall be left to arbitration to determine what (if any) additional amount of purchase money shall be paid to it with reference to its "prospects."

In the case of those railways, or portions of them, which are not yet purchaseable under the Act of 1844, the companies would, if dealt with before the period of 21 years shall have expired, appear to be entitled to a similar arbitration with reference to the prospects of an increased development of traffic during the unexpired portion of that period.

We find that in the 39 railways comprised in Table C. (Class III.), the progress of earnings compared with the length of miles carrying traffic in the three years (the accounts of which have been under examination and analysis) has been as follows:—

Table M.

Progress of Traffic Earnings from 1864–5 to 1866–7.

Year.	Average Number of Miles carrying Traffic.	Total Capital Expenditure at End of each Year.	Total Gross Earnings.	Gross Earnings per Mile per Annum.	Percentage of Gross Earnings to Capital Expenditure.	Increase in Gross Earnings.	Increase Per Cent.	Increase Per Mile.	Increase in Percentage of Gross Earnings to Capital Expenditure per Cent.
	Miles	£	£	£	£	£	£	£	£
1864–5	1,774½	[illegible]	1,547,217	[illegible]	6·119		—	—	—
1865–6	[illegible]	[illegible]	[illegible]	[illegible]	6·370	[illegible]	[illegible]	[illegible]	[illegible]
1866–7	[illegible]	[illegible]	[illegible]	[illegible]	[illegible]	[illegible]	[illegible]	[illegible]	[illegible]
Mean Increase per annum from 1864–5 to 1866–7						[illegible]	[illegible]	[illegible]	[illegible]

It is difficult to say if this rate of increase be more or less than what may be considered the natural growth of the traffic on the railways in Ireland; although it has been continuous during the last three years, it may be assumed that under present conditions, having reference to cost of management and the charges and accommodation for traffic, the probability is not great that for the future the average net revenue of the railways of Ireland will be materially augmented.

If these conditions, however, should become changed by the economy and greater efficiency which would result from concentration of management and more harmonious working of the whole system, and by the adoption of much lower fares for passengers, and rates for carriage of goods and cattle, it is probable that a considerable impetus might be given to the traffic without permanent loss, but in the present state of their credit and finances, the Companies could not afford to run the risk of a period of diminished profit for the chance of any ultimate advantage.

In connexion with the subject of the "prospects" of Irish railways, a reference to future extensions can scarcely be avoided. The history of the efforts made during the last few years to give the benefit of railway communication to districts hitherto unaccommodated, has shown that the limit of unaided undertakings (except in a few trifling cases) has been reached, if not passed.

It will be admitted that few, if any, of the later enterprises have been launched on a sound basis of capital *bonâ fide* subscribed; but the necessity for extensions and additional railways has been so strongly felt that the most strenuous local efforts have been made, and every conceivable financial expedient submitted to, in order to accomplish the much desired result.

It may be desirable to repress the irregular "financing" of the past, but the necessity will still remain for dealing with districts of country in which railways would be of great local benefit, but which cannot be carried out without extraneous aid. Whether such assistance can best be afforded by local assessment, or otherwise, will, of course, require careful consideration. We do not believe, however, that in a matter of such recognised necessity much difficulty would be found in maturing some plan for the purpose, and, as before stated, we have felt the question too important to be left altogether unnoticed in this report.

In conclusion we desire to state that, should any matter connected with the inquiry appear to your Lordships to require elucidation we shall doubtless, from the ample material we have collected, be able to supply any additional information which may be desired.

We have the honour to be,
Your Lordships' obedient Servants,

(Signed) A. Y. SPEARMAN.
JOHN MULHOLLAND.
JOHN FOWLER.
SEYMOUR CLARKE.
C. JOHNSTONE.

The [illegible]th of April 1868.

(Signed) W. NEILSON HANCOCK,
Secretary.

RAILWAYS (IRELAND) COMMISSION.

APPENDIX.

PART I.—TABLES COMPILED BY THE COMMISSION.

TABLE (AA.)—LENGTH and CAPITAL of RAILWAYS, CLASS I., authorised but not commenced.

Referred to in Appendix and on Map: Main Lines.	Branches and Extensions.	Name of Company.	Length of authorised Line.	Capital authorised: Shares.	Loans.	Total.
		1.—Lines not commenced.		£	£	£
1	—	Bray and Enniskerry	3½	35,000	12,000	[illegible]
2	—	Central Ireland (Maryborough to Mullingar)	35	250,000	71,200	[illegible]
3	—	Clonmel, Lismore, and Dungarvan	30	300,000	100,000	400,000
4	—	Dublin Metropolitan (in the city of Dublin)	2½	160,000	53,000	213,000
5	—	Dublin, Rathmines, Rathgar, Roundtown, Rathfarnham, and Rathcoole (Dublin to Poulaphouca Bridge)	24	450,000	140,000	590,000
6	—	Dundalk and Greenore (Co. Louth)	15	160,000	53,300	213,300
7	—	Limerick and North Kerry (Newcastle to Listowel)	23	130,000	43,300	173,300
8	—	Navan and Kingscourt	20	160,000	10,000	160,000
9	—	Sligo and Ballaghaderreen (Kilfree Junction to Ballaghaderreen)	9½	50,000	16,600	66,600
10	—	Waterford, Lismore, and Fermoy (Waterford to Dungarvan and Lismore to Fermoy)	42½	400,000	133,000	533,000
11	—	Waterford and Passage (from Ballytruckle Junction to River Suir at Passage)	9½	80,000	26,600	106,600
12	—	Waterford and Wexford (from Ballyhack to Wexford and Greenore)	33½	330,000	110,000	440,000
		Length of Lines not commenced	254½	2,425,000	820,800	3,245,800
		2.—Branches and Extensions not commenced belonging to Lines (included in Class II.) commenced but not completed.				
	21 a.	Meelick Extension of Midland Counties, &c. (Banagher to Meelick)	4½	Capital included under Class II.		
	24 a.	Collieries Branch of Southern (Graystown Junction to the Collieries)	9½			
	25 a.	Waterford Extension (Ballywilliam to Waterford) and } of Waterford, New Ross, and Wexford	19			
	25 b.	Ballyhoge Branch (Ballywilliam to Ballyhoge) } of Waterford, New Ross, and Wexford	14½			
		Length of Branches and Extensions, Class II., not commenced	48½			
		3.—Branches and Extensions not commenced belonging to Lines (included in Class III.) completed and carrying traffic.				
	29 c.	Kingstown connecting Branch of the Dublin, Wicklow, and Wexford	2	Capital included under Class III.		
	41 a.	Sligo Extension of the Enniskillen, Bundoran, and Sligo	22			
	30 b.	Ballina Extension, and	9½			
	30 c.	Westport Quay Extension of the Great Northern and Western	1¾			
		Length of Branches and Extensions (Class III.) not commenced	36			
		Total Mileage authorised but not commenced	338½			
		Total authorised Share and Loan Capital of the 12 Main Lines forming the first division		2,425,000	820,800	3,245,800

Table (BB).—Capital and Financial Position with Total estimated Cost of Completing the Works of Railways, Class II., commenced but not completed.

No.	[illegible]	Name of Railway	Length	Shares	Loans	Total	Ordinary Share Capital	[illegible]	Settlement Loans	Floating Liabilities	Total
		1.—Lines where after some Expenditure made, the Works are not completed.		£	£	£	£ s. d.	£	£ s. d.	£ s. d.	£ s. d.
16	—	[illegible] (Banbridge to Ballyroney)	[illegible]	[illegible]	[illegible]	[illegible]	[illegible]	—	—	[illegible]	[illegible]
17	—	[illegible] and Antrim Junction ([illegible] to Antrim)	[illegible]	[illegible]	[illegible]	[illegible]	[illegible]	—	—	Cr. [illegible]	[illegible]
[illegible]	—	[illegible] and [illegible]	[illegible]	[illegible]	[illegible]	[illegible]	—	—	—	[illegible]	[illegible]
[illegible]	—	[illegible] ([illegible])	[illegible]	[illegible]	[illegible]	[illegible]	[illegible]	—	—	[illegible]	[illegible]
[illegible]	—	[illegible] Counties and [illegible] Junction ([illegible])	[illegible]	[illegible]	[illegible]	[illegible]	[illegible]	—	[illegible]	[illegible]	[illegible]
[illegible]	—	[illegible] ([illegible])	[illegible]	[illegible]	[illegible]	[illegible]	[illegible]	—	—	[illegible]	[illegible]
	[illegible]	[illegible] Extension of the West Cork.	10	Capital included in Class III.							
		2.—Lines which may be expected to be completed by the Companies to which they belong.									
[illegible]	—	[illegible] and [illegible]	[illegible]	[illegible]	[illegible]	[illegible]	[illegible]	[illegible]	[illegible]	[illegible]	[illegible]
[illegible]	—	Belfast Central (in the town of Belfast)	[illegible]	[illegible]	[illegible]	[illegible]	[illegible]	—	—	[illegible]	[illegible]
[illegible]	—	[illegible], [illegible], and [illegible] (County Down), ([illegible])	[illegible]	[illegible]	[illegible]	[illegible]	[illegible]	—	—	Cr. [illegible]	[illegible]
[illegible]	—	[illegible] and [illegible] Bridge	[illegible]	[illegible]	[illegible]	[illegible]	[illegible]	[illegible]	[illegible]	Cr. [illegible]	[illegible]
	[illegible]	[illegible] Branch of the Great Northern and Western	[illegible]	Capital included in Class III.							
	[illegible]	[illegible] Extension of the Limerick and [illegible]	[illegible]	Capital included in Class III.							
		3.—Lines closed for Three Years which would require to be put in order before being re-opened.									
[illegible]	—	Waterford, New Ross, and Wexford ([illegible] to [illegible])	[illegible]	[illegible]	[illegible]	[illegible]		—			Nil.
		4.—Over [illegible] on 1st May [illegible] (the Period of [illegible] under the Treasury [illegible]), but never opened for Traffic.									
	[illegible]	[illegible] Extension of the [illegible] Junction ([illegible] to [illegible])	[illegible]	Capital included in Class III.							
			[illegible]	[illegible]	[illegible]	[illegible]	[illegible]	[illegible]	[illegible]	[illegible]	[illegible]
		5.—Lines where only a small amount of Works completed until the entire Undertaking has been arranged.									
[illegible]	—	Dublin Trunk Connecting (in the City of Dublin).	[illegible]	[illegible]	[illegible]	[illegible]	[illegible]	—	—	[illegible]	[illegible]
[illegible]	—	[illegible] and [illegible] (County Louth)	[illegible]	[illegible]	[illegible]	[illegible]	[illegible]	—	—	[illegible]	[illegible]
	[illegible]	Wexford Extension of the Dublin, Wicklow, and Wexford.	[illegible]	Capital included in Class III.							
			[illegible]								
		Total Mileage commenced but not completed	[illegible]								
		Total Share and Loan Capital authorised and expended of the [illegible] Main lines included in above Table	—	[illegible]	[illegible]	[illegible]	[illegible]	[illegible]	[illegible]	[illegible]	[illegible]

* [illegible]

TABLE (CC.)—LENGTH and CAPITAL EXPENDITURE as per COMPANY'S ACCOUNTS in each YEAR of the THREE YEARS' PERIOD embraced in the TREASURY MINUTE, of RAILWAYS, CLASS III., completed and carrying TRAFFIC.

No. in Appendix and on Map.	NAME OF RAILWAY.	Mileage. Mileage at Commencement.	Mileage. Miles opened during 3 Years.	Mileage. Mileage at close of 3 Years.	Capital Expenditure per Company's Accounts. At Commencement of Period.	During the Three Years. [illegible]	During the Three Years. [illegible]	During the Three Years. [illegible]	During the Three Years. Total.	Total at close of Three Years' Period.
	PART I.—Revenue computed on the Three Years' average.—				£	£	£	£	£	£
[illegible]	Belfast and County Down	[illegible]	Less 4½*	44½	[illegible]	[illegible]	Cr. [illegible]	11,618	Cr. [illegible]	[illegible]
[illegible]	Belfast & Northern Counties	[illegible]	—	[illegible]	[illegible]	4,[illegible]	17,610	[illegible]	[illegible]	[illegible]
[illegible]	Londonderry and Coleraine	[illegible]	—	[illegible]	[illegible]	-	-	[illegible]	[illegible]	[illegible]
[illegible]	Cork and Bandon	[illegible]	—	[illegible]	[illegible]	[illegible]	[illegible]	[illegible]	[illegible]	[illegible]
[illegible]	Cork and Kinsale	[illegible]	—	[illegible]	[illegible]	[illegible]	[illegible]	[illegible]	[illegible]	[illegible]
[illegible]	Cork, Blackrock, & Passage	[illegible]	—	[illegible]	[illegible]	[illegible]	[illegible]	[illegible]	[illegible]	[illegible]
[illegible]	Dublin and Belfast Junction	[illegible]	—	[illegible]	[illegible]	[illegible]	[illegible]	[illegible]	[illegible]	[illegible]
[illegible]	Banbridge Junction	[illegible]	—	[illegible]	[illegible]	[illegible]	[illegible]	Cr. [illegible]	[illegible]	[illegible]
[illegible]	Dublin and Drogheda	[illegible]	—	[illegible]	[illegible]	[illegible]	[illegible]	[illegible]	[illegible]	[illegible]
[illegible]	Dublin and Meath	[illegible]	—	[illegible]	[illegible]	[illegible]	[illegible]	[illegible]	[illegible]	[illegible]
[illegible]	Dublin, Wicklow, & Wexford	[illegible]	[illegible]	[illegible]	[illegible]	[illegible]	[illegible]	[illegible]	[illegible]	[illegible]
[illegible]	Dublin and Kingstown	[illegible]	—	[illegible]	[illegible]	-	-	-	-	[illegible]
[illegible]	Great Southern and Western / Cork and Youghal†	[illegible]	—	[illegible]	[illegible]	[illegible]	[illegible]	[illegible]	[illegible]	[illegible]
[illegible]	Irish North-Western	[illegible]	—	[illegible]	[illegible]	[illegible]	[illegible]	[illegible]	[illegible]	[illegible]
[illegible]	Finn Valley	[illegible]	—	[illegible]	[illegible]	[illegible]	[illegible]	[illegible]	[illegible]	[illegible]
[illegible]	Londonderry & Enniskillen	[illegible]	—	[illegible]	[illegible]	[illegible]	[illegible]	Cr. [illegible]	Cr. [illegible]	[illegible]
[illegible]	Midland Great Western	[illegible]	—	[illegible]	[illegible]	[illegible]	[illegible]	[illegible]	[illegible]	[illegible]
[illegible]	Athenry and Tuam	[illegible]	—	[illegible]	[illegible]	[illegible]	[illegible]	-	[illegible]	[illegible]
[illegible]	Newry, & Warrenpoint, including Connecting Line	[illegible]	—	[illegible]	[illegible]	[illegible]	[illegible]	Cr. [illegible]	[illegible]	[illegible]
[illegible]	Ulster	[illegible]	—	[illegible]	[illegible]	[illegible]	[illegible]	[illegible]	[illegible]	[illegible]
[illegible]	Portadown, Dungannon, and Omagh	[illegible]	[illegible]	[illegible]	[illegible]	Cr. [illegible]	[illegible]	[illegible]	[illegible]	[illegible]
[illegible]	Waterford and Kilkenny	[illegible]	—	[illegible]	[illegible]	[illegible]	[illegible]	[illegible]	[illegible]	[illegible]
[illegible]	Waterford and Limerick	77	[illegible]	[illegible]	[illegible]	[illegible]	[illegible]	[illegible]	[illegible]	[illegible]
[illegible]	Limerick and Ennis	[illegible]	—	[illegible]	[illegible]	Cr. [illegible]	Cr. [illegible]	-	Cr. [illegible]	[illegible]
[illegible]	Waterford and Tramore	[illegible]	—	[illegible]	[illegible]	-	-	-	-	[illegible]
	Total	[illegible]	[illegible]	[illegible]	[illegible]	[illegible]	[illegible]	[illegible]	[illegible]	[illegible]
	PART II.—Revenue not computed on the Three Years' average.									
[illegible]	Belfast, Holywood, & Bangor	—	[illegible]	[illegible]	[illegible]	[illegible]	[illegible]	[illegible]	[illegible]	[illegible]
[illegible]	Carrickfergus and Larne	[illegible]	—	[illegible]	[illegible]	[illegible]	[illegible]	[illegible]	[illegible]	[illegible]
[illegible]	Cork and Macroom Direct	—	[illegible]	[illegible]	[illegible]	[illegible]	[illegible]	[illegible]	[illegible]	[illegible]
[illegible]	Cork and Limerick Direct	[illegible]	—	[illegible]	[illegible]	[illegible]	[illegible]	[illegible]	[illegible]	[illegible]
[illegible]	Enniskillen, Bundoran, and Sligo	—	[illegible]	[illegible]	[illegible]	[illegible]	[illegible]	[illegible]	[illegible]	[illegible]
[illegible]	Londonderry & Lough Swilly	9	[illegible]	[illegible]	[illegible]	[illegible]	[illegible]	[illegible]	[illegible]	[illegible]
[illegible]	Great Northern and Western	[illegible]	[illegible]	[illegible]	[illegible]	[illegible]	[illegible]	[illegible]	[illegible]	[illegible]
[illegible]	Newry and Armagh	[illegible]	[illegible]	[illegible]	[illegible]	[illegible]	[illegible]	[illegible]	[illegible]	[illegible]
[illegible]	Banbridge, Lisburn, & Belfast	15	—	15	[illegible]	[illegible]	[illegible]	[illegible]	[illegible]	[illegible]
[illegible]	Killarney Junction	[illegible]	[illegible]	[illegible]	[illegible]	[illegible]	[illegible]	[illegible]	[illegible]	[illegible]
[illegible]	Limerick, Castleconnell, & Killaloe	[illegible]	—	[illegible]	[illegible]	[illegible]	[illegible]	[illegible]	[illegible]	[illegible]
[illegible]	Limerick and Foynes	[illegible]	—	[illegible]	[illegible]	[illegible]	[illegible]	[illegible]	[illegible]	[illegible]
[illegible]	Rathkeale and Newcastle	—	[illegible]	[illegible]	[illegible]	[illegible]	[illegible]	[illegible]	[illegible]	[illegible]
[illegible]	West Cork	—	[illegible]	[illegible]	[illegible]	-	-	[illegible]	[illegible]	[illegible]
	Total	[illegible]	[illegible]	[illegible]	[illegible]	[illegible]	[illegible]	[illegible]	[illegible]	[illegible]
	Gross of Parts I. and II.	[illegible]	[illegible]	[illegible]	[illegible]	[illegible]	[illegible]	[illegible]	[illegible]	[illegible]

* Belfast and Holywood line (4½ miles) sold to Belfast, Holywood, and Bangor Company, [illegible] August 18[illegible].
† Cork and Youghal purchased on 1st July 18[illegible], under Statute [illegible] & [illegible] Vict. c. [illegible].

TABLE (DD.)—FINANCIAL POSITION at the date of the last published Accounts prior to

Name of Railway	Mileage: Single	Mileage: Double	Mileage: Total	Capital authorised: Shares	Capital authorised: Loans	Capital authorised: Total	Ordinary Share Capital	Preference Share Capital: Amount	Rate per Cent.	Yearly Dividend payable
PART I.—[illegible]										
Belfast and County Down	[illegible]	[illegible]	[illegible]	[illegible]	[illegible]	[illegible]	[illegible]	[illegible]	[illegible]	[illegible]
Belfast and Northern Counties	[illegible]	[illegible]	[illegible]	[illegible]	[illegible]	[illegible]	[illegible]	[illegible]	[illegible]	[illegible]
Londonderry and Coleraine	[illegible]	[illegible]	[illegible]	[illegible]	[illegible]	[illegible]	[illegible]	[illegible]	[illegible]	[illegible]
Cork and Bandon	[illegible]	[illegible]	[illegible]	[illegible]	[illegible]	[illegible]	[illegible]	[illegible]	[illegible]	[illegible]
Cork and Kinsale	[illegible]	[illegible]	[illegible]	[illegible]	[illegible]	[illegible]	[illegible]	[illegible]	[illegible]	[illegible]
Cork, Blackrock, and Passage	[illegible]	[illegible]	[illegible]	[illegible]	[illegible]	[illegible]	[illegible]	[illegible]	[illegible]	[illegible]
Dublin and Belfast Junction	[illegible]	[illegible]	[illegible]	[illegible]	[illegible]	[illegible]	[illegible]	[illegible]	[illegible]	[illegible]
Banbridge Junction	[illegible]	[illegible]	[illegible]	[illegible]	[illegible]	[illegible]	[illegible]	[illegible]	[illegible]	[illegible]
Dublin and Drogheda	[illegible]	[illegible]	[illegible]	[illegible]	[illegible]	[illegible]	[illegible]	[illegible]	[illegible]	[illegible]
Dublin and Meath	[illegible]	[illegible]	[illegible]	[illegible]	[illegible]	[illegible]	[illegible]	[illegible]	[illegible]	[illegible]
Dublin, Wicklow, and Wexford	[illegible]	[illegible]	[illegible]	[illegible]	[illegible]	[illegible]	[illegible]	[illegible]	[illegible]	[illegible]
Dundalk and Enniskillen	[illegible]	[illegible]	[illegible]	[illegible]	[illegible]	[illegible]	[illegible]	[illegible]	[illegible]	[illegible]
Great Southern and Western	[illegible]	[illegible]	[illegible]	[illegible]	[illegible]	[illegible]	[illegible]	[illegible]	[illegible]	[illegible]
Irish North Western	[illegible]	[illegible]	[illegible]	[illegible]	[illegible]	[illegible]	[illegible]	[illegible]	[illegible]	[illegible]
Finn Valley	[illegible]	[illegible]	[illegible]	[illegible]	[illegible]	[illegible]	[illegible]	[illegible]	[illegible]	[illegible]
Londonderry and Enniskillen	[illegible]	[illegible]	[illegible]	[illegible]	[illegible]	[illegible]	[illegible]	[illegible]	[illegible]	[illegible]
Midland Great Western	[illegible]	[illegible]	[illegible]	[illegible]	[illegible]	[illegible]	[illegible]	[illegible]	[illegible]	[illegible]
Athenry and Tuam	[illegible]	[illegible]	[illegible]	[illegible]	[illegible]	[illegible]	[illegible]	[illegible]	[illegible]	[illegible]
Newry, Warrenpoint, and Rostrevor; Town of Newry Connecting Line	[illegible]	[illegible]	[illegible]	[illegible]	[illegible]	[illegible]	[illegible]	[illegible]	[illegible]	[illegible]
Ulster	[illegible]	[illegible]	[illegible]	[illegible]	[illegible]	[illegible]	[illegible]	[illegible]	[illegible]	[illegible]
Portadown, Dungannon, and Omagh	[illegible]	[illegible]	[illegible]	[illegible]	[illegible]	[illegible]	[illegible]	[illegible]	[illegible]	[illegible]
Waterford and Kilkenny	[illegible]	[illegible]	[illegible]	[illegible]	[illegible]	[illegible]	[illegible]	[illegible]	[illegible]	[illegible]
Waterford and Limerick	[illegible]	[illegible]	[illegible]	[illegible]	[illegible]	[illegible]	[illegible]	[illegible]	[illegible]	[illegible]
Limerick and Ennis	[illegible]	[illegible]	[illegible]	[illegible]	[illegible]	[illegible]	[illegible]	[illegible]	[illegible]	[illegible]
Waterford and Tramore	[illegible]	[illegible]	[illegible]	[illegible]	[illegible]	[illegible]	[illegible]	[illegible]	[illegible]	[illegible]
Total	[illegible]	[illegible]	[illegible]	[illegible]	[illegible]	[illegible]	[illegible]	[illegible]	[illegible]	[illegible]
PART II.—[illegible]										
Belfast, Holywood, and Bangor	[illegible]	[illegible]	[illegible]	[illegible]	[illegible]	[illegible]	[illegible]	[illegible]	[illegible]	[illegible]
Carrickfergus and Larne	[illegible]	[illegible]	[illegible]	[illegible]	[illegible]	[illegible]	[illegible]	[illegible]	[illegible]	[illegible]
Cork and Macroom Direct	[illegible]	[illegible]	[illegible]	[illegible]	[illegible]	[illegible]	[illegible]	[illegible]	[illegible]	[illegible]
Cork and Limerick Direct	[illegible]	[illegible]	[illegible]	[illegible]	[illegible]	[illegible]	[illegible]	[illegible]	[illegible]	[illegible]
Enniskillen, Bundoran, and Sligo	[illegible]	[illegible]	[illegible]	[illegible]	[illegible]	[illegible]	[illegible]	[illegible]	[illegible]	[illegible]
Londonderry and Lough Swilly	[illegible]	[illegible]	[illegible]	[illegible]	[illegible]	[illegible]	[illegible]	[illegible]	[illegible]	[illegible]
Great Northern and Western	[illegible]	[illegible]	[illegible]	[illegible]	[illegible]	[illegible]	[illegible]	[illegible]	[illegible]	[illegible]
Newry and Armagh	[illegible]	[illegible]	[illegible]	[illegible]	[illegible]	[illegible]	[illegible]	[illegible]	[illegible]	[illegible]
Banbridge, Lisburn, and Belfast	[illegible]	[illegible]	[illegible]	[illegible]	[illegible]	[illegible]	[illegible]	[illegible]	[illegible]	[illegible]

...the 11th of October 1867, of RAILWAYS, CLASS III. COMPLETED AND CARRYING TRAFFIC.

[illegible]	[illegible]	[illegible]	[illegible]	[illegible]	[illegible]	[illegible]	[illegible]	[illegible]	[illegible]	[illegible]	[illegible]	[illegible]	[illegible]	[illegible]
[illegible]	[illegible]	[illegible]	[illegible]	[illegible]	[illegible]	[illegible]	[illegible]	[illegible]	[illegible]	[illegible]	[illegible]	[illegible]	[illegible]	[illegible]
[illegible]	[illegible]	[illegible]	[illegible]	[illegible]	[illegible]	[illegible]	[illegible]	[illegible]	[illegible]	[illegible]	[illegible]	[illegible]	[illegible]	[illegible]
[illegible]	[illegible]	[illegible]	[illegible]	[illegible]	[illegible]	[illegible]	[illegible]	[illegible]	[illegible]	[illegible]	[illegible]	[illegible]	[illegible]	[illegible]
[illegible]	[illegible]	[illegible]	[illegible]	[illegible]	[illegible]	[illegible]	[illegible]	[illegible]	[illegible]	[illegible]	[illegible]	[illegible]	[illegible]	[illegible]
[illegible]	[illegible]	[illegible]	[illegible]	[illegible]	[illegible]	[illegible]	[illegible]	[illegible]	[illegible]	[illegible]	[illegible]	[illegible]	[illegible]	[illegible]
[illegible]	[illegible]	[illegible]	[illegible]	[illegible]	[illegible]	[illegible]	[illegible]	[illegible]	[illegible]	[illegible]	[illegible]	[illegible]	[illegible]	[illegible]
[illegible]	[illegible]	[illegible]	[illegible]	[illegible]	[illegible]	[illegible]	[illegible]	[illegible]	[illegible]	[illegible]	[illegible]	[illegible]	[illegible]	[illegible]
[illegible]	[illegible]	[illegible]	[illegible]	[illegible]	[illegible]	[illegible]	[illegible]	[illegible]	[illegible]	[illegible]	[illegible]	[illegible]	[illegible]	[illegible]
[illegible]	[illegible]	[illegible]	[illegible]	[illegible]	[illegible]	[illegible]	[illegible]	[illegible]	[illegible]	[illegible]	[illegible]	[illegible]	[illegible]	[illegible]
[illegible]	[illegible]	[illegible]	[illegible]	[illegible]	[illegible]	[illegible]	[illegible]	[illegible]	[illegible]	[illegible]	[illegible]	[illegible]	[illegible]	[illegible]
[illegible]	[illegible]	[illegible]	[illegible]	[illegible]	[illegible]	[illegible]	[illegible]	[illegible]	[illegible]	[illegible]	[illegible]	[illegible]	[illegible]	[illegible]

TABLE (III.)—RAILWAYS, CLASS III.

Progress of Traffic during Three Years,

Name of Railway	Mileage: [illegible]	Mileage: [illegible]	Mileage: [illegible]	Traffic [illegible]: Passengers [illegible]	Traffic [illegible]: Goods [illegible]	Traffic [illegible]: Total	[illegible] per Mile [illegible]
Part I.—[illegible] Three Years' Averages.	Miles.	Miles.	Miles.	£	£	£	£
[illegible]	[illegible]	[illegible]	[illegible]	[illegible]	[illegible]	[illegible]	[illegible]
[illegible]	[illegible]		[illegible]	[illegible]	[illegible]	[illegible]	[illegible]
[illegible]	[illegible]		[illegible]	[illegible]	[illegible]	[illegible]	[illegible]
[illegible]	[illegible]		[illegible]	[illegible]	[illegible]	[illegible]	[illegible]
[illegible]	[illegible]		[illegible]	[illegible]	[illegible]	[illegible]	[illegible]
[illegible]	[illegible]		[illegible]	[illegible]		[illegible]	[illegible]
[illegible]	[illegible]		[illegible]	[illegible]	[illegible]	[illegible]	[illegible]
[illegible]	[illegible]		[illegible]	[illegible]	[illegible]	[illegible]	[illegible]
[illegible]	[illegible]		[illegible]	[illegible]	[illegible]	[illegible]	[illegible]
[illegible]	[illegible]		[illegible]	[illegible]	[illegible]	[illegible]	[illegible]
[illegible]	[illegible]	[illegible]	[illegible]	[illegible]	[illegible]	[illegible]	[illegible]
[illegible]	[illegible]						
[illegible]	[illegible]		[illegible]	[illegible]	[illegible]	[illegible]	[illegible]
[illegible]	[illegible]		[illegible]	[illegible]	[illegible]	[illegible]	[illegible]
[illegible]	[illegible]		[illegible]	[illegible]	[illegible]	[illegible]	[illegible]
[illegible]	[illegible]						
[illegible]	[illegible]		[illegible]	[illegible]	[illegible]	[illegible]	[illegible]
[illegible]	[illegible]		[illegible]	[illegible]	[illegible]	[illegible]	[illegible]
[illegible]	[illegible]		[illegible]	[illegible]	[illegible]	[illegible]	[illegible]
[illegible]	[illegible]		[illegible]	[illegible]	[illegible]	[illegible]	[illegible]
[illegible]	[illegible]		[illegible]	[illegible]	[illegible]	[illegible]	[illegible]
[illegible]	[illegible]		[illegible]	[illegible]	[illegible]	[illegible]	[illegible]
[illegible]	[illegible]	[illegible]	[illegible]	[illegible]	[illegible]	[illegible]	[illegible]
[illegible]	[illegible]		[illegible]	[illegible]	[illegible]	[illegible]	[illegible]
[illegible]	[illegible]		[illegible]	[illegible]	[illegible]	[illegible]	[illegible]
Total Part I.	[illegible]	[illegible]	[illegible]	[illegible]	[illegible]	[illegible]	
Average Part I.							[illegible]
Part II.—[illegible] Three Years' Average.							
[illegible]	[illegible]	[illegible]	[illegible]				
[illegible]	[illegible]		[illegible]	[illegible]	[illegible]	[illegible]	[illegible]
[illegible]		[illegible]	[illegible]				
[illegible]	[illegible]		[illegible]	[illegible]	[illegible]	[illegible]	[illegible]
[illegible]		[illegible]	[illegible]				
[illegible]	[illegible]	[illegible]	[illegible]	[illegible]	[illegible]	[illegible]	[illegible]
[illegible]	[illegible]	[illegible]	[illegible]	[illegible]	[illegible]	[illegible]	[illegible]
[illegible]	[illegible]	[illegible]	[illegible]	[illegible]	[illegible]	[illegible]	[illegible]
[illegible]	[illegible]		[illegible]	[illegible]	[illegible]	[illegible]	[illegible]
[illegible]		[illegible]	[illegible]				
[illegible]	[illegible]		[illegible]	[illegible]	[illegible]	[illegible]	[illegible]
[illegible]	[illegible]		[illegible]	[illegible]	[illegible]	[illegible]	[illegible]
[illegible]		[illegible]	[illegible]				
[illegible]		[illegible]	[illegible]				
Total Part II.	[illegible]	[illegible]	[illegible]	[illegible]	[illegible]	[illegible]	[illegible]
Average Part II.							
Total of both Parts	[illegible]	[illegible]	[illegible]	[illegible]	[illegible]	[illegible]	
Average							[illegible]

* [illegible]

† [illegible]

[illegible]PLACED AND CARRYING TRAFFIC

[illegible]uding Rents and Miscellaneous Receipts

[illegible]

Table (FF.), showing Position of Railways in Ireland with respect to their liability to be purchased under the Act of 1844. (7 & 8 Vict. c. 85.)

Lines, Parts of which are not purchasable under the Act of 1844, having been authorised before that Date.

No. in Appendix and on Map.	Name of Railway.	Length of part not purchasable, under Act of 1844.	Length of part at once purchasable under Act of 1844.	Total Length.
		Miles.		
40	Dublin and Kingstown	6	[illegible]	[illegible]
43	Ulster	24[illegible]	40	[illegible]
57	Dublin and Drogheda	31[illegible]	43	74[illegible]
	Total	[illegible]	[illegible]	147[illegible]

Lines entirely purchasable under the Act of 1844, on the 1st of January [illegible].

No. in Appendix and on Map.	Name of Railway.	Length.	Total Share Capital and Borrowed Money.
		Miles.	£
31	Cork and Bandon	20	340,814
32	Cork, Blackrock, and Passage	6[illegible]	154,[illegible]
35	Dublin and Belfast Junction	[illegible]	1,100,1[illegible]
48	Waterford and Kilkenny	[illegible]	731,442
60	Limerick and Ennis	24	193,5[illegible]
	Total	184[illegible]	2,541,816

Lines partly purchasable under the Act of 1844, on the 1st of January [illegible].

No. in Appendix and on Map.	Name of Railway.	Length of part purchasable 1st January [illegible].	Length of part subsequently purchasable, with Dates when Right of Purchase arises		Length of part authorised prior to 1844.	Total Length.	Total Share Capital and Borrowed Money.
		Miles.	Miles.	Date.	Miles.	Miles.	£
[illegible]	Waterford & Limerick	77	[illegible]	[illegible]	—	77[illegible]	1,[illegible],316
[illegible]	Newry, Warrenpoint, & Rostrevor	[illegible]	[illegible]*	1879	—	6[illegible]	1[illegible],[illegible]
[illegible]	Londonderry and Coleraine	[illegible]	[illegible]	1878	—	[illegible]	370,[illegible]
41	Great Southern & Western	[illegible]	[illegible]	1875–[illegible]	—	[illegible]	6,[illegible],13[illegible]
[illegible]	Midland Great Western	[illegible]	[illegible]	[illegible]	—	[illegible]	[illegible],[illegible]77
57	Dublin and Drogheda	[illegible]	[illegible]	[illegible]	31[illegible]	7[illegible]	1,[illegible],810
[illegible]	Belfast & Northern Counties	[illegible]	61[illegible]	187[illegible]–[illegible]	—	[illegible]	1,[illegible],190
[illegible]	Portadown, Dungannon, and Omagh	[illegible]	[illegible]	1879	—	41	[illegible]
[illegible]	Dublin, Wicklow, & Wexford	[illegible]	[illegible]	1879–1885	—	[illegible]	1,[illegible]
[illegible]	Dublin and Kingstown	[illegible]	—	—	6	[illegible]	11[illegible],[illegible]
[illegible]	Irish North-Western	[illegible]	[illegible]	1874–18[illegible]	—	[illegible]	1,011,[illegible]
[illegible]	Belfast, Holywood, & Bangor	[illegible]	7[illegible]	[illegible]	—	[illegible]	[illegible]
[illegible]	Belfast and County Down	[illegible]	[illegible]	1877–[illegible]	—	[illegible]	61[illegible],540
[illegible]	Londonderry & Enniskillen	14[illegible]	[illegible]	1878–[illegible]	—	60	[illegible],[illegible]14
[illegible]	Newry and Armagh	[illegible]	17[illegible]	1875–1879	—	[illegible]	[illegible]
[illegible]	Ulster	11	[illegible]	1877–[illegible]	[illegible]	[illegible]	1,[illegible]
	Total	[illegible]	[illegible]		[illegible]	1,[illegible]	[illegible]

* Town of Newry connecting Line.

LINES PURCHASEABLE WHOLLY OR IN PART UNDER THE ACT OF 1844, BETWEEN 1870–1878.

No. in Appendix and on Map.	Name of Railway.	Date when purchaseable.	Length of part purchaseable before 1878.	Length of part not purchaseable before 1878.	Total Length.	Total Share Capital and Borrowed Money.
			Miles.	Miles.	Miles.	£
62	Waterford and Tramore	1873	7¼	—	7¼	77,[illegible]
38	Banbridge Junction	1873	6¾	—	6¾	57,[illegible]
61	Limerick and Foynes	1873	26¾	—	26¾	[illegible]
47	Londonderry and Lough Swilly	1873	8¾	6	14¾	107,[illegible]
39	Limerick and Castleconnell	1877	5¾	7½	13	[illegible]
	Total		54½	13½	68	[illegible]

LINES PURCHASEABLE UNDER THE ACT OF 1844 BETWEEN 1878–1889.

No. in Appendix and on Map.	Name of Railway.	Date.	Length purchaseable before 1889.	Total Share Capital and Borrowed Money.
			Miles.	£
30	Carrickfergus and Larne	1887	13¾	194,[illegible]
[illegible]	Cork and [illegible] Junction	1881	10¾	[illegible]
34	Cork and Macroom Direct	[illegible]	[illegible]	141,77[illegible]
[illegible]	Dublin and Meath	[illegible]	[illegible]	[illegible]
[illegible]	Cork and Limerick Direct	[illegible]	17	[illegible]
[illegible]	Enniskillen, Bundoran, and Sligo	[illegible]	[illegible]	[illegible]
[illegible]	Finn Valley	[illegible]	[illegible]	[illegible]
[illegible]	Athenry and Tuam	[illegible]	[illegible]	[illegible],417
50	Great Northern and Western	1879–1883	[illegible]	[illegible]
54	Banbridge, Lisburn, and Belfast	[illegible]	15	197,444
57	Kilkenny Junction	[illegible]	19	277,545
[illegible]	Rathkeale and Newcastle	[illegible]	10	73,046
64	West Cork	[illegible]	17½	317,[illegible]
	Total	—	311	[illegible]

SUMMARY OF FOREGOING TABLES.

—	Length	Total Share Capital and Borrowed Money
	Miles	
Purchaseable on 1st of January 1889:		
Five entire lines	134¾	
Sixteen lines partly purchaseable	[illegible]	
Total	[illegible]	
Purchaseable after 1st of January 1889:		
Parts of 16 lines above mentioned	[illegible]	
Five lines wholly or in part purchaseable between 1870–1878	54½	
Parts of same lines subsequently purchaseable	13½	
Thirteen lines purchaseable between 1878–1889	311	
Total length ultimately purchaseable	[illegible]	
Parts of three lines not purchaseable as having been authorised prior to 1844	[illegible]	
Total	[illegible]	[illegible]

TABLE (GG).—NUMBER of the DIRECTORS, and of the different CLASSES of

Name of Railway.	[illegible]	[illegible]	General Manager's Office.		Secretary's Office.		Accountant's Office [illegible]		Traffic [illegible] Office.		Goods Manager's Office.	
			[illegible]	[illegible]	[illegible]	[illegible]	[illegible]	[illegible]	[illegible]	[illegible]	[illegible]	[illegible]
Belfast and County Down	[illegible]	[illegible]	[illegible]	[illegible]	[illegible]	[illegible]	[illegible]	[illegible]	—	—	[illegible]	[illegible]
Belfast, Holywood, and Bangor	[illegible]	[illegible]	[illegible]	[illegible]	[illegible]	—	[illegible]	—	—	—	—	—
Belfast and Northern Counties	[illegible]	[illegible]	[illegible]	[illegible]	[illegible]	—	[illegible]	[illegible]	—	—	[illegible]	[illegible]
Carrickfergus and Larne	[illegible]	[illegible]	—	—	[illegible]	—	—	—	—	Staff supplied by the		
Londonderry and Coleraine	[illegible]	[illegible]	—	—	—	—	—	—	—	Staff supplied by the		
Cork and Bandon	[illegible]	[illegible]	[illegible]	[illegible]	[illegible]	[illegible]	—	—	—	—	—	—
Cork and Kinsale	[illegible]	[illegible]	—	—	[illegible]	—	—	—	—	Staff supplied by the		
Cork, Blackrock, and Passage	[illegible]	[illegible]	—	—	[illegible]	—	[illegible]	—	—	—	—	—
Cork and Macroom Direct	[illegible]	[illegible]	[illegible]	—	[illegible]	—	[illegible]	[illegible]	—	—	—	—
Dublin and Belfast Junction	[illegible]	[illegible]	[illegible]	—	[illegible]	[illegible]	[illegible]	[illegible]	[illegible]	[illegible]	—	—
Banbridge Junction	[illegible]	[illegible]	—	—	[illegible]	—	—	—	—	Staff supplied by the		
Dublin and Drogheda	[illegible]	[illegible]	1 collector		[illegible]	[illegible]	[illegible]	[illegible]	—	—	—	—
Dublin and Meath	[illegible]	[illegible]	[illegible]	[illegible]	[illegible]	—	[illegible]	[illegible]	—	—	—	—
Dublin, Wicklow, and Wexford	[illegible]	[illegible]	—	—	[illegible]	[illegible]	[illegible]	[illegible]	[illegible]	[illegible]	—	—
Dublin and Kingstown	[illegible]	—	—	—	[illegible]	—	—	—	—	Staff supplied by the		
Great Southern and Western	[illegible]	[illegible]	—	—	[illegible]	[illegible]	[illegible]	[illegible]	[illegible]	[illegible]	—	—
Cork and Limerick Direct	[illegible]	[illegible]	—	—	[illegible]	—	—	—	—	Staff supplied by the		
Irish North Western	[illegible]	[illegible]	—	—	[illegible]	[illegible]	[illegible]	[illegible]	[illegible]	[illegible]	—	—
Enniskillen, Bundoran, and Sligo	[illegible]	[illegible]	—	—	[illegible]	[illegible]	—	—	—	Staff supplied by the		
Finn Valley	[illegible]	[illegible]	—	—	[illegible]	—	—	—	—	Staff supplied by the		
Londonderry and Enniskillen	[illegible]	[illegible]	—	—	—	—	—	—	—	Staff supplied by the		
Londonderry and Lough Swilly	[illegible]	[illegible]	[illegible]	—	[illegible]	—	[illegible]	[illegible]	—	—	—	—
Midland Great Western	[illegible]	[illegible]	[illegible]	[illegible]	[illegible]	[illegible]	[illegible]	[illegible]	—	—	[illegible]	[illegible]
Athenry and Tuam	[illegible]	[illegible]	—	—	[illegible]	[illegible]	—	—	—	Staff supplied by the		
Great Northern and Western	[illegible]	[illegible]	—	—	[illegible]	—	—		…	Staff supplied by the		
Newry and Armagh	[illegible]	[illegible]	[illegible]	[illegible]	—	—	[illegible]	[illegible]	[illegible]	[illegible]	—	—
Newry, Warrenpoint, and Rostrevor	[illegible]	[illegible]	[illegible]	—	[illegible]	[illegible]	[illegible]	—	—	…	…	—
Ulster	[illegible]	[illegible]	[illegible]	[illegible]	[illegible]	[illegible]	[illegible]	[illegible]	—	—	[illegible]	[illegible]
Banbridge, Lisburn, and Belfast	[illegible]	[illegible]	—	—	[illegible]	—	—	—	—	Staff supplied by the		
Portadown, Dungannon, and Omagh	[illegible]	[illegible]	—	—	[illegible]	—	—	—	—	Staff supplied by the		
Waterford and Kilkenny	[illegible]	[illegible]	—	—	[illegible]	[illegible]	—	—	—	—	—	—
Kilkenny Junction	[illegible]	[illegible]	—	—	—	—	—	—	—	Staff supplied by the		
Waterford and Limerick	[illegible]	[illegible]	—	—	[illegible]	[illegible]	[illegible]	[illegible]	[illegible]	[illegible]	—	—
Limerick and Castleconnell	[illegible]	[illegible]	—	—	[illegible]	—	—	—	—	Staff supplied by the		
Limerick and Ennis	[illegible]	[illegible]	—	—	[illegible]	—	—	—	—	Staff supplied by the		
Limerick and Foynes	[illegible]	[illegible]	—	—	[illegible]	—	—	—	—	Staff supplied by the		
[illegible]	[illegible]	—	—	—	[illegible]	—	—	—	—	Staff supplied by the		
Waterford and Tramore	[illegible]	[illegible]	—	—	[illegible]	[illegible]	—	—	—	—	—	—
West Cork	[illegible]	[illegible]	[illegible]	—	[illegible]	—	—	—	—	—	—	—
	[illegible]	[illegible]	15	[illegible]	[illegible]	[illegible]	11	[illegible]	6	[illegible]	4	[illegible]

OFFICERS and MEN employed on the several RAILWAYS completed and carrying TRAFFIC.

Traffic Department.						Engineer's Office.		Locomotive Department.					Permanent Way Department.							
[illegible]	[illegible]	[illegible]	[illegible]	[illegible]	[illegible]	Clerks.	[illegible]	[illegible]	Clerks.	[illegible]	[illegible]	[illegible]	[illegible]	Clerks.	[illegible]	[illegible]	[illegible]	[illegible]	[illegible]	[illegible]
6	13	8	8	65	1	1	—	1	1	30	31	35	1	1	24	61	285	—	289	34
10	1	2	9	40	—	—	—	Work done by Belfast and County Down Company.							5	{ 14 / 8 }	71	4	83	37
[illegible]	65	30	33	330	5	1	3	1	4	[31 / 1]	60	[63 / 9]	8	1	[19 / 7]	301 / 129	924	127	971	38
Belfast and Northern Counties Company.						—	—	—	—	—	—	—	—	—	—	—	15	—	15	39
Belfast and Northern Counties Company.						—	—	—	—	—	—	—	—	—	—	—	7	—	7	40
3	19	8	1	71	—	—	—	1	1	6	19	33	—	—	14	61	299	—	299	41
Cork and Bandon Company.						—	—	—	—	—	—	—	—	—	—	—	8	—	8	[illegible]
—	3	—	9	17	—	1	1	1	—	4	{ 16 / 8 }	3	—	—	6	{ 10 / 8 }	79	4	83	35
—	6	1	2	17	—	—	—	1	1	4	1	4	—	—	11	36	95	—	95	36
3	30	2	7	70	1	1	6	1	—	30	60	36	8	—	9	130	398	—	348	[illegible]
Dublin and Belfast Junction Company.						—	—	—	—	—	—	—	—	—	—	—	7	—	7	[illegible]
1	33	38	15	144	1	—	9	8	8	65	65	36	1	—	30	90	435	—	435	[illegible]
—	8	—	4	70	1	—	—	1	—	8	8	8	—	—	13	30	113	—	113	[illegible]
—	60	26	10	301	1	1	5	1	1	40	14	60	1	1	44	230	741	—	741	[illegible]
Dublin, Wicklow, and Wexford Company.						—	—	—	—	—	—	—	—	—	—	—	10	—	10	43
—	67	74	43	633	1	15	1	2	25	165	445	350	3	6	{ 160 / 18 }	{ 240 / 664 }	[illegible]	712	[illegible]	41
Great Southern and Western Company.						—	—	—	—	—	—	—	—	—	—	—	10	—	10	[illegible]
—	41	35	17	300	1	1	8	5	—	43	130	65	1	8	5	386	1,076	—	1,074	[illegible]
Irish North-western Company.						—	—	—	—	—	—	—	—	—	—	—	10	—	10	44
Irish North-western Company.						—	—	—	—	—	—	—	—	—	—	—	11	—	11	45
Irish North-western Company.						—	—	—	—	—	—	—	—	—	—	—	7	—	7	46
—	3	—	1	12	—	—	—	5	—	7	1	1	—	—	—	30	40	—	40	47
18	30	16	33	453	1	9	8	1	1	76	343	133	1	1	{ 110 / 18 }	{ 163 / 343 }	1,111	383	[illegible]	48
Midland Great Western Company.						—	—	—	—	—	—	—	—	—	—	—	10	—	10	49
Midland Great Western Company.						—	—	—	—	—	—	—	—	—	—	—	15	—	13	50
4	4	—	4	34	—	—	—	1	—	3	16	3	—	—	10	30	143	—	143	51
1	—	1	2	{ 10 / 9 }	—	—	—	—	—	3	{ 4 / 1 }	5	—	—	1	6	45	3	48	52
15	43	67	35	361	1	1	3	1	8	43	131	47	1	1	54	184	790	—	790	53
Ulster Company.						—	—	—	—	—	—	—	—	—	—	—	11	—	11	54
Ulster Company.						—	—	—	—	—	—	—	—	—	—	—	3	—	3	55
3	8	—	4	34	1	—	—	1	8	18	46	75	—	—	30	33	130	1	[illegible]	56
Waterford and Kilkenny Company.						—	—	—	—	—	—	—	—	—	—	—	11	—	11	57
30	30	—	14	163	1	1	1	1	9	33	115	30	1	8	30	{ 130 / 30 }	[illegible]	30	118	58
Waterford and Limerick Company.						—	—	—	—	—	—	—	—	—	—	—	9	—	9	59
Waterford and Limerick Company.						—	—	—	—	—	—	—	—	—	—	—	14	—	14	60
Waterford and Limerick Company.						—	—	—	—	—	—	—	—	—	—	—	17	—	17	61
Waterford and Limerick Company.						—	—	—	—	—	—	—	—	—	—	—	6	—	6	62
—	6	—	1	6	—	—	—	1	—	9	—	6	1	—	8	8	39	—	39	63
—	9	—	8	10	—	—	—	1	—	9	1	9	—	6	5	15	56	—	56	64
54	335	348	276	2,873	13	35	48	35	65	833	1,477	903	14	15	645	2,369	[illegible]	[illegible]	[illegible]	

* Temporary when ballasting the line. † Permanent servants.

TABLE (III.)—NUMBER of LOCOMOTIVE ENGINES and TENDERS, and of CARRIAGE and WAGON STOCK belonging to the several RAILWAY COMPANIES in IRELAND on 30th June 1867.

Number in Appendix and Map.	NAME OF RAILWAY COMPANY.	Locomotive Engines and Tenders. Passenger Engines.	Goods Engines.	Tank Engines.	Total Number of Engines.	Carriage Stock. First Class.	Second Class.	Third Class.	Composite.	Luggage Vans.	Mail and Sorting Vans.	Horse Boxes.	Carriage Trucks.	Saloon Carriages.	Passenger Brake Vans.	Total Number of Carriage Stock.
36	Belfast and County Down	8	3	0	11	8	7	18	14	8	—	5	—	—	—	45
37	Belfast, Holywood, and Bangor	—	—	5	7	10	22	—	5	—	—	—	—	—	5	39
39	Belfast and Northern Counties	19	11	8	38	11	6	33	35	—	—	16	5	—	11	135
31	Cork and Bandon	[illegible]	[illegible]	[illegible]	6	1	—	7	5	—	—	2	1	—	6	[illegible]
42	Cork, Blackrock, and Passage	—	—	5	5	8	1	6	2	—	—	—	—	—	8	15
34	Cork and Macroom	—	—	3	3	8	3	5	—	—	—	—	—	—	8	21
35	Dublin and Belfast Junction	11	6	2	19	7	6	18	20	6	—	10	10	—	—	61
37	Dublin and Drogheda	19	5	2	26	8	10	24	21	—	—	10	17	—	12	[illegible]
38	Dublin and Meath	6	3	—	[illegible]	3	4	10	4	—	—	6	—	—	1	[illegible]
39	Dublin, Wicklow, and Wexford	8	15	27	[illegible]	22	20	50	6	30	8	8	4	—	—	173
41	Great Southern and Western	55	39	11	[illegible]	63	34	82	15	42	18	42	30	1	—	[illegible]
45	Irish North-Western	18	13	2	33	—	6	25	20	15	—	8	4	—	—	[illegible]
47	Londonderry and Lough Swilly	—	—	2	2	—	—	6	2	—	—	—	—	—	1	7
48	Midland Great Western	33	27	4	[illegible]	5	8	56	17	25	—	30	12	1	—	159
51	Newry and Armagh	1	6	1	7	3	2	5	6	—	—	5	1	—	3	[illegible]
52	Newry, Warrenpoint, and Rostrevor	—	—	4	4	[illegible]	1	2	—	1	—	—	—	—	—	10
53	Ulster	23	13	—	36	14	12	31	11	20	5	10	6	—	—	[illegible]
55	Waterford and Kilkenny	3	3	1	7	6	11	4	2	6	—	4	5	—	—	[illegible]
56	Waterford and Limerick	9	14	1	24	7	8	31	12	—	—	9	7	—	2	71
63	Waterford and Tramore	—	—	1	4	6	—	7	1	—	—	—	—	—	1	[illegible]
64	West Cork	—	—	3	3	1	—	4	1	—	—	2	2	—	3	17
	Total	[illegible]	[illegible]	104	461	180	[illegible]	[illegible]	207	150	37	179	116	6	80	1,[illegible]

—continued.

Number in Appendix and on Map.	NAME OF RAILWAY COMPANY.	Total Number of Carriage Stock.	Wagon Stock. Flat or Low-sided.	Open Box.	High-sided.	Covered.	Cattle.	Timber.	Mineral.	Powder Vans.	Ballast.	[illegible]	[illegible]	[illegible]	Goods Brakes.	Total Number of Wagon Stock.	Total Carriage and Wagon Stock.
36	Belfast and County Down	45	53	18	—	38	30	2	—	—	11	—	—	—	5	217	272
37	Belfast, Holywood, and Bangor	39	—	—	—	5	—	—	—	—	—	—	—	—	—	5	[illegible]
39	Belfast and Northern Counties	135	—	[illegible]	—	161	11	16	—	—	20	—	8	—	16	727	[illegible]
31	Cork and Bandon	[illegible]	[illegible]	—	—	[illegible]	—	2	—	—	—	—	—	—	—	[illegible]	66
42	Cork, Blackrock, and Passage	15	—	—	—	—	—	—	—	—	2	—	—	—	—	2	17
34	Cork and Macroom	21	—	10	—	24	—	—	—	—	8	—	—	—	—	42	[illegible]
35	Dublin and Belfast Junction	61	103	5	—	119	—	6	—	—	10	—	—	—	—	[illegible]	[illegible]
37	Dublin and Drogheda	[illegible]	16	—	15	164	47	30	—	—	20	—	—	—	1	[illegible]	[illegible]
38	Dublin and Meath	[illegible]	10	—	—	21	20	—	—	—	—	—	—	—	—	51	[illegible]
39	Dublin, Wicklow, and Wexford	173	140	71	—	163	—	6	111	—	30	31	—	—	—	[illegible]	[illegible]
41	Great Southern and Western	[illegible]	—	[illegible]	—	1,217	70	60	—	—	163	—	—	—	30	1,794	[illegible]
45	Irish North-Western	94	—	140	—	[illegible]	70	6	—	—	30	—	—	—	—	[illegible]	[illegible]
47	Londonderry and Lough Swilly	7	18	—	—	1	4	—	—	—	—	—	—	—	—	[illegible]	[illegible]
48	Midland Great Western	159	23	—	—	[illegible]	[illegible]	30	—	8	40	—	—	—	11	1,1[illegible]	1,[illegible]
51	Newry and Armagh	[illegible]	—	71	—	75	4	10	—	—	5	—	—	—	—	[illegible]	[illegible]
52	Newry, Warrenpoint, and Rostrevor	10	—	—	11	11	4	—	—	—	2	—	—	—	—	[illegible]	73
53	Ulster	[illegible]	143	—	[illegible]	117	40	22	—	—	30	—	—	—	10	[illegible]	[illegible]
55	Waterford and Kilkenny	[illegible]	—	6	—	71	22	6	—	—	30	—	—	—	3	[illegible]	[illegible]
56	Waterford and Limerick	71	—	176	—	[illegible]	[illegible]	[illegible]	—	—	[illegible]	—	—	6	7	[illegible]	[illegible]
63	Waterford and Tramore	[illegible]	4	—	—	—	—	—	—	—	4	—	—	—	—	8	[illegible]
64	West Cork	17	—	10	—	20	—	3	—	—	—	—	—	—	7	[illegible]	51
	Total	1,[illegible]	[illegible]	1,[illegible]	[illegible]	[illegible]	713	[illegible]	118	[illegible]	[illegible]	[illegible]	[illegible]	[illegible]	[illegible]	[illegible]	[illegible]

APPENDIX, PART II.—DOCUMENTS AND RETURNS.

1.—Copy of Treasury Minute, dated the 14th of October 1867, addressed to Railway Companies in Ireland.

My Lords read the Railways (Ireland) Act 1867, 30 & 31 Vict. c. 104. s. 1.

In accordance with the powers therein contained, and in the terms thereof, my Lords are now pleased to direct that every railway company in Ireland do, on the 15th November next, furnish to them a full and true account of all moneys received and paid during a period of three years previous to the date of the last half-yearly account of such company on account of such railway, or of any undertaking connected therewith (distinguishing, if the said railway should be a branch railway, or one worked in common with other railways, the receipts, and giving an estimate of the expenses, on account of the said railway, from those on account of the trunk line, or other railways), by the directors of the company to whom such railway belongs, or by whom the same may be worked; and also an account of the assets and liabilities of such company at the commencement of each of the said three years, and at the expiration of the last of the said three years, such accounts to be duly audited and certified under the hands of two or more of the directors of such company.

Transmit a copy of the above Minute to each of the companies named in the schedule,* and state that it appears to my Lords that their Lordships will carry into effect the intentions of Parliament with the least inconvenience to the companies, and with the greatest advantage to the inquiry, by requiring that the accounts to be rendered in the first instance shall be, as far as possible, the accounts furnished by the directors to their shareholders at each yearly or half-yearly meeting during the three years previous to the date of the last half-yearly account, but including that account; and that any further information required by their Lordships to be given, as directed in this Minute, which may not be contained in such accounts as furnished to the shareholders, shall be given in a supplementary statement accompanying such accounts.

Should these accounts and statements, when so rendered, appear to their Lordships to be insufficient in substance, or inconvenient in form, my Lords will direct a further communication to be made to the directors of the company by whom they have been furnished, so that they may comply in all respects with what their Lordships require.

2.—Copy of Letter from the Secretary of the Treasury to the Secretary of the Commissioners extending the Inquiries of the Commission to Canal Companies.

Treasury Chambers,
Nov. 1, 1867.

Sir,

In reply to your letter of this day's date, I am directed by the Lords Commissioners of Her Majesty's Treasury to request that you will acquaint the Railways (Ireland) Commissioners that my Lords are desirous of having an investigation by them of the accounts of any canal company who are willing to submit them to the Commissioners, and whose undertaking can be considered in any way competing with any railway company's line in the transmission of goods or passengers, and also an examination of the works of such canal company should like consent be given.

I am, Sir,
Your obedient Servant,
(Signed) George Ward Hunt.

W. N. Hancock, Esq., LL.D.

3.—Copy of Letter from the Secretary of the Treasury to the Commissioners, dated the 4th of April 1868, directing particulars to be furnished in the Report, with respect to agreements for limiting the charges for traffic.

Treasury Chambers,
April 4, 1868.

Gentlemen,

I am directed by the Lords Commissioners of Her Majesty's Treasury to inform you that the Marquis of Clanricarde lately stated in the House of Lords, that the Irish railway companies had entered into agreements among themselves and with canal companies regulating the tariff to be charged for the transport of goods; that in consequence goods are now conveyed at higher rates than were paid before the construction of railways, and that the public has no means of checking or controlling the monopolies thus created.

It appears to my Lords that it would be very desirable to take steps for ascertaining, as far as may be practicable, whether the agreements in force between the companies in question are of a nature to justify the charges put forward by Lord Clanricarde, and I am therefore to instruct you to include in your forthcoming report the particulars of all such agreements with respect to limiting the charges for traffic, the accommodation to the public, or the assistance to be given to railway extensions or new railways in cases where there was a competition between routes of communication for the traffic of any district or place.

I am, Gentlemen,
Your obedient Servant,
(Signed) G. Sclater Booth.

The Commissioners of Inquiry
into Irish Railways,
8, Victoria Street.

4.—Return of the Particulars of all Agreements that Irish Railway Companies have entered into among themselves or with Canal Companies with respect to limiting the Charges for Traffic, the Accommodation to the Public, or the Assistance to be given to Railway Extensions or new Railways in cases where there was a competition between routes of communication for the traffic of any district or place.

I.—*Abstract of Award of Messrs. Watkin and Hawkshaw of the 8th of February 1850, applicable to the Midland Great Western and Great Southern and Western Railway Companies.*

Application to be made to Parliament for a lease of the Royal Canal for 250,000*l.*, half to each company, to be worked by a joint committee. Canal to be worked under agreement in the meantime.

Award accompanied by a map upon which a line is drawn, thus:—

From Dublin west through Edenderry to Athlone; thence following the course of the Shannon to the

* The schedule included 30 companies. The Minute was afterwards extended to all the companies included in the report, 36 in all.

middle of Lough Derg; thence west through Ennis to a point between Kilrush and Kilkee, terminating at the mouth of the Shannon, equidistant between Loop Head and Kerry Head.

North, north-west, and north-east of this line to be considered the district of the Midland Great Western Company. South, south-east, and south-west that of the Great Southern and Western Company.

Midland Great Western to assign to the Great Southern and Western their share interest in the Castleconnell Railway Company.

Neither company shall make, promote, assist, or encourage any lines of railway or branch canal to any point beyond the boundary line now awarded or intended to join a portion of a line in contravention of such boundary, nor in the event of any lines being made by other parties shall either of the companies directly or indirectly enter into any alliance or arrangement to or from any point which can fairly be considered as within the scope and intention of this award.

Traffic between Ennis and Dublin to be common to both, and equal fares and rates by each, and in case of the opening of the Ennis and Athenry Railway the traffic from Ennis shall be equally divided.

Traffic between Dublin and Athlone to be divided thus:—

From 1860 to 1866.

—	Passengers.	Goods and Cattle.
Midland Great Western	45 per cent.	55 per cent.
Great Southern and Western	55 " "	45 " "

From 1866 to 1870 inclusive and thereafter in perpetuity.

—	Passengers.	Goods and Cattle.
Midland Great Western	50 per cent.	55 per cent.
Great Southern and Western	50 " "	45 " "

30 per cent. allowed for working. Neither company to evade these provisions by re-booking, charging lower proportionate rates at consignment at intermediate places, or by bonuses, drawbacks, undue credits, or the like.

Dublin and Clara traffic to be put into a common fund, equal fares and rates to be charged by both companies. To be divided as under:—

—	Passengers.	Goods and Cattle.
For first five years after [illegible] *—*		
Midland Great Western	37 per cent.	45 per cent.
Great Southern and Western	63 " "	55 " "
After first five years in perpetuity —		
Midland Great Western	40 " "	45 " "
Great Southern and Western	60 " "	55 " "

Provisions of award not to be evaded. *See* Dublin and Athlone *supra*.

Companies shall interchange through rates and fares between non-competitive points. Local traffic not to be interfered with.

Steamers to be worked on the Shannon between Athlone and Killaloe (after the purchase of the canal) under the superintendence of the Joint Committee. Companies to book through from all towns and places on their line to towns and places on the Shannon. Steamboats, &c., required for and now used by Midland Great Western shall, after purchase of canal, be worked by the Joint Committee, who shall fix the payment to be allowed to Midland Great Western Company for use and maintenance of plant, and settle the proportion of profit or loss to be borne by each company.

Award subject to a further award to be made on or before 1st October next.

II.—*Abstract of Final Award dated* [illegible] *September 18*[illegible]*, applicable to Midland Great Western and Great Southern and Western Railway Companies.*

Refers to previous award and recites its provisions.

States that the railway companies did apply to Parliament for the purchase of the Grand Canal, but the House of Lords decided on certain toll clauses proposed by the Board of Works, Ireland, which were considered to be unremunerative, and the bill was withdrawn.

Companies to observe the provisions of the previous award, notwithstanding the failure of the Grand Canal Leasing Bill, which they are capable of performing irrespective of the canal.

Map or plan to be observed.

So much of award confirmed as prohibits the making or assisting in the formation of or alliance with any lines of railway by either of the said companies in the district assigned to the other of them.

Transfer of Castleconnell shares also confirmed.

Ennis, Athlone, Clara traffic divisions also confirmed.

Neither company to enter into treaty for the lease or purchase of the Grand Canal without the consent of the other company, but either may enter into working arrangements with the canal for traffic affected by canal.

As companies have failed to obtain the canal they shall not be required to work the steamboat traffic on the Shannon in manner settled by former award; but the steamboats, barges, vessels, and other plant belonging to the Midland Great Western Company, and hitherto used by that company in working the Shannon traffic shall be valued* by Mr. Martin Simonds of Hull, and the Great Southern and Western Company shall pay to the Midland Great Western Company 55 per cent. of such certified value, and become joint owners of such plant; plant to be used jointly or otherwise dealt with from time to time as the said two companies may agree.

Disputes to be settled by arbitration.

III.—*Abstract of an Agreement between Great Southern and Western, Waterford and Limerick, Cork and Limerick, and London and North-western Railway Companies, Waterford and Steam Ship Company, Cork and Liverpool Steam Ship Company, City of Dublin Steam Packet Company.*

Agreement to take effect from 1st June 1864 for 18 months, and afterwards terminable by three months' notice.

Provides for through rates on traffic arising at or destined for places on these lines by way of Cork, Waterford, Dublin and Liverpool, and Dublin and Holyhead, and for the division thereof.

Rates to be the same by all routes, and not to be altered except by consent.

Traffic to and from Limerick, Limerick Junction, and Tipperary with Liverpool, and stations in England north of Birmingham inclusive, to form a common fund. The Cork route having an interest in Limerick traffic only.

Unconsigned traffic from the Great Southern and Western Company line to be given exclusively to the City of Dublin Company, and for places common to that company and the London and North-western Company to be equally divided between them. The City of Dublin Company booking such traffic and all other unconsigned traffic to the London and North-

* Note.—By an award dated 25th December 1865, Mr. Simonds valued the plant at £5,000

western Company at Liverpool. The Cork and Waterford Steam Companies to hand to London and North-western Company at Liverpool all traffic not otherwise specially consigned. In like manner the City of Dublin Company and the London and North-western Company shall deliver to the Great Southern and Western Company all unconsigned traffic for their district.

No allowance, privilege, or bonus to be given to induce goods to be sent by any route.

The Waterford and Limerick and the Cork and Limerick Direct Railway Companies undertake that all traffic consigned through them by other routes than *via* Liverpool or Holyhead between places in England and the places in Ireland, to which this agreement refers, shall not be booked through, and shall be charged the ordinary local rates.

IV.—Abstract of Agreement between the Glasgow and Londonderry Steam Packet Company, Belfast and Northern Counties, Londonderry and Coleraine, Ulster, Portadown, Dungannon, and Omagh, and Irish North-western Railway Companies.

To pay John Cameron, of Glasgow, acting for the Steam Packet Company, for four years, from 1st December 1858, the sum of 400*l.* a year, in consideration of his discontinuing the calling of his steam-packets at the port of Belfast, either on the outward or return voyage to or from Morecambe to Londonderry for four years from the above date.

V.—Abstract of Agreement between the City of Dublin Steam Packet Company, and the Dublin and Drogheda, Dublin and Belfast Junction, and Ulster Railway Companies for traffic between Dublin and Belfast.

Under an award by Mr. E. Marion, of London, dated 16th January 1858.

To apply for two years from date and afterwards subject to three months notice.

The sailings of the steamboats to be reduced to one trip each way between Dublin and Belfast per week.

The companies to pay to the steamboat company for passenger traffic 1,000*l.* per annum clear, and the receipts of the steamboat company to be handed over to the railway companies without deduction.

The goods traffic to be divided one half to the steamboat company, and one half to the railway companies, 25 per cent. to be allowed to the company carrying the stream. Railway companies have power to fix the fares.

VI.—Abstract of Agreement between the Midland Great Western Railway Company, and the Grand Canal Company.

The traffic to and from Dublin and Lanesboro', Carrick on Shannon, and all places above Athlone, and all traffic conveyed to Athlone by any other means than the Shannon below Athlone to be given to the Midland Great Western Company.

The river trade between Limerick and Carrick on Shannon and intermediate places to be considered as belonging to the Grand Canal.

Provides for differential rates in favour of canal. The Midland Company fixing rate from Dublin to Woodlawn station proportionately higher than the rates to Ballinasloe.

Dated, 2nd January 1854.

The Great Southern and Western Company to cease plying boats on the Shannon during the continuance of this agreement.

VII.—Abstract of award of Captain Heath, dated 15th October 1861, between the Irish North-western and the Ulster Railway Companies.

For the prevention of undue competition between the Ulster Company as lessees of the Portadown, Dungannon, and Omagh Railway and the Irish North-western Company as lessees of the Londonderry and Enniskillen Railway for traffic between Omagh and Londonderry and Omagh and Belfast.

That the Irish North-western Company shall book through by their Enniskillen route traffic arriving at stations between Londonderry and Omagh, and destined for places to which they have through booking south of Dundalk as far as Dublin, based on the mileage by the Portadown route.

The Portadown route being 18 miles shorter than the Enniskillen route.

That the public be left to choose either route, and trains be arranged to accommodate them by either route.

That the Irish North-western Company take on by their first train the traffic by the Portadown route passing southward, but their express trains be not required to stop more than five minutes, and ordinary trains more than ten minutes.

That carriages and waggons be taken through by the Irish North-western Company, providing they contain a certain number of passengers or weight of goods.

Similar clauses for dealing with traffic southward by the Ulster Company.

The same mileage rates charged by the Irish North-western for passengers and goods between Omagh and Londonderry shall be the mileage rates charged by the company using the line *vid* Portadown to Belfast, except by mutual consent. Each company to book through between Londonderry *vid* Omagh, Portadown, and Belfast and intermediate places at such rates as, having reference to the rates of the Northern Counties Railway, might be agreed on.

That this award shall not be evaded by either company by making private arrangements with foreign companies, steam packet companies, or others. Local rates between Omagh and Belfast and Omagh and Londonderry to be so fixed as not to encroach upon or nullify the mileage rate arrangement already awarded.

VIII.—Abstract of Agreement between the Midland Great Western Company and the Athenry and Tuam Company. Dated April 23, 1860.

The Athenry and Tuam Company shall not during the period of this agreement extend or apply for powers to extend their line of railway beyond Tuam to or towards or in the direction of Castlebar, Westport, or Ballina, nor assist or encourage others to do so, without the consent in writing of the Midland Great Western Company.

This agreement is set out in the Schedule of the Company's Leasing Act of 1860 (Stat. 23rd and 24th Vict. cap. 162).

IX.—Abstract of an Agreement, dated 1st August 1859, between the Midland Great Western, and the Great Southern and Western Companies.

Provides for through booking between all stations on the Great Southern and Western line and the Midland line. The fares to be the sum of the two companies rates.

No rates from Tuam or from any station on the Athenry and Tuam line to any station on the Midland line or vice versa to be fixed at a lower mileage rate than the joint rates fixed as above.

This agreement was approved by the Board of Trade on the 16th of August 1859.

1. Return of Advances made by the Public Works Loan Commissioners to Railway Companies in Ireland [illegible] made, Rate of Interest, Principal repaid, Principal unpaid, Interest in arrear,

Name of Railway.		Total Advances.	Date of Security.	Period for which the Loan was made.	Rate of Interest.
Dublin and Drogheda:—	£	£			
1st loan—1st advance	[illegible]		18th Dec [illegible]	20 years - - -	5 per cent., reduced to 4 per cent.
2nd "	10,[illegible]		14th July [illegible]	" - - -	"
3rd "	1[illegible]		[illegible] Aug "	" - - -	"
4th "	14,[illegible]		22 Sept "	" - - -	"
5th "	10,[illegible]		1st Dec "	20 years, but wholly repaid with interest in two years from date of advance	5 per cent.
6th "	1[illegible]		1st March [illegible]		"
7th "	15,000		31st May "		"
2nd loan—1st "	[illegible]		14th Sept [illegible]	20 years - - -	5 per cent., reduced to 4 per cent.
2nd "	[illegible]	[illegible]	[illegible] Feb [illegible]	" - - -	"
Irish North-Western:—					
1st advance	[illegible]		[illegible] Oct [illegible]	20 years, extended to 30 years by Treasury Warrant.	4 per cent.
2nd "	70,[illegible]		7th July [illegible]	" [illegible] "	"
3rd "	[illegible]		7th Sept [illegible]	" [illegible] "	"
4th "	[illegible]		2nd May [illegible]	" [illegible] "	"
5th "	[illegible]	[illegible]	1st July [illegible]	" [illegible] "	"
Waterford and Kilkenny:—					
1st loan—1st advance	[illegible]		27th Aug [illegible]	Each of the sums was made repayable in 20 years from date of advance, but by Treasury Warrant of [illegible] June [illegible], the balances unpaid were consolidated, and made repayable, with interest at [illegible] per cent. in [illegible] years from [illegible] July [illegible].	5 per cent., reduced to 4 per cent., and subsequently to [illegible] per cent.
2nd "	[illegible]		[illegible] Nov "		
3rd "	[illegible]		[illegible] Aug [illegible]		
4th "	[illegible]		31st Oct [illegible]		
2nd loan—1st "	[illegible]		2nd April [illegible]		
2nd "	[illegible]		[illegible] Sept "		
3rd "	[illegible]		[illegible] Jan [illegible]		
4th "	[illegible]	[illegible]	[illegible] July "		
[illegible] Southern and Western:—					
1st advance	[illegible]		31st Aug [illegible]	20 years, wholly repaid in [illegible]	5 per cent. reduced to 4 per cent.
2nd "	[illegible]		5th Nov. "	" " "	"
3rd "	[illegible]		[illegible] April [illegible]	" " [illegible]	"
4th "	[illegible]		[illegible] Sept "	" " "	"
5th "	[illegible]	[illegible]	[illegible] Jan [illegible]	" " "	"
Midland Great Western (of Ireland):—					
1st advance	[illegible]		[illegible] Oct [illegible]	[illegible] years - -	[illegible] per cent., half yearly
2nd "	[illegible]		[illegible] Sept [illegible]	" - -	"
3rd "	[illegible]		[illegible] Feb [illegible]	" - -	"
4th "	[illegible]		[illegible] June "	" - -	"
5th "	[illegible]		2nd [illegible] "	" - -	"
6th "	[illegible]	[illegible]	[illegible] April [illegible]	" - -	"

showing as to each the Name of the Railway, Total Advances, Date of Security, Period for which the Loan was ... and Costs paid to the Solicitor of the Commissioners up to the 31st of January 1856.

Principal repaid.	Total repaid by each Railway.	Principal unrepaid.	Total unrepaid by each Railway.	Interest in Arrear.	Total Interest due by each Railway.	Costs paid to Solicitor.	Total Costs paid by each Railway.
£ s. d.	£ s. d.	£ s. d.	£ s. d.	£ s. d.	£ s. d.	£ s. d.	£ s. d.
[illegible] 0 0						1[illegible] 7 6	
[illegible] 0 0						79 0 10	
[illegible] 0 0						82 19 9	
[illegible] 0 0						82 19 6	
[illegible] 0 0						36 16 8	
[illegible] 0 0						405 9 8	
[illegible] 0 0						36 [illegible] 11	
[illegible] 0 0						387 9 6	
16,736 17 3		1,255 7 9				108 9 4	
	136,706 19 3		1,275 7 9				1,[illegible] 8 7
9,[illegible] 15 8		10,[illegible] 5 7		4[illegible] 16 5		5[illegible] 16 7	
8,974 7 6		11,350 [illegible] 6				837 0 7	
7,386 0 5		12,665 19 7		381 13 8		[illegible] 10 11	
[illegible] 10 7		11,160 0 6				323 13 9	
4,[illegible] 4 4		15,160 16 6				573 0 6	
	36,[illegible] 9 0		60,666 11 9		[illegible]		1,[illegible] 16 6
						614 10 9	
						79 15 0	
						483 18 10	
79,117 6 10		13,[illegible] 11 8				326 19 8	
	79,117 6 10		63,[illegible] 11 7			605 19 8	
						389 10 8	
						[illegible] 9 11	
						[illegible] 4 4	
							1,[illegible] 9 1
125,000 0 0						3[illegible] 9 6	
132,000 0 0						139 4 0	
124,000 0 0						642 1 7	
108,000 0 0						360 0 4	
75,000 0 0						308 3 0	
	5[illegible],000 0 0						1,[illegible] 6 1
13,718 8 8		60,206 16 4				878 11 0	
11,747 8 0		55,917 16 0				253 0 6	
14,[illegible] 0 0		63,187 11 4				867 0 8	
9,814 17 0		70,651 8 0				476 8 7	
6,[illegible] 11 6		65,496 0 5				480 0 11	
4,[illegible] 11 8		65,684 0 0				367 10 1	
	6[illegible] 17 10		3[illegible],734 8 9				[illegible] 14 8
4,160 0 0		631 0 0				171 10 8	
4,160 0 0		631 0 0				112 8 7	
3,328 0 0		664 0 0				592 7 7	
1,664 0 0		444 0 0				143 11 8	
	13,[illegible] 0 0		2,770 0 0				760 9 10
8,[illegible] 0 0		7,[illegible] 0 0		48 3 11		758 1 11	
7,500 0 0		8,[illegible] 0 0		116 0 0		173 18 9	
7,[illegible] 10 0		8,[illegible] 4 0		189 11 8		483 16 8	
8,[illegible] 0 0		1,[illegible] 13 0		82 9 11		148 3 1	
	3[illegible] 4 0		4,[illegible] 14 0		4[illegible] 10 9		1,[illegible] 14 0
7,000 0 0		2,000 0 0				873 10 8	
7,[illegible] 0 0		2,000 0 0				140 17 1	
7,000 0 0		2,000 0 0				[illegible] 4 8	
4,000 0 0		2,100 0 0				[illegible] 6 8	
	26,[illegible] 0 0		8,[illegible] 0 0				[illegible] 7 4
25,000 0 0						645 0 6	
25,000 0 0						843 1 5	
25,000 0 0						[illegible] 6 11	
	7[illegible],000 0 0						7[illegible] 11 6

Name of Railway.		Total Advances.	Date of Advance.	Period for which the Loan was made.	Rate of Interest.
Londonderry and Coleraine:—	£	£			
1st advance	14,000		6th July 18[illegible]	15 years; wholly repaid in 1[illegible]	5 per cent., reduced to 4 per cent.
2nd "	[illegible]		14th Nov. "		
3rd "	14,000		2nd May 18[illegible]		
4th "	[illegible]	70,000	19th July "		
Waterford and Limerick:—				Each of these advances was made repayable in 20 years from date of advance, but by Treasury Warrant of [illegible] August 18[illegible], the balance remaining unpaid was consolidated, and made repayable, with interest at [illegible] per cent., in [illegible] years from 1[illegible] May 18[illegible].	5 per cent., reduced to 4 per cent., and subsequently to 3½ per cent.
1st "	[illegible]		14th April 18[illegible]		
2nd "	[illegible]		31st Oct. "		
3rd "	[illegible]		14th April 18[illegible]		
4th "	[illegible]		10th Aug. "		
5th "	[illegible]		[illegible] Dec. "		
6th "	[illegible]	1[illegible]	[illegible] July 18[illegible]		
[illegible] and [illegible]:—					
1st "	[illegible]		[illegible] April 18[illegible]	"	"
2nd "	[illegible]		1[illegible] July "		
3rd "	[illegible]	[illegible]	[illegible] Dec. "		
[illegible] and [illegible]:—					
1st "	[illegible]		[illegible] Nov. 18[illegible]	"	"
2nd "	[illegible]		[illegible] March 18[illegible]		
3rd "	[illegible]	[illegible]	[illegible] May "		
Killarney Junction:—					
1st advance	[illegible]		[illegible] Feb. 18[illegible]	[illegible] years	5 per cent., reduced to 4 per cent.
2nd "	[illegible]		[illegible] Nov. "	"	"
3rd "	[illegible]		[illegible] April 18[illegible]	"	"
4th "	[illegible]	1[illegible]	[illegible] Aug. "	"	"
Londonderry and Enniskillen:—					
1st advance	1[illegible]		[illegible] Feb. 18[illegible]	1[illegible] years, extended to [illegible] years	"
2nd "	[illegible]		[illegible] May "	"	"
3rd "	[illegible]		[illegible] Nov. "	"	"
4th "	[illegible]	[illegible]	[illegible] Dec. "	"	"
Dublin and Wicklow:—					
1st advance	[illegible]		[illegible] Dec. 18[illegible]	[illegible] years	"
2nd "	[illegible]		1st May 18[illegible]	"	"
3rd "	[illegible]		[illegible] July "	"	"
4th "	[illegible]	1[illegible]	[illegible] March 18[illegible]	"	"
Portadown, Dungannon, and Omagh Junction:—					
1st advance	[illegible]		[illegible] June 18[illegible]	[illegible] years	
2nd "	[illegible]		1[illegible] Oct. "	"	
3rd "	[illegible]	[illegible]	[illegible] July 18[illegible]	"	
Tralee and Killarney:—					
1st advance	[illegible]		[illegible] Nov. 18[illegible]	[illegible] years	
2nd "	[illegible]		1[illegible] April 18[illegible]	"	
3rd "	[illegible]	[illegible]	[illegible] July "	"	
Great Southern and Western (of Ireland):—					
1st loan—1st advance	[illegible]		[illegible] June 18[illegible]	[illegible] years, extended to [illegible] years	"
2nd "	[illegible]		2nd July "	"	"
3rd "	[illegible]		3rd Jan. 18[illegible]	"	"
4th "	[illegible]		[illegible] Aug. "	"	"
2nd loan	[illegible]		[illegible] July 18[illegible]	"	"
3rd loan	[illegible]	1[illegible]	17th Sept. 18[illegible]	"	"
Dublin, Wicklow, and Wexford:—					
1st loan—1st advance	[illegible]		[illegible] Aug. 18[illegible]	[illegible] years	[illegible] per cent.
2nd "	[illegible]		[illegible] April 18[illegible]	"	"
3rd "	[illegible]		17th Sept. "	"	"
2nd loan	[illegible]	1[illegible]	[illegible] Sept. 18[illegible]	"	"
Finn Valley:—					
1st advance	[illegible]		[illegible] Sept. 18[illegible]	[illegible] years	"
2nd "	[illegible]	[illegible]	[illegible] Jan. 18[illegible]	"	"
Londonderry and Lough Swilly:—					
1st advance	[illegible]		1[illegible] Dec. 18[illegible]	15 years	"
2nd "	[illegible]	1[illegible]	[illegible] Oct. 18[illegible]	"	"
[illegible] and [illegible] Bridge:—					
1st advance	[illegible]		31st Jan. 18[illegible]	[illegible] years	"
2nd "	[illegible]	1[illegible]	[illegible] Aug. "	"	"
Athenry and Ennis Junction:—					
1st advance	[illegible]	[illegible]	17th May 18[illegible]	[illegible] years	"
		[illegible]			

Principal unpaid.	Total unpaid by each Railway.	Principal unpaid.	Total unpaid by each Railway.	Interest in Arrear.	Total Interest due by each Railway.	Costs paid to Solicitors.	Total Costs paid by each Railway.
£ s. d.	£ s. d.	£ s. d.	£ s. d.	£ s. d.	£ s. d.	£ s. d.	£ s. d.
[illegible]	[illegible]	[illegible]	[illegible]	[illegible]	[illegible]	[illegible]	[illegible]

Name of Railway.	Total Advance.	Date of Security.	Period for which the Loan was made.	Rate of Interest.
Advances under "The Railway Companies (Ireland) Temporary Advances Act,"—				
*Dublin, Wicklow, and Wexford:—	£			
1st advance [illegible]	-	[illegible] Oct. [illegible]	[illegible] years	[illegible] per cent.
2nd " [illegible]	[illegible]	[illegible] April 1867	"	"
*Newry, Warrenpoint, and Rostrevor	[illegible]	[illegible] Nov 1866	"	"
*Waterford and Kilkenny	14,[illegible]	[illegible] Nov 1866	"	"
*Athenry and Tuam	[illegible]	7th Nov. 1866	"	"
Dublin and Meath: 1st advance	[illegible]	[illegible] Jan. 1867	"	"
*Rathkeale and Newcastle	[illegible]	31st Dec 1866	"	"
Waterford and Limerick:—				
1st loan 14,120	-	[illegible] June 1867	"	"
2nd " [illegible]	[illegible]	15th July 1867	"	"
	[illegible]			

* Time extended to 11th July [illegible] by Treasury Letter of [illegible] October 1867.

Public Works Loan Office,
8, Bank Buildings, E.C.
3rd January 1868.

6.—Return* of all Advances made by the Commissioners of Public Works to Railways in Ireland, for which such Loan was made, the Rate of Interest charged, the Amount of Principal now paid off of the Board of Works by the Company applying for such Loans, with Totals in the Case of each.

Name of Company.	Amount Advanced. £ s. d.	[illegible] £ s. d.	Year advanced.	Period for which the Loan was made.
Dublin and Kingstown	[illegible] 0 0	-	[illegible]	[illegible] years
Do. do.	[illegible] 0 0	-	[illegible]	[illegible] years
Do. do. (Dalkey Branch)	[illegible] 0 0	-	[illegible]	[illegible] years
		[illegible] 0 0	-	-
Ulster Railway	[illegible] 0 0	[illegible] 0 0	[illegible]	[illegible] years
Waterford and Limerick†	[illegible] 13 6	[illegible] 13 6	[illegible]-7	-
		[illegible] 13 6	-	-

* Reprinted from Parliamentary Paper, [illegible], No. [illegible]

† This sum was advanced in [illegible] out of the Labour Rate Fund, Act 9 & 10 Vict. c. 107, on the security of the [illegible]

Office of Public Works, Dublin, 5 March 1867.

7.—Return showing the Amount of Railway Deposits standing in the Name of the Accountant-General of the Court of Chancery, Ireland, on the 1st October 1867:—

—	Cash. £ s. d.	Government New 3 per cent. Stock. £ s. d.
[illegible] and [illegible] Railway	[illegible] 0 0	—
[illegible], [illegible], and [illegible]	[illegible] 0 1	[illegible] 0 0
Dublin Metropolitan Railway	[illegible] 1 6	[illegible] 15 6
Dublin Trunk Connecting (Deposits)	[illegible] 15 9	[illegible] 0 0 Exchequer bills.
Waterford, Dungarvan, and Lismore	[illegible] 3 9	[illegible] 0 3
Dublin, Rathdrum, and [illegible]	—	[illegible] 9 8
Waterford and Passage Railway and Ferry	[illegible] 0 [illegible]	—
Dublin, [illegible], and [illegible]	—	[illegible] 0 0 Consols.
[illegible] and [illegible]	[illegible] 0 0	—

Totals		£ s. d.
Cash	-	[illegible] 15 9
Government New 3 per cent. Stock	-	[illegible] 16 1
Government 3 per cent. Consols	-	[illegible] 0 [illegible]
Exchequer bills	-	[illegible] 0 0
		[illegible] 15 6

(Signed) [illegible] P. [illegible], Accountant-General.

W. Neilson Hancock, Esq.,
Secretary Railways (Ireland) Commission,
3, Victoria Street, Westminster.

Principal repaid.	Total repaid by each Railway.	Principal unpaid.	Total unpaid by each Railway.	Interest in Arrear.	Total Interest due by each Railway.	Costs paid to Solicitor.	Total Costs paid by each Railway.
£ s. d.	£ s. d.	£ s. d.	£ s. d.	£ s. d.	£ s. d.	£ s. d.	£ s. d.
- - -	- - -	[illegible] 0 0				[illegible] 16 0	
- - -	- - -	15,[illegible] 0 0				[illegible] 0 0	
			87,[illegible] 0 0				[illegible] 10 0
- - -	- - -	[illegible] 0 0				[illegible] 10 0	
			[illegible] 0 0				[illegible]
- - -	- - -	13,776 0 0				[illegible] 14 0	
			13,776 0 0				[illegible] 10 0
- - -	- - -	[illegible] 0 0				[illegible] 0 4	
			[illegible] 0 0				[illegible] 0 4
- - -	- - -	15,[illegible] 0 0				87 7 0	
			15,[illegible] 0 0				87 7 0
- - -	- - -	16,[illegible] 0 0				[illegible] 0 0	
			16,[illegible] 0 0				[illegible] 0 0
- - -	- - -	14,[illegible] 0 0				87 6 4	
- - -	- - -	3,[illegible] 0 0				8 6 7	
			[illegible] 0 0				[illegible] 12 0
- - -	1,117,416 17 6		[illegible] 0 0		13,000 13 10		[illegible] 17 0

(Signed) W. W. W[illegible],
Secretary.

---

specifying the Name of the Company, the Amount advanced and the Year in which advanced, the Period the Amount remaining due, the Amount of Interest now due, and the Cost paid in each case to the Solicitor Railway, and also Gross Totals.

Rate of Interest.	Amount of Principal paid off.		Amount remaining due. Principal.	Amount remaining due. Interest.	Cost paid to Solicitor of Board of Works.
	£ s. d.	£ s. d.	£ s. d.	£ s. d.	£ s. d.
[illegible] per cent. -	7[illegible] 0 0				
[illegible] per cent. -	[illegible] 0 0				
[illegible] per cent. -	[illegible] 0 0				
- - -		[illegible] 0 0	- - -	- - -	[illegible] 10 6
[illegible] per cent. -	- - -	[illegible] 0 0	- - -	- - -	[illegible] 0 0
[illegible] per cent. -	- - -	[illegible] 13 6	—	—	—
- - -	- - -	[illegible] 13 6	- - -	- - -	[illegible] 19 4

[illegible] of the Baronies of Clanwilliam, [illegible] and [illegible] East, and [illegible] and [illegible] West, in the County of Tipperary.

W. B. S[illegible], A[illegible].

RAILWAYS (IRELAND) COMMISSION.

APPENDIX, PART III., CLASS I.—LINES AUTHORIZED BUT NOT COMMENCED.

No. in Appendix and on Map. Main Lines.	Branches and Extensions.	RAILWAYS, CLASS I.—LINES AUTHORIZED BUT NOT COMMENCED.	Length of Line authorized. Miles.	Miles.	Appendix Page.
		1st.—Lines not commenced.			
1.		Bray and Enniskerry	3¾		42
2.		Central Ireland (Maryborough to Mullingar)	30		43
3.		Clonmel, Lismore, and Dungarvan (main line)	30		44
	3 a.	Dungarvan branch of the Clonmel, Lismore, and Dungarvan			
4.		Dublin Metropolitan (in the City of Dublin)	3½		44
5.		Dublin, Rathmines, Rathgar, Roundtown, Rathfarnham, and Rathcoole (Dublin to Poulaphouca Bridge)	24		46
6.		Dundalk and Greenore (Co. Louth)	13		47
7.		Limerick, and North Kerry (Newcastle to Listowel)	22		48
8.		Navan and Kingscourt	20		49
9.		Sligo and Ballaghaderreen (Kilfree Junction to Ballaghaderreen)	9½		50
10.		Waterford, Lismore, and Fermoy (Waterford to Dungarvan, and Lismore to Fermoy)	43¾		51
11.		Waterford and Passage (Ballytruckle Junction to River Suir, at Passage)	9½		52
12.		Waterford and Wexford (Ballyhack to Wexford)	43¼		53
	12 a.	Greenore (Co. Wexford) branch of the Waterford and Wexford			
		Length of lines not commenced		254¼	
		2nd.—Branches and Extensions not commenced belonging to lines (included in Class II.) commenced but not completed.			
	31 a.	Meelick Extension of the Midland Counties, &c. Railway (Banagher to Meelick)	5¼		60
	34 a.	Colliery Branches of the Southern (Graystown Junction to the Collieries)	8½		65
	35 a.	Waterford Extension (Ballywilliam to Waterford) } of Waterford, New Ross, and Wexford	19		67
	35 b.	Ballyhoge Branch (Ballywilliam to Ballyhoge) } of Waterford, New Ross, and Wexford	14½		67
		Length of branches and extensions connected with railways in Class II., but not commenced		48¾	
		3rd.—Branches and Extensions not commenced belonging to lines (included in Class III.) completed and carrying traffic.			
	39 c.	Kingstown connecting branch of the Dublin, Wicklow, and Wexford	2		94
	44 a.	Sligo Extension of the Enniskillen, Bundoran, and Sligo	22		111
	60 b.	Ballina Extension } of the Great Northern and Western	9½		124
	50 c.	Westport Quay Extension } of the Great Northern and Western	1½		124
		Length of branches and extensions connected with railways in Class III., but not commenced		35	
		Total mileage authorized but not commenced		338¼	

1. THE BRAY AND ENNISKERRY RAILWAY.

LENGTH OF AUTHORIZED LINE.

	Miles.
BRAY to ENNISKERRY	3¾

CAPITAL.

Capital authorised :—

	£
Shares	36,000
Borrowing Powers	12,000
Total	£48,000

No capital has been raised, and no particulars have been ascertained of the cost of obtaining the Act.

This railway will, if made, connect Enniskerry with the Dublin, Wicklow, and Wexford line at Bray.

THE LINE.

The line was authorized in 1866.

No land has been taken; the compulsory powers for acquiring it will expire on the 6th August 1868; and no bill has been applied for in the present session for extending the time. The powers for completing the works will expire on the 6th August 1869.

RELATIONS OF THE BRAY AND ENNISKERRY WITH OTHER RAILWAY COMPANIES.

Name of Railway Company.	Point of Junction.	Page of Report.
The Dublin, Wicklow, and Wexford	Bray	94

The Dublin, Wicklow, and Wexford Railway.

The Dublin, Wicklow, and Wexford Company is empowered to subscribe 15,000*l.* to the undertaking.

---

2. THE CENTRAL IRELAND RAILWAYS (promoted by the Waterford and Kilkenny and the Kilkenny Junction Railway Companies).

MARYBOROUGH to MULLINGAR.

LENGTH OF AUTHORIZED LINE.

MARYBOROUGH to MULLINGAR, including connecting lines at Maryborough and Geashill - 36 miles.

CAPITAL.

Capital authorized :—

	£
Shares—	
To be found by the Waterford and Kilkenny Company	110,000
" " Kilkenny Junction Company	110,000
Borrowing Powers—	
To be exercised by the Waterford and Kilkenny Company	36,600
" " Kilkenny Junction Company	36,600
Total	£293,200

No capital has been raised. The expenses of the Act (for which the promoting Companies are jointly liable) amount to 6,924*l.* 11*s.* 2*d.*

This railway, if made, will be an extension of the line of the Kilkenny Junction from Maryborough to the Athlone branch of the Great Southern and Western Railway at Geashill, and thence to the Midland Great Western Railway at Mullingar.

THE LINE.

The line was authorized in 1866, with the usual limit of three years for compulsory purchase of lands, and five years for the completion of the works. No land has yet been taken.

RELATIONS OF THE CENTRAL IRELAND RAILWAYS WITH OTHER RAILWAY COMPANIES.

The lines in connexion with the Central Ireland Railways are stated in the following table :—

Name of Railway Company.	Point of Junction.	Page of Report.
The Great Southern and Western	At Maryborough and at Geashill	100
The Midland Great Western	Near Mullingar	118

The Great Southern and Western Railway.

The line of the Central Ireland crosses under the Great Southern and Western main line near Maryborough, and over the Athlone branch near Geashill, with connecting lines to near the stations at those towns, but without power to use any part of the Great Southern and Western Railway, or any stations thereon.

The Midland Great Western Railway.

The Waterford and Kilkenny and the Kilkenny Junction Companies, as promoters and owners of the Central Ireland Railway, are authorised to make an agreement with the Midland Great Western Company for the use of the Mullingar station, and of the line between the junction and the station.

---

8. THE CLONMEL, LISMORE, AND DUNGARVAN RAILWAY.

CLONMEL to LISMORE, with branch to Dungarvan.

LENGTH OF AUTHORIZED LINE.

MAIN LINE.

	Miles.
CLONMEL to LISMORE - - - - -	32¼

BRANCH.

(a.) THE DUNGARVAN BRANCH (from the Junction with the Main Line to Dungarvan)	5¾
Total length of main line and branch - - - -	38

CAPITAL.

Capital authorised :—	£
Shares - - - - -	300,000
Borrowing Powers - - -	100,000
Total - -	£400,000

Financial position on the 30th of June as ascertained by the Commission:

Capital raised :—	
Ordinary Shares - - - - -	£5,079
Floating liabilities - - - -	£6,969

This railway would, if made, connect the towns of Lismore and Dungarvan and a portion of the county of Waterford, with the Waterford and Limerick line at Clonmel.

THE LINE.

The line was authorised in 1865. No land has been taken; the power of taking it will expire on the 5th of July 1868; and no bill has been applied for in the present session for extending the time.

RELATIONS OF THE CLONMEL, LISMORE, AND DUNGARVAN WITH OTHER RAILWAY COMPANIES.

The lines in connexion with the Clonmel, Lismore, and Dungarvan Railway are stated in the following table:—

Name of Railway Company.	Point of Junction.	Page of Report.
Completed Line.		
The Waterford and Limerick - - -	Clonmel - - -	140
Line authorized but not commenced.		
The Waterford, Lismore, and Fermoy - -	Lismore and Dungarvan -	41

The Waterford, Lismore, and Fermoy Railway.

Power is conditionally reserved by the Act of incorporation to the Waterford, Lismore, and Fermoy Company to continue the line between Dungarvan and Lismore if the Clonmel, Lismore, and Dungarvan Company shall not before 5th July 1869 have made that portion of the line.

The Waterford and Limerick Railway.

By the same Act the Waterford and Limerick Company is authorised to make working agreements with the Clonmel, Lismore, and Dungarvan Company.

---

4. THE DUBLIN METROPOLITAN JUNCTION RAILWAY.

Dublin Metropolitan Junction Railway.

Connecting the GREAT SOUTHERN AND WESTERN, the DUBLIN AND RATHMINES, &c. and the DUBLIN, WICKLOW, AND WEXFORD LINES.

LENGTH OF AUTHORIZED LINE.

JUNCTION with GREAT SOUTHERN AND WESTERN RAILWAY to JUNCTION with the DUBLIN AND RATHMINES, &c. RAILWAY (including a short connecting line between the Dublin and Rathmines, &c. and the Dublin, Wicklow, and Wexford lines) - - - -	2¼ miles.

CAPITAL.

	£
Capital authorized :—	
Shares - - - -	160,000
Borrowing Powers - -	58,000
Total - -	£218,000

No capital has been raised by the Company.

THE LINE.

The line was authorized in 1865. No land has been taken; the power of taking it will expire on the 6th of July 1868, and no bill has been applied for in the present session for extending the time for compulsory purchase. 28 & 29 Vict. c. [illegible]

RELATIONS OF THE DUBLIN METROPOLITAN JUNCTION WITH OTHER RAILWAY COMPANIES.

The lines in connexion with the Dublin Metropolitan Junction are stated in the following table :—

Name of Railway Company	Point of Junction	Page of Report.
Completed Lines.		
The Great Southern and Western - -	Near Island Bridge Barracks -	100
The Dublin, Wicklow, and Wexford - -	In the Harcourt Street Terminus	94
Line authorized but not constructed.		
The Dublin and Rathmines, &c. - -	Camden Row - - -	46

The Dublin Metropolitan Junction Railway would, if made, connect the Dublin, Wicklow, and Wexford line (including the Kingstown Connecting branch), with the Great Southern and Western, and with the proposed central station of the Dublin and Rathmines, &c. Railway, and it will also connect the Dublin, Wicklow, and Wexford with the Great Southern and Western Railway.

Dublin, Rathmines, &c. Railway.

5. THE DUBLIN, RATHMINES, RATHGAR, ROUNDTOWN, RATHFARNHAM, AND RATHCOOLE RAILWAY.

From Dublin to Poulaphuca Bridge.

LENGTH OF AUTHORIZED LINE.

	Miles.
Dublin to Poulaphuca Bridge - - -	24

CAPITAL.

Capital authorized :—	£
Shares - - - - - -	450,000
Borrowing Powers - - - -	149,000
Total - - -	£599,000

Financial position, on the 30th of June 1867, as ascertained by the Commission :—

Capital raised by the Company :—	£
Ordinary Shares - - - -	7,136
Floating Liabilities, less Floating Assets - - -	9,860

This railway would, if made, connect the towns of Blessington, Rathcoole, Rathfarnham, and the suburbs of Rathmines, Rathgar, and Roundtown, with a central station in Dublin.

THE LINE.

27 & 28 Vict. c. 301. 28 & 29 Vict. c. 365.

The line as far as Tallaght was authorized in 1864, and the extension to Blessington and Poulaphuca Bridge in 1865.

There is not the usual limit of time for the power of taking land as far as Tallaght, but the power of completing the works terminates on 29th July 1869.

Power for taking land for the extension to Poulaphuca Bridge will expire on 5th July 1868. 400*l*. only has been expended for land and compensation, and no application has been made for extension of time for purchase.

Relations of the Dublin, Rathmines, Rathgar, Roundtown, Rathfarnham, and Rathcoole with other Railway Companies.

The lines in connexion with this railway are stated in the following table :—

Name of Railway Company.	Point of Junction.	Page of Report.
Completed Line.		
The Dublin, Wicklow, and Wexford - -	Near the Terminus in Dublin - -	94
Line authorized but not commenced.		
The Dublin Metropolitan Junction Railway -	Two Junctions near Camden Row -	45

The Dublin, Wicklow, and Wexford Railway.

The Dublin, Rathmines, &c. Railway would, if made, connect the Dublin, Wicklow, and Wexford Railway with the proposed central station in Dublin.

The Dublin Metropolitan Junction Railway.

This line would, if made, connect the Great Southern and Western Railway with the central station of the Dublin, Rathmines, &c. Railway, and would give a shorter connexion between the Dublin, Wicklow, and Wexford line and the proposed central station than the authorized connecting line of the Dublin, Rathmines, &c. Railway.

6. THE DUNDALK AND GREENORE RAILWAY.

Dundalk and Greenore Railway.

LENGTH OF AUTHORIZED LINE.

	Miles.
Dundalk to Greenore Harbour (Co. Louth) - -	15

CAPITAL.

Capital authorized :—	£
Shares - - - - -	160,000
Borrowing Powers - - - - -	53,200
Total - - - -	£213,200

Financial position, on the 30th of August 1867, as ascertained by the Commission :—

Capital raised by the Company :—	£
Ordinary Shares - -	5,345
Total Capital -	£5,345
Floating Liabilities, less Floating Assets - -	£10,187

All the land has been taken, but the works are not commenced.

This railway would, if made, connect the Irish North Western line with the proposed harbour at Greenore.

THE LINE.

The line was authorized in 1863, and the two connecting lines at Dundalk in 1867; in that year the time for completing the works was extended to the 19th of August 1870. 26 & 27 Vict. c. 215. 30 & 31 Vict. c. 165.

RELATIONS OF THE DUNDALK AND GREENORE WITH OTHER RAILWAY COMPANIES.

The lines in connexion with the Dundalk and Greenore are stated in the following table :—

Name of Railway Company	Point of Junction	Page of Report
Completed Line.		
The Irish North Western - - - -	At the Goods Station and at the Quay Extension at Dundalk.	106
Line commenced but not completed.		
The Newry and Greenore - - - -	Near Greenore - - -	84

The Irish North Western Railway.

By the Act of 1867 the Irish North Western Company sold land to the Dundalk and Greenore Company for an extension to the Quay of Dundalk. The Companies have Parliamentary power to enter into agreements for working and maintaining the line.

The Newry and Greenore Railway.

The Act of 1863 provides that the pier and works at Greenore, and the line between Greenore Harbour and the junction between the Dundalk and Greenore and Newry and Greenore lines, shall be made by the Newry and Greenore Company, and become the joint property of both Companies; but owing to some default on the part of the Newry and Greenore Company, the Dundalk and Greenore Company has been authorized to execute the joint works at Greenore.

The London and North Western Railway.

This Company is authorized to subscribe 130,000*l.* to the Dundalk and Greenore Railway, and to enter into arrangements for working and maintaining the line. The Company has advanced 7,590*l.* towards the undertaking.

The Ulster Railway.

Certain facilities for traffic between Belfast and English ports are secured by the Act of 1867 to the Ulster Company in case the London and North Western and Irish North Western Companies enter into traffic arrangements with the Dundalk and Greenore line.

The Midland Great Western Railway.

Equal facilities for traffic in the like event, are secured by the Act of 1867 to the Midland Great Western of Ireland Railway.

---

7. THE LIMERICK AND NORTH KERRY JUNCTION RAILWAY

NEWCASTLE (County of Limerick) to LISTOWEL.

LENGTH OF AUTHORIZED LINE.

	Miles.
NEWCASTLE (County of Limerick) to LISTOWEL . .	23

CAPITAL.

Capital authorized :—	£
Shares	130,000
Borrowing Powers	43,300
Total . . .	£173,300

No capital has been raised, but the expenses already incurred amount to about 5,000*l.*, which has been paid by the promoters.

This railway would, if made, give the town of Listowel and the north part of the county of Kerry railway communication with Limerick.

THE LINE.

The line was authorized in 1865; the time to take the land will expire on the 5th July 1866, but a bill is being promoted in the present session of Parliament to extend the time for four years. No land has been taken.

RELATIONS OF THE LIMERICK AND NORTH KERRY WITH OTHER RAILWAY COMPANIES.

Name of Railway Company.	Points of Junction.	Page of Report.
The Rathkeale and Newcastle . .	Newcastle	148

The Rathkeale and Newcastle Railway.

The Limerick and North Kerry Railway is an extension of the Rathkeale and Newcastle Railway.

---

6. THE NAVAN AND KINGSCOURT RAILWAY.

LENGTH OF AUTHORIZED LINE.

	Miles.
Navan to Kingscourt - - - -	20

CAPITAL.

Capital authorized :—	£
Shares - - - - -	120,000
Borrowing Powers - - - -	40,000
Total - - - -	£160,000

Financial position, on the 30th of June 1867, as ascertained by the Commission :—
No capital has been raised.
12,000*l*. has been spent for Parliamentary and engineering expenses. No information has been furnished to the Commission as to how this sum or any portion of it has been raised.

This railway is an extension of the Dublin and Meath Railway to the town of Kingscourt.

THE LINE.

The line was authorized in 1865, but in 1867 the time for completing it was extended to the 15th July 1871. No land has been taken.

RELATIONS OF THE NAVAN AND KINGSCOURT WITH OTHER RAILWAY COMPANIES.

Name of Railway Company.	Point of Junction.	Page of Report.
The Dublin and Meath - - - -	Navan - - - -	[illegible]
The Dublin and Drogheda - - - -	Navan - - - -	[illegible]

The Dublin and Meath Railway.

The Dublin and Meath Company is empowered to enter into working agreements with the Navan and Kingscourt Company, and to subscribe 40,000*l*.; but no money has yet been subscribed.

The Dublin and Drogheda Railway.

One of the deviations authorized in 1867 will connect the Navan and Kingscourt line with the Oldcastle branch of the Dublin and Drogheda line at Navan.

---

9. THE SLIGO AND BALLAGHADERREEN JUNCTION RAILWAY.

From Junction with the Sligo Branch of the Midland Great Western Railway to Ballaghaderreen.

LENGTH OF AUTHORIZED LINE.

	Miles
Kilfree Junction to Ballaghaderreen -	9½

CAPITAL.

Capital authorized :—	£
Shares -	50,000
Borrowing Powers -	16,600
Total -	£66,600

Financial position, on the 30th of June 1867, as ascertained by the Commission :—

Capital raised by the Company :—	£
Ordinary Shares -	978
Total Capital -	£978
Cr. Floating Assets -	£94

This railway would, if made, connect the town of Ballaghaderreen, in the county of Mayo, with the Sligo branch of the Midland Great Western Railway.

THE LINE.

The line was authorized in 1863; the time for exercising powers for the purchase of lands has been extended to the 10th of August 1868, and for completing the works to August 1869.

No land has been taken or any works contracted for, but the proprietor through whose estate the greater part of the line is to pass has applied to the Commissioners of Public Works to sanction a loan for 10,000*l.* as a Railway Estate Improvement, under Stat. 27 & 28 Vict. c. 114.

Relations of the Sligo and Ballaghaderreen Junction with other Railway Companies.

Name of Railway Company.	Point of Junction.	Page of Report.
The Midland Great Western -	Kilfree Junction -	116

The Midland Great Western Railway.

Power is given for making working agreements with the Midland Great Western Company.

10. THE WATERFORD, LISMORE, AND FERMOY RAILWAY.

Waterford, Lismore, and Fermoy Railway.

WATERFORD to DUNGARVAN, and LISMORE to FERMOY (with right of using or making under certain contingencies the line of the Clonmel, Lismore, and Dungarvan Railway between Dungarvan and Lismore).

LENGTH OF AUTHORIZED LINE.

	Miles.
WATERFORD to DUNGARVAN - - - - -	27¾
LISMORE to FERMOY - - - - - -	14½
Total length authorized - - -	42¼

CAPITAL.

Capital authorized :—	£
Shares - - - - - - -	400,000
Borrowing Powers - - - - -	133,000
Total - - -	£533,000

No capital has been raised, and the expenses incurred in obtaining the Act of Parliament have not been ascertained.

This railway, if completed, will connect the towns of Dungarvan, Lismore, and Fermoy with Waterford.

THE LINE.

The line was authorized in 1863. The time for taking land will expire on the 5th of July 1868, and the time for completing the works on the 5th of July 1870. No land has been taken; the works are not commenced, and no bill has been applied for in the present session for extension of time. 26 & 27 Vict. c. 161.

RELATIONS OF THE WATERFORD, LISMORE, AND FERMOY WITH OTHER RAILWAY COMPANIES.

The lines in connexion with the Waterford, Lismore, and Fermoy are stated in the following table:—

Name of Railway Company.	Point of Junction.	Page of Report.
Completed Line.		
The Great Southern and Western - -	Fermoy - -	100
Line authorized but not commenced.		
The Clonmel, Lismore, and Dungarvan -	Dungarvan and Lismore -	44

The Great Southern and Western Railway.

The Waterford, Lismore, and Fermoy Railway joins the Fermoy branch of the Great Southern and Western Company, and power is given to the Companies to make traffic arrangements.

The Clonmel, Lismore, and Dungarvan Railway.

Power to use part of the line between Dungarvan and Lismore is reserved to the Waterford, Lismore, and Fermoy Company; also a contingent power of constructing this part of the railway, if not made before 5th July 1868 by the Clonmel, Lismore, and Dungarvan Company, and if the Waterford, Lismore, and Fermoy Company shall have then made the line from Waterford to Dungarvan.

---

11. THE WATERFORD AND PASSAGE RAILWAY.

(From Junction at Ballytruckle with Waterford and Tramore Railway to the shore of the River Suir near Passage.)

LENGTH OF AUTHORIZED LINE.

	Miles.
Ballytruckle Junction to River Suir at Passage - -	9½

CAPITAL.

Capital authorized:—	£
Shares - - - - - -	80,000
Borrowing Powers - - - -	26,600
Total - - - - -	£106,600

Financial position, on the 30th of June 1867, as ascertained by the Commission:—
No capital has been raised.

All expenses up to this time have been borne by the promoters.

THE LINE.

The line from Ballytruckle, near Waterford, to Passage, was authorized in 1862, and the short extension from Passage to the south-west shore of the estuary of the River Suir in 1863. By the Act of 1863 the Company was authorized to make a pier on the shore of the River Suir at the end of the railway and also a pier on the opposite side of the estuary at Ballyhack, in the county of Wexford. The Company was authorized to acquire the property and rights of the Passage and Ballyhack ferry and to work it by steamboats.

The valuator's final award under the Railways, Ireland, Act, 1851, as to the land, has been delivered, but no land has been taken.

In 1865 the Company obtained an extension of two years to complete the works, and in 1867 a further extension to the 25th July 1869.

RELATIONS OF THE WATERFORD AND PASSAGE RAILWAY WITH OTHER RAILWAY COMPANIES.

Name of Railway Company.	Point of Junction.	Page of Report
Completed Lines.		
The Waterford and Tramore - -	Ballytruckle, near Waterford -	180
The Waterford and Wexford - -	Pier at Wexford side of Ballyhack Ferry -	53

The Waterford and Tramore Railway.

The Waterford and Passage Railway will join the Waterford and Tramore line at Ballytruckle, about half a mile from Waterford, and the Company has power to lay down an additional line of rails into the Waterford station, and to use it on terms to be settled by arbitration in case of difference.

The Waterford and Wexford Railway.

This railway would, if made, connect the pier at Ballyhack with the proposed harbour at Greenore (Co. Wexford), and with the Wexford Extension of the Dublin, Wicklow, and Wexford line at Wexford.

19. THE WATERFORD AND WEXFORD RAILWAY.

From Ballyhack to Wexford, with Branch to Greenore Bay (Co. Wexford).

Waterford and Wexford Railway.

LENGTH OF AUTHORIZED LINE.

MAIN LINE.

	Miles.
Ballyhack to Wexford - - -	26¾

BRANCH.

(a) The Greenore (Co. Wexford) Branch - From Junction to Greenore (Co. Wexford).	6½
Total number of miles authorized -	33¼

CAPITAL.

Capital authorized:—	£
Shares - - - - -	330,000
Borrowing Powers - - -	110,000
Total - - -	£440,000

No capital has been raised.

As the promoters of the Act of 1864 failed to raise the capital, some influential proprietors of land in Wexford promoted the Act of 1867 for the extension of time, but no land has been taken or capital raised by them.

This line will connect Wexford with the steam ferry across the Suir to the authorized Waterford and Passage line, proposed to be established by that Company.

THE LINE.

The line was authorized in 1864, and the time for purchase of land was extended in 1867 to the 15th of July 1869. 27 & 28 Vict. c. 214. 30 & 31 Vict. c. 160.

Relations of the Waterford and Wexford with other Railway Companies.

The lines in connexion with the Waterford and Wexford are stated in the following table:—

Name of Railway Company.	Point of Junction.	Page of Report.
Extension commenced but not completed.		
The Wexford Extension of the Dublin, Wicklow, and Wexford.	Wexford - - -	54
Line authorized but not commenced.		
The Waterford and Passage - - -	Pier at the Wexford side of the Ballyhack Ferry.	53

The Dublin, Wicklow, and Wexford Railway.

The Wexford Extension of this line will meet the commenced extension of the Dublin, Wicklow, and Wexford Railway at Wexford, and so connect it with Dublin.

The Waterford and Passage Railway.

This Railway, when made, will establish railway communication from the Waterford side of the Ballyhack Ferry to Waterford.

RAILWAYS (IRELAND) COMMISSION.

APPENDIX, PART III., CLASS II.—LINES COMMENCED BUT NOT COMPLETED.

No. in Appendix and on Map. Main Lines.	No. in Appendix and on Map. Branches and Extensions.	—	Length of Line authorised and in part commenced. Miles.	Length of Line authorised and in part commenced. Total Miles.	Page.
		A.—Lines commenced but not completed.			
13		Athenry and Ennis - - - - - -	36½		55
14		Banbridge Extension (Banbridge to Ballyroney) - - -	9½		56
15		Belfast Central (in the town of Belfast) - - - -	3		57
16		Downpatrick, Dundrum, and Newcastle (County Down) (Downpatrick to Newcastle) - - - - - -	11		58
17		Dublin and Antrim Junction (Knockmore Junction to Antrim) -	18½		59
18		Dublin Trunk Connecting (in the city of Dublin) - - -	7		60
19		Kilrush and Kilkee - - - - - - -	8¼		61
20		Letterkenny (Letterkenny to Farland) - - - -	16¼		62
21		Midland Counties and Shannon Junction (from Clara to Banagher) -	17¼		63
	21(a)	Meelick Extension of the Midland Counties Railway (Banagher to Meelick) - - - - -	Vide Cl. I.		63
22		Newry and Greenore (Co. Louth) - - - - -	14		64
23		Parsonstown and Portumna Bridge - - - - -	12½		65
24		Southern (Thurles Junction to Clonmel) - - - -	3¾		65
	24(a)	Colliery Branches of the Southern (Graystown Junction to the Collieries - - - - - -	Vide Cl. I.		66
25		Waterford, New Ross, and Wexford (Bagenalstown to Ballywilliam)	20½		67
	25(a)	Waterford Extension (Ballywilliam to Waterford) - - - } of Waterford, New Ross, and Wexford	Vide Cl. I.		67
	25(b)	Ballyhoge Branch (Ballywilliam to Ballyhoge) - - - } of Waterford, New Ross, and Wexford	Vide Cl. I.		67
		Mileage of lines commenced but not completed -		180¼	
		B.—Extensions and Branches commenced but not completed belonging to Lines completed and carrying traffic. (Class III.)			
	28(d)	Wexford Extension of the Dublin, Wicklow, and Wexford - -	15		91
	50(a)	Foxford Branch of the Great Northern and Western - -	11½		124
	57(a)	Maryborough Extension of the Kilkenny Junction (from Abbeyleix to Maryborough), since completed - - - -	9½		135
	59(a)	Shannon Extension of the Limerick and Castleconnell - -			142
	64(a)	Skibbereen Extension of the West Cork - - - - -	16		151
		Mileage of Extensions and Branches commenced but not completed - - - - -		53½	
		Total mileage commenced but not completed -		233	

The lines included in this class may be subdivided as follows:—

1st. Those railways where after some expenditure has been made the works are at a standstill.

2nd. Those railways which may be expected to be completed by the companies to which they belong.

3rd. One railway which having been closed for three years would require to be put in order before being re-opened.

4th. The Maryborough Extension of the Kilkenny Junction, which was incomplete at the period named in the Treasury Minute, but has been since opened for traffic.

5th. Those railways where only a small amount of work compared with the entire undertaking has been executed.

Under the first division may be classed—

(14.) The Banbridge Extension.
(17.) The Dublin and Antrim Junction.
(19.) The Kilrush and Kilkee.
(20.) The Letterkenny.
(21.) The Midland Counties and Shannon Junction.
(24.) The Southern.

Under the second division may be classed—

(13.) The Athenry and Ennis.
(15.) The Belfast Central.
(16.) The Downpatrick, Dundrum, and Newcastle.
(23.) The Parsonstown and Portumna Bridge.
(50a.) The Foxford Branch of the Great Northern and Western.
(59a.) The Shannon Extension of the Limerick and Castleconnell.

The third division consists of (25) the Bagenalstown and Ballywilliam part of the Waterford, New Ross, and Wexford Railway, which has been closed for the three years, and would require to be put in order before it could be safely used.

The fourth division consists of (57a) the Maryborough Extension of the Kilkenny Junction.

Under the fifth division may be classed—

(18.) The Dublin Trunk Connecting.
(22.) The Newry and Greenore.
(39d.) The Wexford Extension of the Dublin, Wicklow, and Wexford.

---

13. THE ATHENRY AND ENNIS JUNCTION RAILWAY.

LENGTH OF AUTHORIZED LINE.

Ennis to Athenry - - 35¾ miles.

CAPITAL.

Capital authorized :—	£
Shares - - - - - -	230,000
Borrowing Powers - - - - -	76,600
Total - - - -	£306,600

Financial Position on the 30th of June 1867, as ascertained by the Commission :—

Capital raised by the Company :—	£
Ordinary Shares - - - -	54,990
Preference Shares - - -	65,790
Debentures - - - -	16,600
Total Capital - -	£137,380

Floating Liabilities, less Floating Assets - - - £16,597

This railway will connect part of the counties of Galway and Clare with the Midland Great Western line at Athenry, and also with the Limerick and Ennis Railway at Ennis.

THE LINE.

The line was authorized in 1860. The time for completing the works was extended in 1863, and again in 1867, and will terminate on the 20th of August 1869.

The works are in a forward state, and about 11 miles of permanent way are laid.

The original contractor failed, but the works have been re-let to two sub-engineers, who, under the engineer-in-chief, execute the work on payment for the portions completed by them, without responsibility to complete the whole work. The land for the entire line has been taken and paid for or included in floating liabilities.

RELATIONS OF THE ATHENRY AND ENNIS WITH OTHER RAILWAY COMPANIES.

The lines in connexion with the Athenry and Ennis Junction are stated in the following table :—

Name of Railway Company.	Point of Junction.	Page of Report.
The Midland Great Western - - -	Near Athenry - - -	118
The Limerick and Ennis - - -	Near Ennis - - -	143

The Midland Great Western Railway.

The Athenry and Ennis Company and any Company using that line have, under the Act of 1867, the right to use the Athenry station of the Midland Great Western Company, and the portion of line between the junction and the station.

The Limerick and Ennis Railway.

The Athenry and Ennis Company and any Company using that line have the power to use the Ennis station of the Limerick and Ennis Company, and the portion of line between the junction and the station.

The Waterford and Limerick Railway.

The Waterford and Limerick Company has subscribed 4,000*l.* to the Athenry and Ennis Railway, under an agreement of 27th May 1863, sanctioned by the Act of that year, and has undertaken to work and maintain the Athenry and Ennis line until the 22nd of April 1881, or (at the option of the Waterford and Limerick Company), until 20 years after the opening of the entire line, at the following rates, per train mile:—2*s.* 6*d.* for one train; 2*s.* for two trains; 1*s.* 10*d.* for three trains, and 1*s.* 9*d.* for more than three trains daily.

---

14. THE BANBRIDGE EXTENSION RAILWAY.

BANBRIDGE to BALLYROONEY.

LENGTH OF AUTHORIZED LINE.

	Miles.
Banbridge to Ballyrooney - - - -	9¾

CAPITAL.

	£
Capital authorized :—	
Shares - - - - - - -	90,000
Borrowing Powers - - - - -	30,000
Total - - - -	120,000

Financial position on the 30th of June 1867, as ascertained by the Commission :—

	£
Capital raised by the Company :—	
Ordinary Shares - - - - - -	51,114
Total Capital - - -	£51,114
Floating Liabilities, less Floating Assets - - -	£23,382

The Company's affairs are in the Bankruptcy Court.

This line, if completed, would afford railway communication to a portion of the County Down, and connect it with the railways now working to Banbridge.

THE LINE.

The line was authorized in 1861, and considerable progress was made on the first nine miles until the year 1865, when the Company was made bankrupt under the Irish Bankruptcy and Insolvent Act, 1857. The statutable powers of completing the works expired in June 1866, but the land has all been taken and paid for, except £7,198, which is included in present floating liabilities.

The powers of making a branch to Rathfryland were allowed to expire without any land being taken.

RELATIONS OF THE BANBRIDGE EXTENSION WITH OTHER RAILWAY COMPANIES.

Name of Railway Company.	Point of Junction.	Page of Report.
The Banbridge, Lisburn, and Belfast - -	Banbridge - - - -	183

The Banbridge, Lisburn, and Belfast Railway.

The Banbridge Extension Railway continues this line into a part of the county of Down.

The Ulster Railway.

The Ulster Company was authorized to make working arrangements with the Banbridge Extension Company, and has subscribed 9,000*l.* to the line.

---

15. THE BELFAST CENTRAL RAILWAY.

Belfast Central Railway.

For connecting the ULSTER, the BELFAST AND COUNTY DOWN, the BELFAST, HOLYWOOD, AND BANGOR, and the BELFAST AND NORTHERN COUNTIES RAILWAYS, with a Central station in Belfast.

LENGTH OF AUTHORIZED LINE.

From the ULSTER, the BELFAST AND COUNTY DOWN, the BELFAST, HOLYWOOD, AND BANGOR, and the BELFAST AND NORTHERN COUNTIES RAILWAYS, to the CENTRAL STATION, including all the connecting lines - } 3 miles.

CAPITAL.

Capital authorized :—	£
Shares - - - - - -	300,000
Borrowing Powers - - - -	100,000
Total - - - - -	£400,000

Financial position on the 30th of June 1867, as ascertained by the Commission :—

Capital raised by the Company :—	£
Ordinary Shares - - - - - -	65,930
Floating Liabilities, less Floating Assets - - -	187,354

THE LINE.

The principal part of this railway was authorized in 1864, and the connecting line with the Belfast and County Down Railway in 1865. The time for completing the part authorized in 1865 will expire on the 25th of July 1869, and for that authorized in 1864, on the 25th of July 1869. 27 & 28 Vict. c. 324. 28 & 29 Vict. c. 229.

The Company is promoting a bill in the present session, for placing the Central Station in the Pork Market, for abandoning the proposed railway under Corporation Street, and for modifying the plan for connecting the central station with the different railways. The works have been commenced between the river and the Belfast and County Down Railway, and in the direction of the Ulster Railway.

RELATIONS BETWEEN THE BELFAST CENTRAL RAILWAY AND OTHER RAILWAY COMPANIES.

The lines in connexion with the Belfast Central Railway are stated in the following table :—

Name of Railway Company.	Point of Junction.	Page of Report.
The Ulster - - -	Near the Ulster Terminus and Ulster Goods Station.	180
The Belfast and County Down -	At Junction between Belfast and County Down, and Belfast, Holywood, and Bangor Railway.	70
The Belfast, Holywood, and Bangor -		78
The Belfast and Northern Counties - -	Near the York Street Terminus	71

Running powers are granted to the above Companies over the railway to the new Station, and the Belfast Central Company has running powers to the terminus and goods station in Belfast of each of them.

RELATIONS OF THE BELFAST CENTRAL RAILWAY WITH THE BELFAST HARBOUR COMMISSIONERS.

By the Act of 1865, the Belfast Harbour Commissioners are authorised to make a tramway in connexion with the Belfast Central Railway, and the Company is authorised to enter into contracts with the Commissioners for the maintenance and use of any tramway constructed by them which may communicate with any railway or tramway of the Company.

---

16. THE DOWNPATRICK, DUNDRUM, AND NEWCASTLE (Co. DOWN) RAILWAY.

LENGTH OF AUTHORIZED LINE.

	Miles
Downpatrick to Newcastle (Co. Down) -	11

CAPITAL.

Capital authorized :—	£
Shares - - - - -	75,000
Borrowing Powers - - - -	25,000
Total - - -	£100,000

Financial position on the 30th of June 1867, as ascertained by the Commission.

Capital raised by the Company :—	£
Ordinary Shares - - - - -	2,016
Total capital - - -	£2,016
Cr. Floating Assets, less Floating Liabilities - - -	£764

This railway connects Newcastle with Downpatrick and Belfast.

THE LINE.

The line was authorized in 1866. A portion of the land has been acquired and the works are in progress. As no land was taken or paid for on the 30th of June 1867, no purchase money is included in the floating liabilities at that date.

RELATIONS OF THE DOWNPATRICK, DUNDRUM, AND NEWCASTLE WITH OTHER RAILWAY COMPANIES.

Name of Railway Company.	Point of Junction.	Page of Report.
The Belfast and County Down - -	Downpatrick - - -	70

The Belfast and County Down Railway.

The Downpatrick, Dundrum, and Newcastle Railway will form a junction with the Belfast and County Down line at Downpatrick. A bill has been applied for in the present session to enable the Company to use the Downpatrick station of the Belfast and County Down Railway, to make traffic arrangements, to authorize a subscription to the line by the Belfast and County Down Company, and to reduce the capital to 80,000*l*.

17. THE DUBLIN AND ANTRIM JUNCTION RAILWAY.

From Knockmore Junction near Lisburn to Antrim.

LENGTH OF AUTHORIZED LINE.

	Miles.
Knockmore Junction to Antrim - -	18½

CAPITAL.

Capital authorized :—	£
Shares - - - - -	120,000
Borrowing Powers - - -	40,000
Total - -	£160,000

Financial position on 30th of June 1867, as ascertained by the Commission :—

Capital raised by the Company :—	£
Ordinary Shares - - - -	59,363
Cr. Floating Assets, less Floating Liabilities - -	635

This railway, when completed, will make a shorter route than the present one between Dublin and that portion of the Northern Counties line that lies to the north of Antrim.

THE LINE.

The line was authorized in 1861, and in 1866 the time for completing the works was extended to the 11th of July 1869. The land has all been taken and paid for from Knockmore to within a mile of Antrim. The cost of land for that mile is not included in the floating liabilities.

Relations of the Dublin and Antrim Junction with other Railway Companies.

The lines in connexion with the Dublin and Antrim Junction are stated in the following table :—

Name of Railway Company.	Points of Junction.	Page of Report.
The Ulster - - -	Lisburn -	120
The Belfast and Northern Counties -	Antrim -	74

The Ulster Railway.

By the Act of 1861 the Ulster Company was authorized to subscribe 10,000*l.* to the Dublin and Antrim Company, but it has not exercised that power.

The Dublin and Antrim Junction Company is empowered to lease its undertaking for 21 years, to either the Ulster or the Belfast and Northern Counties Company, or to both jointly.

The Belfast and Northern Counties Railway.

This Company is also authorized to subscribe 10,000*l.* to the Dublin and Antrim Company, but the power has not been exercised. The Belfast and Northern Counties Company is protected against undue competition for traffic between Antrim and Belfast by the Dublin and Antrim Company being restricted from charging lower tolls and rates from Antrim than are in force on the Belfast and Northern Counties line.

---

16. THE DUBLIN TRUNK CONNECTING RAILWAY.

In the City and Suburbs of Dublin, connecting the Dublin and Kingstown, Dublin and Drogheda, Midland Great Western, and Great Southern and Western Railways.

LENGTH OF AUTHORIZED LINE.

	Miles.
Junction with Kingstown Line to the Junction with the Great Southern and Western Line (including connecting lines with the Dublin and Drogheda, and with the Midland Great Western) - - - -	7½

CAPITAL.

Capital authorized:—	£
Shares - - - - - -	279,000
Borrowing Powers - - - -	93,000
Total - - - - -	£372,000

Financial position on the 30th of June 1867, as ascertained by the Commission.

Capital raised by the Company:—	£
Ordinary Shares* - - - - -	70,904
Total Capital - - - -	£70,904

Floating Liabilities, less Floating Assets - - - £16,305

From the small amount of works executed the line may be considered as almost in the position of a line authorized but not commenced.

This railway is intended to connect four out of the five railways which have a terminus in Dublin.

THE LINE.

The line was authorized in 1864, and a connecting line and some deviations sanctioned in 1865; in 1867 the time for completing the works was extended to the 15th of August 1870.

A very small portion only of the works has been executed, viz., a shaft sunk at each side of the Liffey for the proposed tunnel under that river. An application has been made to the Board of Trade for leave to abandon the undertaking.

Relations of the Dublin Trunk Connecting with other Railway Companies.

The lines in connexion with the Dublin Trunk Connecting Railway are stated in the following table:—

Name of Railway Company.	Point of Junction.	Page of Report.
The Dublin and Kingstown (worked by the Dublin, Wicklow, and Wexford Company).	A short distance from the Westland Row terminus.	99
The Dublin and Drogheda - - - -	Two points at a short distance from the Amiens Street terminus.	69
The Midland Great Western - - - -	Two points at a short distance from the Broadstone terminus, and one with the Liffey Branch, near the junction.	118
The Great Southern and Western - - -	A short distance from the Kings Bridge terminus.	100

The Dublin Trunk Connecting Railway would, if made, give a through route from Kingstown to the railways in the north, west, and south of Ireland, and connect all the railways mentioned in the table with one another.

---

* This does not include the amount recovered by judgment creditors, of which no particulars have been received.

19. THE KILRUSH AND KILKEE RAILWAY AND POULNASHERRY RECLAMATION.

LENGTH OF AUTHORIZED LINE.

	Miles.
Kilrush to Kilkee - - - -	$8\frac{1}{4}$

CAPITAL.

Capital authorized :—	£
Shares - - - - -	60,000
Borrowing Powers - - -	20,000
Total - - -	£80,000

Financial position on the 30th of June 1867, as ascertained by the Commission.

No capital has been raised.

Floating Liabilities, less Floating Assets - - £23,436

Money has been advanced by the promoters, but no books of accounts have been kept, and Lloyd's bonds to the amount of 23,433*l*. were issued to the contractor, which are now overdue, and in the hands of a Financial Company.

This railway will connect Kilkee, a sea-bathing place on the Atlantic, with Kilrush harbour on the Shannon, from which steamers ply to Foynes on the Limerick and Foynes Railway. The reclamation part of the project is the enclosure of 950 acres of slob land in Poulnasherry Bay by an embankment, on which the railway would be carried.

THE LINE.

The line was authorized under an Act of 1860, with certain deviations sanctioned in 1861, the time for completing the works was extended in 1865 for two years, which expired on the 19th June 1867, and no bill is being promoted in the present session for extending the time. The embankment was at one time nearly completed, but has been much damaged by the action of the tide.

---

20. THE LETTERKENNY RAILWAY.

LETTERKENNY to FARLAND.

LENGTH OF AUTHORIZED LINE.

	Miles.
LETTERKENNY to FARLAND - - - -	16¼

CAPITAL.

	£
Capital authorized :—	
Shares - - - - - - -	150,000
Borrowing Powers - - - -	49,800
Total - - - -	£199,800

Financial position on the 30th of June 1867, as ascertained by the Commission :—

	£
Capital raised by the Company—	
Ordinary Shares - - - - - -	55,869
Floating Liabilities, less Floating Assets - - - -	26,355

This railway, if completed, would connect Letterkenny and the north part of Donegal with Londonderry.

THE LINE.

The line as far as Pluck was authorized in 1860, and to Burt Junction in 1863. In 1866 the time for completing the works was extended to the 11th June 1869. All the land has been taken, and if not paid for added to capital expenditure, with the exception of 3,000*l.* which is included as a present liability.

RELATIONS OF THE LETTERKENNY WITH OTHER RAILWAY COMPANIES.

Name of Railway Company.	Point of Junction.	Page of Report.
The Londonderry and Lough Swilly -	Near Farland Station - -	116

The Londonderry and Lough Swilly Railway.

The original line authorized in 1860 was intended to form a junction with the Londonderry and Enniskillen line at Cuttymanhill; the portion from Pluck to Cuttymanhill was abandoned in 1863, and the new line to join the Londonderry and Lough Swilly Railway in the parish of Burt sanctioned.

Power is given to the Letterkenny Company to purchase the Londonderry and Lough Swilly line in case any persons other than the Londonderry and Lough Swilly Company become entitled to sell it, and to raise the capital required for such purchase.

21. THE MIDLAND COUNTIES AND SHANNON JUNCTION RAILWAY.

Midland Counties and Shannon Junction Railway.

From Clara to Meelick, with a Bridge across the Shannon.

LENGTH OF AUTHORIZED LINE.

MAIN LINE

	Miles.
Clara to Banagher - - - - - - - about	17¾

EXTENSION AUTHORIZED BUT NOT COMMENCED.

	Miles.
(a.) The Meelick Extension (from Banagher to Meelick) - -	5½
Total mileage authorized - - - - - -	23¼

CAPITAL.

Capital authorized :—	£
Shares - - - - - - -	115,000
Borrowing Powers - - - - -	38,300
Total - -	£153,300

Financial position on the 31st of December 1865, as ascertained by the Commission :—

Capital raised by the Company :—	£
Ordinary Shares - - - - - -	47,711
Debentures - - - - - -	100
Total Capital - - - -	£47,811

	£
Floating Liabilities, less Floating Assets - - - - -	27,477

This railway, when completed, will accommodate the district between King's County and Tipperary on the one side and Galway on the other.

THE MAIN LINE.

Clara to Banagher (17¾ miles).

The line was authorized in 1861; the time to complete the works was extended in 1866 to the 16th of July 1869. The land has all been taken on the main line and paid for or included in the floating liabilities, but during the last three years no progress has been made on the main line.

EXTENSION AUTHORIZED BUT NOT COMMENCED.

(a.) *The Meelick Extension.*

Banagher to Meelick (5½ miles).

The works on the extension have not been commenced though authorized in 1861, and no land has been taken.

Relations of the Midland Counties and Shannon Junction with other Railway Companies.

Name of Railway Company.	Point of Junction.	Page of Report.
The Great Southern and Western - -	Near Clara - - -	100

The Great Southern and Western Railway.

The Midland Counties and Shannon Junction Company has a right to use the Clara station of the Great Southern and Western Company, and intervening portions of the line, at a rent of 300*l.* a year, and to have traffic forwarded by the Clara and Streamstown branch of the Midland Great Western to all stations on that railway except Dublin or any place within 19 miles of Dublin.

---

23. THE NEWRY AND GREENORE (Co. LOUTH) RAILWAY.

LENGTH OF AUTHORIZED LINE.

	Miles.
Newry to Greenore (Co. Louth) - - -	14

CAPITAL.

	£
Capital authorized :—	
Shares - - - - -	202,000
Borrowing Powers - - - -	67,300
Total - - -	£269,300

Financial position on the 30th of June 1867, as ascertained by the Commission :—

	£
Capital raised by the Company :—	
Ordinary Shares - - -	31,879
Floating Liabilities, less Floating Assets - -	60,134

This railway will connect the Newry and Armagh line with the proposed pier at Greenore.

THE LINE.

The line was authorized in 1863. In the year 1867 the time for completing the works was extended to June 1870. Land has been taken for 11 miles, but only a short tunnel commenced at Carlingford and a station platform at Newry.

Relations of the Newry and Greenore with other Railway Companies.

The lines in connexion with the Newry and Armagh are stated in the following table:—

Name of Railway Company.	Point of Junction.	Page of Report.
Completed Line.		
The Newry and Armagh - -	Newry - -	125
Line authorized but not commenced.		
The Dundalk and Greenore - - -	Near Greenore - - -	47

The Newry and Armagh Railway.

Traffic arrangements are sanctioned between the Newry and Armagh and the Newry and Greenore Companies.

The Dundalk and Greenore Railway.

The power to make the pier at Greenore has lapsed to the Dundalk and Greenore Company, but the Newry and Greenore Company retains a right of using the works and of becoming joint owners on certain terms, so that the line is nearly in the position of one authorized but not completed.

23. THE PARSONSTOWN AND PORTUMNA BRIDGE RAILWAY.

LENGTH OF AUTHORIZED LINE.

	Miles.
PARSONSTOWN to PORTUMNA BRIDGE - -	12¾

CAPITAL.

Capital authorized :—

	£
Shares - - - - - -	65,000
Borrowing Powers - - - -	21,600
Total - - -	£86,600

Financial position on the 4th of May 1867, as ascertained by the Commission :—

Capital raised by the Company :—

	£
Ordinary Shares - - - -	32,363
Preference Shares - - - -	12,400
Debentures - - - - -	7,878
Loan Commissioners - - - -	6,000
Total Capital - - -	£58,641

Cr. Floating Assets, less Floating Liabilities - - - £5,054

This railway is an extension of the Parsonstown branch of the Great Southern and Western Railway to the River Shannon.

The Parsonstown and Portumna Bridge Extension Company obtained powers in 1864 to erect a railway bridge across the River Shannon, and to continue its railway to the town of Portumna, but these powers expired in July 1867 without having been exercised.

The line will connect the Great Southern and Western Railway with the Shannon, and the Parsonstown and Portumna Bridge Company is authorized to purchase steamers to work on that river, between Portumna Bridge and Killaloe.

THE LINE.

The line was authorized in 1861, and in 1866 the time for completing the works was extended to the 11th of June 1868; the line is nearly ready for traffic. The whole of the land has been taken, and the sum for payment of it has been included either in the capital expended or in floating liabilities.

RELATIONS OF THE PARSONSTOWN AND PORTUMNA BRIDGE WITH OTHER RAILWAY COMPANIES.

Name of Railway Company.	Point of Junction.	Page of Report.
The Great Southern and Western - -	Near Parsonstown - -	100

The Great Southern and Western Railway.

The Great Southern and Western Company has subscribed 12,000*l.* towards the undertaking, and powers are reserved to that Company for working, leasing, or purchasing the Parsonstown and Portumna Bridge Railway.

24. THE SOUTHERN RAILWAY.

From Junction with the Great Southern and Western Railway near THURLES to CLONMEL, with Branches to Collieries at Ballingarry.

LENGTH OF AUTHORIZED LINE.

MAIN LINE.

	Miles.
THURLES JUNCTION to CLONMEL - - - - -	24

(a.) THE COLLIERIES BRANCHES.

Graystown Junction to Capper Colliery in Ballingarry, and lines to Ballynastic and Earlshill Collieries - - -	9¼
Total number of miles authorized - -	33¼

CAPITAL.

Capital authorized :—	£
Shares - - - - - -	231,000
Borrowing Powers - - - -	77,000
Total - - - - -	£308,000

Financial position on the 30th of June 1867, as ascertained by the Commission :—

Capital raised by the Company :—	
Ordinary Shares - - - -	£86,458
Total - - - - -	£86,458

Floating Liabilities, less Floating Assets - - -	£28,079

This railway, when completed, will establish a second route from Clonmel to Dublin, and from Thurles to the seaport of Waterford.

THE MAIN LINE.

THURLES JUNCTION to CLONMEL - - - - 24 miles.

The main line was authorized in 1865, and a deviation in 1866.

The works of the line for eight miles (from Thurles Junction to Laffan's Bridge) are in a forward state.

(a.) *The Collieries Branches.*

GRAYSTOWN JUNCTION to the COLLIERIES, near BALLINGARRY - - 9¼ miles.

The branch to Capper Colliery in Ballingarry, with two short lines to Ballynastic and Earlshill Collieries, were authorized in 1866. The powers for compulsory purchase of land expire on the 23rd of July 1869.

RELATIONS OF THE SOUTHERN WITH OTHER RAILWAY COMPANIES.

The lines in connexion with the Southern are stated in the following table :—

Name of Railway Company.	Point of Junction.	Page of Report.
The Great Southern and Western - - -	Thurles - - - - - -	100
The Waterford and Limerick - - - -	Clonmel - - - - - -	140

The Great Southern and Western Railway.

The Southern Railway joins this line one mile south of Thurles station, and working agreements between the Companies are authorized.

The Waterford and Limerick Railway.

The Southern Railway joins the Waterford and Limerick line at the Clonmel station; provision is made for the use of the station and for working agreements between the two Companies.

25. THE WATERFORD, NEW ROSS, AND WEXFORD JUNCTION RAILWAY.

Waterford, New Ross, and Wexford Railway.

LENGTH OF AUTHORIZED LINE.

MAIN LINE.

	Miles.
Bagenalstown to Ballywilliam - -	20¾

EXTENSION AND BRANCH AUTHORIZED BUT NOT COMMENCED.

(a.) The Waterford Extension (Ballywilliam to Waterford)	19
(b.) The Ballyhoge Branch (Ballywilliam to Ballyhoge Junction) - - - - - -	14¼
Total number of miles authorized - -	54

CAPITAL.

Capital authorized :—	£
Shares - - - - - -	330,000
Borrowing Powers - - - -	110,000
Total - - - -	£440,000

Financial position as ascertained by the Commission :—

Up to the 7th December 1867 no capital had been raised by the issue of shares (excepting for Directors' qualification), or by loan, the promoters having borne the Engineering, Parliamentary, and other expenses.

This Company has purchased the Bagenalstown and Wexford railway, which line had been completed from Bagenalstown to Ballywilliam, and which after being worked for a short time by the Great Southern and Western Company, was closed to public traffic in 1863. The Company proposes an extension to New Ross and Waterford, and a branch to the Dublin, Wicklow, and Wexford line between Enniscorthy and Wexford.

THE MAIN LINE.

Bagenalstown to Ballywilliam - - - 20¾ miles.

The line from Bagenalstown to Ballywilliam was constructed under an Act of 1854 by the Bagenalstown and Wexford Company, subject to certain alterations and deviations sanctioned in 1856 and 1859. On the 27th May 1864 the Bagenalstown and Wexford Company was adjudged bankrupt under the provision of the Irish Bankrupt and Insolvent Act of 1857 (since repealed), the bond and share capital and judgment debts amounting to between 200,000*l.* and 300,000*l.* Under an Act of 1865, the railway was sold in bankruptcy for a sum of 25,000*l.*

17 & 18 Vict. c. 1[illegible].
19 & 20 Vict. c. 1[illegible].
20 & 21 Vict. c. 60.
28 & 29 Vict. c. [illegible].

In the Act of 1866 it is recited that the purchaser Mr. Motte was willing to sell the line to the Waterford, New Ross, and Wexford Company for 25,000*l.* if paid before the 10th of February 1867. In the Act of 1867 it is recited that the Bagenalstown and Wexford line had not been purchased by that Company, but would be so at a valuation to be made by a valuator appointed by the Board of Public Works in Ireland. The amount fixed in November 1867 was 179,760*l.*, one fourth to be paid in cash, and the rest in shares. The Company not having paid the cash, the valuator, by a further award in January 1868, declared Mr. Motte entitled to rentcharge at five per cent. on 44,940*l.*, to 44,940*l.* five per cent. debenture stock in perpetuity, to 44,940*l.* in preference shares, and to 44,940*l.* in ordinary shares.

I 2

The following table shows the dates when the works were authorised, and the several portions of the line opened for traffic:—

Date of Act.	Date of opening and closing of Line.			
	From	To	Distance.	Date.
			Miles.	
3rd July 1854 - -	Bagenalstown - -	Borris - - - -	9	11 Dec. 1858.
" " - -	Borris - - -	Ballywilliam - -	13	18 March 1862.
	The line was closed for traffic	- - - -		1863.

The main line having been so long closed would require repairs before being again opened.

(a.) *The Waterford Extension.*

Ballywilliam to Waterford (19 miles).

This extension was authorized in 1866, subject to deviations in 1867. The usual time of three years from 1866 is allowed for taking land, and five years for completing the works. No land for this extension has yet been taken.

(b.) *The Ballyhoge Branch.*

Ballywilliam to Ballyhoge Junction (14½ miles.)

This branch was authorized in 1868, and the usual time of three years allowed for taking land, but no land has yet been taken.

RELATIONS OF THE WATERFORD, NEW ROSS, AND WEXFORD JUNCTION WITH OTHER RAILWAY COMPANIES.

The lines in connexion with the Waterford, New Ross, and Wexford are stated in the following table:—

Name of Railway Company.	Point of Junction.	Page of Report.
The Great Southern and Western - -	Bagenalstown.	100
The Dublin, Wicklow, and Wexford -	Ballyhoge Junction.	94

The Great Southern and Western Railway.

The main line of the Waterford, New Ross, and Wexford Company is an extension of the Great Southern and Western railway. Authority is given to enter into traffic arrangements.

The Dublin, Wicklow, and Wexford Railway.

The Ballyhoge branch, if made, would connect the main line with the authorized extension of the Dublin, Wicklow, and Wexford line between Enniscorthy and Wexford. Authority is given for traffic arrangements.

RAILWAYS, CLASS III.—LINES COMPLETED AND CARRYING TRAFFIC.

No. in Appendix and on Map.	Railways, Class III.—Lines Completed and Carrying Traffic.	Mileage.			Appendix.
		Single.	Double.	Total.	Page.
26.	Belfast and County Down	44¼	—	44¼	70
27.	Belfast, Holywood, and Bangor	12¼	—	12¼	73
28.	Belfast and Northern Counties	92½	6¼	98¾	74
29.	*Carrickfergus and Larne*	14½	—	14½	77
30.	*Londonderry and Coleraine*	36½	—	36½	78
31.	Cork and Bandon	20	—	20	80
32.	*Cork and Kinsale*	10½	—	10½	83
33.	Cork, Blackrock, and Passage	6¼	—	6¼	88
34.	Cork and Macroom Direct	23½	—	23½	91
35.	Dublin and Belfast Junction	—	33¼	33¼	85
36.	*Banbridge Junction*	6¾	—	6¾	87
37.	Dublin and Drogheda	43	31½	74½	89
38.	Dublin and Meath	36½	—	36½	93
39.	Dublin, Wicklow, and Wexford	[illegible]	27	[illegible]	94
40.	*Dublin and Kingstown*	6	6	6	98
41.	Great Southern and Western	298½	120¼	418¾	100
42.	*Cork and Limerick Direct*	17	—	17	106
43.	Irish North Western	66	—	66	108
44.	*Enniskillen, Bundoran, and Sligo*	35½	—	35½	111
45.	*Finn Valley*	13¼	—	13¼	112
46.	*Londonderry and Enniskillen*	50	9¾	60	114
47.	Londonderry and Lough Swilly	14½	—	14½	116
48.	Midland Great Western	131	115¼	246¼	119
49.	*Athenry and Tuam*	15½	—	15½	123
50.	*Great Northern and Western*	32½	—	32½	124
51.	Newry and Armagh	21	—	21	125
52.	Newry, Warrenpoint, and Rostrevor	6¼	—	6¼*	126
53.	Ulster	16	48½	64½	130
54.	*Banbridge, Lisburn, and Belfast*	16	—	15	133
55.	*Portadown, Dungannon, and Omagh*	41	—	41	134
56.	Waterford and Kilkenny	30	—	30	135
57.	*Kilkenny Junction*	19	—	19	139
58.	Waterford and Limerick	55	22½	77½	140
59.	*Limerick and Castleconnell*	12	—	12	143
60.	*Limerick and Ennis*	24	—	24	145
61.	*Limerick and Foynes*	25½	—	25½	146
62.	*Rathkeale and Newcastle*	10	—	10	148
63.	Waterford and Tramore	7¼	—	7¼	150
64.	West Cork	17½	—	17½	151
	Total	1,409	500¾	1,909¾	

The lines leased or worked by other companies are marked in italics, immediately below the names of the company by which they are worked.

* Including [illegible] of Newry connecting line, [illegible] of a mile, joint property between this company and Newry and Armagh.

26. THE BELFAST AND COUNTY DOWN RAILWAY.

Belfast to Downpatrick, with branches to Donaghadee and Ballynahinch.

LENGTH OF LINE

—	Single.	Double.	Total.
MAIN LINE.	Miles.	Miles.	Miles.
Belfast to Downpatrick - - - - -	26¾	—	26¾
BRANCHES.			
(a.) The Donaghadee Branch (from Comber to Donaghadee) - -	14	—	14
(b.) The Ballynahinch Branch (from Ballynahinch Junction to Ballynahinch)	3½	—	3½
Total number of miles owned by the Company - - -	44¼	—	44¼

Length of main line - - - 26¾ miles.
Length of branches - - - 17½ „
Total length of main line and branches — - 44¼ miles.

CAPITAL.

Capital authorised :—

	£
Shares - - - - - -	515,000
Borrowing Powers - - - - -	166,666
Total - - - -	£681,666

Financial position on the 31st of July 1867, as ascertained by the Commission :—

Capital raised by the Company :—

	£
Ordinary Shares - - - - -	237,287
Preference Shares - - - - -	193,400
Debentures - - - - -	166,643
Total Capital - - -	£597,330

Floating liabilities, less floating assets - - - £17,208

Net revenue of each of the three last years, from Company's accounts :—

	£
1864–65 - - - - - -	18,713
1865–66 - - - - - -	20,035
1866–67 - - - - - -	20,337
Average of three years - -	£19,695

Dividend on Ordinary Shares :—

1864–65 }
1865–66 } - - Nil.
1866–67 }

Dividend on Preference Shares :—

*Average of three years ended the 31st of July 1867, 4*l.* 19*s.* 0*d.* per cent.

Interest (average rate on the 31st of July 1867) :—

On Debentures - - - - - 4*l.* 16*s.* 6*d.* per cent.

This line connects Downpatrick, Newtownards, and Comber, and a large part of the county of Down with Belfast. It extends also to Donaghadee, a port on the Irish coast at the narrow part of the Irish Channel, and distant 22½ miles from the small port of Portpatrick, on the Scotch side. Considerable works have been carried out, both at Donaghadee and Portpatrick, with a view of establishing a steamboat route between the two countries, but the Lords Commissioners of Her Majesty's Treasury decided against subsidising the steamboat service, and have by Minute of the 5th of July 1867, signified their intention to propose a measure to Parliament authorising an advance to the Belfast and County Down Railway Company by way of loan of 166,666*l.* at 3½ per cent.

The district of country which may be considered to be accommodated by the line embraces an area of 324,314 acres, with a population of 262,897 persons.

* Besides this the Company has paid, during the three years, arrears amounting to 5,001*l.*, being 2*l.* 18*s.* 11*d.* per cent. on the shares.

Belfast and County Down Railway.

THE MAIN LINE.

Belfast to Downpatrick.

(26¾ miles, single line.)

The main line to Comber was constructed under an Act 1846, and from Comber to Downpatrick under an Act of 1855. 9 & 10 Vict. c. 81. 18 & 19 Vict. c. 11.

The following table shows the dates when the works were authorized, and the several portions of the line sanctioned for traffic:—

Date of Act.	Length sanctioned by Board of Trade, with Date of Sanction.			
	From	To	Distance.	Date.
			Miles.	
26 June 1846 - -	Belfast - - - -	Comber - - - -	8	29 April 1850.
23 May 1855 - -	Comber - - -	Ballynahinch Junction	9¾	8 Sept. 1858.
" " - -	Ballynahinch Junction	Downpatrick - -	9	23 March 1859.

BRANCHES.

(a.) *The Donaghadee Branch.*

Comber to Donaghadee.

(14 miles, single line.)

This branch as far as Newtownards was constructed under the Act of 1846, and from Newtownards to Donaghadee under that of 1856, the time for completing the works having been extended in 1858, and again in 1860. 19 Vict. c. 13. 23 Vict. c. 22.

The following table shews the dates when the works were authorized, and the several portions of the branch sanctioned for traffic:—

Date of Act.	Length sanctioned by Board of Trade, with Date of Sanction.			
	From	To	Distance.	Date.
			Miles.	
26 June 1846 - -	Comber - - -	Scrabo - - - -	4	29 April 1850.
12 July 1856 - -	Scrabo - - -	Donaghadee -	10	27 May 1861.

(b.) *The Ballynahinch Branch.*

Ballynahinch Junction to Ballynahinch.

(3½ miles, single line.)

This branch was constructed under the Act of 1855.

Date of Act.	Length sanctioned by Board of Trade, with Date of Sanction.			
	From	To	Distance.	Date.
			Miles.	
23 May 1855 - -	Ballynahinch Junction	Ballynahinch - -	3½	8 Sept. 1858.

Relations of the Belfast and County Down with other Railway Companies.

The lines in connexion with the Belfast and County Down are stated in the following table:—

Name of Railway Company.	Point of Junction.	Page of Report.
Completed Line.		
The Belfast, Holywood, and Bangor - -	Be[illegible] -	72
Line commenced but not completed.		
The Belfast Central - - - -	Belfast - - - - -	47
The Downpatrick, Dundrum, and Newcastle -	Downpatrick - - - -	38

The Belfast, Holywood, and Bangor Railway.

This line has a terminus in Belfast, irrespective of but adjoining the terminus of the Belfast and County Down Company.

The Belfast and County Down Company supply locomotive power to the Belfast, Holywood, and Bangor Company for 8*d.* per train mile.

The Belfast Central.

This line when completed will connect the Belfast and County Down with Ulster and the Belfast and Northern Counties lines, and with a central station in Belfast.

The Downpatrick, Dundrum, and Newcastle Railway.

This is an extension of the Belfast and County Down line to Newcastle. A Bill has been introduced in the present Session for authorising arrangements between the two Companies.

The Portpatrick Railway.

Under the Act of 1857 the Belfast and County Down Company subscribed 15,000*l.* to this railway.

---

27. THE BELFAST, HOLYWOOD, AND BANGOR RAILWAY.

BELFAST to BANGOR.

LENGTH OF LINE.

	Single.	Double.	Total.
	Miles.	Miles.	Miles.
BELFAST to BANGOR - - - -	12¼	–	12¼
Total number of miles owned by the Company -	12¼	–	12¼

CAPITAL.

Capital authorized :—	£
Shares - - - - -	300,000
Borrowing Powers - - - -	99,000
Total - - - -	£399,000

Financial position on the 30th of June 1867, as ascertained by the Commission :—

Capital raised by the Company :	£
Ordinary Shares - - - -	156,868
Preference Shares - - - -	79,220
Debentures - - - -	38,000
Total Capital - - -	£274,088

Floating liabilities, less floating assets - - -	£60,870

Net revenue of each of the last two years, as returned by the Company :—

	£
1865-66 - - - - -	1,039
1866-67 - - - - -	2,029
Average of two years - -	£1,443

Belfast, Holywood, and Bangor Railway.

Dividend on Ordinary Shares :—

1865–66 } 1866–67 } - -	Nil.

Dividend on Preference Shares :—

Average of three years ended 30th June 1867 - Nil.

Interest (average rate on the 30th of June 1867) : —

On Debentures - - - 5*l.* 0*s.* 0*d.* per cent.

This railway connects the towns of Bangor and Holywood, and intermediate places, with Belfast.

The district of country which may be considered to be accommodated by the line embraces an area of 17,618 acres, with a population of 130,085 persons.

THE LINE.

The line to Holywood was made by the Belfast and County Down Company under an Act of 1846, and sold to the Belfast, Holywood, and Bangor Company in 1865 for 30,000*l.*, and a yearly rental of 5,000*l.*, redeemable. 9 & 10 Vict. c. 97.

The line was extended to Bangor under an Act of 1860, the time for completing the works having been extended in 1863. 23 Vict. c. 61. 26 & 27 Vict. c. 152.

The following table shews the dates when the works were authorized, and the several portions of the line sanctioned for traffic :—

Date of Act.	Length sanctioned by Board of Trade, with Date of Inspection.			
	From	To	Mileage.	Date.
			Miles.	
26 June 1846 - -	Belfast - - -	Holywood - -	3	31 July 1848.
23 May 1860 - -	Holywood - -	Bangor - - -	8	16 May 1865.

RELATIONS OF THE BELFAST, HOLYWOOD, AND BANGOR WITH OTHER RAILWAY COMPANIES.

The lines in connexion with the Belfast, Holywood, and Bangor are stated in the following table : —

Name of Railway Company.	Point of Junction.	Page of Report.
Completed Line.		
The Belfast and County Down - - -	Belfast - - -	70
Line commenced but not completed.		
The Belfast Central - - - -	Belfast - - - -	57

The Belfast and County Down Railway.

The stations of this Company and of the Belfast and County Down Railway in Belfast are contiguous, though not worked as one.

The Belfast Central Railway.

When completed this railway will connect the Belfast, Holywood, and Bangor Railway with the railways on the west side of the river Lagan, and with the proposed central station in Belfast.

	Single.	Double.	Total.
MAIN LINE.	Miles.	Miles.	Miles.
Belfast to Londonderry and Coleraine Line at Coleraine - -	55¾	6¾	62½
BRANCHES.			
(a.) The Carrickfergus Branch (from Carrick Junction to near Carrickfergus).	3¾	—	3¾
(b.) The Cookstown Branch (from Cookstown Junction to Cookstown) -	27	—	27
(c.) The Portrush Branch (from Coleraine to Portrush) - -	6¼	—	6¼
Total number of miles owned by the Company - -	92¾	6¾	99½
LINES WORKED AND MAINTAINED BY THE COMPANY.			
The Carrickfergus and Larne - - - - - -	15¼	—	15¼
The Londonderry and Coleraine - - - - -	35¾	—	35¾
Total mileage, worked and maintained by the Company -	143¾	6¾	150½

Length of main line - - - - - - 62½ miles.
Length of branches - - - - - - 37 „
Total length of main line and branches - —— 99½ miles.
Length of line worked and maintained but not owned by the Company. 51 „
Total mileage worked and maintained - 150½ „

CAPITAL.

Capital authorized :—

	£
Shares - - - - - -	910,000
Borrowing Powers - - - - -	323,833
Total - - - -	£1,233,833

Financial position on the 30th of June 1867, as ascertained by the Commission :—

Capital raised by the Company :.

	£
Ordinary Shares - - - - -	556,703
Preference Shares - - - - -	210,500
Debentures - - - - -	292,184
Debenture Stock - - - - -	110
Total Capital - - -	£1,059,497

Floating liabilities, less floating assets - - - £89,693

Net revenue of each of the last three years, from Company's accounts :—

	£
1864–65 - - - - - -	46,644
1865–66 - - - - - -	51,987
1866–67 - - - - - -	55,293
Average of three years - -	£51,274

Dividend on Ordinary Shares :—

1864–65 - - - -	3*l.* 15*s.* 0*d.* per cent.
1865–66 - - - -	4*l.* 10*s.* 0*d.* „
1866–67 - - - -	5*l.* 0*s.* 0*d.* „

Dividend on Preference Shares :—

Average of three years ended the 30th of June 1867, 4*l.* 1*s.* 3*d.* per cent.

Interest (average rate on 30th June 1867) :— £ s. d.
On Debentures - - - 4 9 5 per cent.
On Debenture Stock - - - 4 0 0 per cent.

This railway connects the counties of Londonderry, Antrim, and part of Tyrone, with Belfast. The district of country which may be considered to be accommodated by the line embraces an area of 906,359 acres, with a population of 441,209 persons.

THE MAIN LINE.

Belfast to Coleraine.

(6¾ miles double line, 55¼ miles single line.)

The main line from Belfast to Ballymena was constructed by the Belfast and Ballymena Company under an Act of 1845.

The extension of the main line to the junction with the Londonderry and Coleraine line at Coleraine was constructed by the Ballymena, Ballymoney, Coleraine, and Portrush Junction Company under Acts of 1853 and 1859, and was purchased by the Belfast and Ballymena Company, which took the name of the Belfast and Northern Counties Company in the year 1860.

The following table shows the dates when the works were authorized, and the several portions of the line sanctioned for traffic :—

Date of Act.	Length sanctioned by Board of Trade, with Date of Sanction.			
	From	To	Distance.	Date.
			Miles.	
21 July 1845 - -	Belfast - -	Ballymena - -	33¾	14 April 1848.
9 July 1853 - -	Ballymena - -	Coleraine - -	[illegible]	27 Nov. 1855.
19 April 1859 -	Coleraine - -	Junction with Londonderry and Coleraine Line.	½	15 Nov. 1860.

BRANCHES.

(a.) *The Carrickfergus Branch.*

Carrick Junction to the Carrickfergus and Larne Line near Carrickfergus.

(2¼ miles, single line.)

This branch was constructed under the Act of 1845. Since the opening of the Carrickfergus and Larne line the Belfast and Northern Counties Company has used the Carrickfergus station of the Carrickfergus and Larne Company.

Date of Act.	Length sanctioned by Board of Trade, with Date of Sanction.			
	From	To	Distance.	Date.
			Miles.	
21 July 1845 -	Carrickfergus Junction.	Carrickfergus - -	2¼	11 April 1848.

(b.) *The Cookstown Branch.*

Cookstown Junction to Cookstown.

(29 miles, single line.)

This branch was constructed as far as Randalstown under the Act of 1845, and was completed under an Act of 1853.

The following table shows the dates when the works were authorised and the several portions of the branch line sanctioned for traffic :—

Date of Act.	Length sanctioned by Board of Trade, with Date of Sanction.			
	From	To	Distance.	Date.
			Miles.	
21 July 1845 - -	Cookstown Junction	Randalstown - -	2	11 April 1848.
28 June 1853 - -	Randalstown - -	Cookstown -	27	16 October 1856.

Belfast and Northern Counties Railway.

(c.) *The Portrush Branch.*

Coleraine to Portrush.

(5¾ miles, single line.)

16 & 17 Vict. c. cl. This branch was constructed under the Act of 1853 by the Ballymena, Ballymoney, Coleraine, and Portrush Junction Company, and purchased by the Belfast and Northern Counties Company under the Act of 1858.

Date of Act.	Length certified by Board of Trade, with Date of Opening.			
	From	To	Distance.	Date.
			Miles.	
8 July 1853 - -	Coleraine - -	Portrush - -	5¾	27 Nov. 1855.

RELATIONS OF THE BELFAST AND NORTHERN COUNTIES WITH OTHER RAILWAY COMPANIES.

The lines in connexion with the Belfast and Northern Counties are stated in the following table:—

Name of Railway Company.	Point of Junction.	Page of Report.
Completed Lines.		
The Carrickfergus and Larne - -	a mile from Carrickfergus -	77
The Londonderry and Coleraine - -	a mile from the Coleraine Station	78
Line commenced but not completed.		
The Belfast Central - - -	York Street Terminus - -	57

The Carrickfergus and Larne Railway.

This railway is a continuation of the Carrickfergus branch of the Belfast and Northern Counties line to the town and harbour of Larne, and is worked under an agreement herein-after mentioned (p. 78) for a minimum rent of 3,000*l.* a year.

The Londonderry and Coleraine Railway.

This railway forms a continuation of the Belfast and Northern Counties line to Londonderry, and is worked under an agreement herein-after mentioned (p. 80) for 2*s.* 2*d.* per train mile, subject to certain conditions and modifications.

The Belfast Central.

The authorized line of the Belfast Central Railway would, if made, connect the Belfast and Northern Counties Railway with the Ulster and the Belfast and County Down lines, and with a central station in Belfast. By the Bill of the present session it is proposed to substitute a tramway, to be laid down by the Belfast Harbour Commissioners as the means of communication.

20. THE CARRICKFERGUS AND LARNE RAILWAY.

Carrickfergus and Larne Railway.

LENGTH OF LINE.

	Single.	Double.	Total.
	Miles.	Miles.	Miles.
Carrickfergus to Larne Pier - - - -	15½	—	15½

The line is worked and maintained by the Belfast and Northern Counties Company.

CAPITAL.

Capital authorized :—

	£
Shares - - - - - -	125,000
Borrowing Powers - - - -	41,500
Total - - -	£166,500

Financial position on the 30th of June 1867, as ascertained by the Commission :—
Capital raised by the Company :—

	£
Ordinary Shares - - - - -	82,529
Debentures - - - - -	41,010
Total Capital - -	£123,539

Floating liabilities, less floating assets - - - £1,348

Net revenue of each of the three last years, as returned by the Company :—

	£
1864–65 - - - - - -	693
1865–66 - - - - - -	1,334
1866–67 - - - - - -	2,245
Average for the three years - -	£1,424

Dividends on Ordinary Shares :—

1864–65 - - - - - -	Nil.
1865–66 - - - - - -	Nil.
1866–67 - - - - - -	Nil.

Interest on Debentures :— £ s. d.
Average rate on the 30th of June 1867 - 4 10 8 per cent.

This railway connects the town and harbour of Larne via Carrickfergus with the Belfast and Northern Counties line.

The district of country which may be considered to be accommodated by the line embraces an area of 66,784 acres, with a population of 27,099 persons.

THE LINE

The line was constructed under an Act of 1860; and the following table shows the dates when the works were authorized and sanctioned for traffic :— 23 Vict. c. 36.

Date of Act.	Length sanctioned by Board of Trade, and Date of Sanction.			
	From	To	Distance.	Date.
			Miles.	
15 May 1860 - -	Carrickfergus -	Larne - - -	15	29 Sept. 1862.

RELATIONS OF THE CARRICKFERGUS AND LARNE WITH OTHER RAILWAY COMPANIES.

Name of Railway Company.	Point of Junction.	Page of Report.
The Belfast and Northern Counties - -	Half a mile from Carrickfergus -	74

The Belfast and Northern Counties Railway.

The Belfast and Northern Counties Company has subscribed 12,500*l.* to the undertaking. The use of the Carrickfergus station and of the intermediate portion of the line is secured to that Company.

By agreement under Parliamentary sanction, dated the 7th February 1866, the line is worked by the Belfast and Northern Counties Company, which receives 3,000*l.* per annum, and 50 per cent. of all excess above 4,500*l.* per annum. The agreement to remain in force for seven years from 1st November 1865.

---

30. THE LONDONDERRY AND COLERAINE RAILWAY.

LONDONDERRY to COLERAINE, with branch to Newtownlimavady.

LENGTH OF LINE.

	Single.	Double.	Total.
MAIN LINE.	Miles.	Miles.	Miles.
LONDONDERRY to COLERAINE - - - - -	32½	—	32½
BRANCH.			
(a.) THE NEWTOWNLIMAVADY BRANCH (from Broharris Junction to Newtownlimavady).	3¼	—	3¼
Total number of miles owned by the Company - - - -	35¾	—	35¾

Length of main line - - - - 32½ miles.
Length of branch - - - - 3¼ "
Total length of main line and branch - 35¾ miles.

The line is worked and maintained by the Belfast and Northern Counties Company.

CAPITAL.

Capital authorized:—

	£
Shares - - - - -	325,775
Borrowing Powers - - - -	262,763
Total - - -	£588,538

Financial position on the 30th of June 1867, as ascertained by the Commission:—
Capital raised by the Company:—

	£
Ordinary Shares - - - -	176,050
Preference Shares - - - -	146,335
Debentures - - - -	236,991
Total Capital - - -	£559,376

Floating liabilities, less floating assets - - - £11,089

Net revenue of each of the last three years, as returned by the Company :—

	£
1864–65 - - - - -	6,679
1865–66 - - - - -	2,672
1866–67 - - - - -	4,992
Average for three years - - -	£5,446

Dividend on Ordinary Shares :—

	£
1864–65 - - - - -	Nil.
1865–66 - - - - -	
1866–67 - - - - -	

Dividend on Preference Shares :—

Average of three years ended the 30th of June 1867 - Nil.

Interest (average rate on the 30th of June 1867) :—

On Debentures - - - - 3*l.* 16*s.* 10*d.* per cent.

The line connects Londonderry with the Belfast and Northern Counties line at Coleraine.

The district of country which may be considered to be accommodated by the line embraces an area of 231,557 acres, with a population of 75,834 persons.

THE MAIN LINE.

Londonderry to Coleraine.

(31½ single miles.)

The main line was constructed under an Act of 1845.

The following table shews the dates when the works were sanctioned, and the several portions of the line opened for traffic :—

Date of Act.	Length sanctioned by Board of Trade, with Date of Opening.			
	From	To	Distance.	Date.
			Miles.	
4 August 1845 -	Londonderry -	Broharris Junction -	14	23 Dec. 1852.
" " -	Broharris Junction -	Coleraine -	17½	18 July 1853.

(a.) *The Newtownlimavady Branch.*

Broharris Junction to Newtownlimavady.

(3½ single miles.)

The Belfast and Northern Counties Railway.

The Belfast and Northern Counties Company works the Londonderry and Coleraine Railway, under an agreement of the 10th of April 1865, for two shillings and twopence per train mile, to be reduced if the mileage exceeds 7,500 miles per month. The Coleraine Company paying for the renewal of the line and half the poor's rates.

---

31. THE CORK AND BANDON RAILWAY.

CORK to BANDON.

LENGTH OF LINE.

	Single.	Double.	Total.
MAIN LINE.	Miles.	Miles.	Miles.
CORK to BANDON - - - - - - - -	20	—	20
Total number of miles owned by the Company - - -	20	—	20
LINE WORKED AND MAINTAINED BY THE COMPANY.			
CORK AND MUSKERRY JUNCTION (from Junction with Cork and Bandon Line to Blarney) - - - - - - - - -	10¾	—	10¾
Total worked and maintained by the Company - - -	30¾	—	30¾

Length of main line - - - - - - 20 miles.
Length of line worked and maintained, but not owned by the Company - - - - - 10¾ „
Total mileage worked and maintained - - 30¾ miles.

CAPITAL.

Capital authorised :—

	£
Shares - - - - - - -	318,000
Borrowing Powers - - - - -	80,000
Total - - - -	£398,000

Financial position on the 30th of June 1867, as ascertained by the Commission :—

Capital raised by the Company :—

		£
Ordinary Shares - - - -		173,241
Preference Shares - - -	No. 1.	48,000
	No. 2.	29,393
Debentures - - - - -		62,586
Debenture Stock - - - -		8,310
Loan Commissioners - - - -		8,912
Total Capital - - - -		£332,652

Floating liabilities, less floating assets - - - £7663

Net revenue of each of the last three years, from Company's accounts :—

	£
1864–65 - - - - - -	7,327
1865–66 - - - - - -	8,115
1866–67 - - - - - -	11,391
Average for three years - - -	£8,944

Dividend on Ordinary Shares :—

1864–65 }
1865–66 } - - Nil.
1866–67 }

Cork and Bandon Railway.

Dividend on Preference Shares :—

		£	s.	d.	
Average of three years ended the 30th of June 1867	No. 1.	5	10	0	per cent.
	No. 2.*	4	0	0	"

Interest (average rate on the 30th of June 1867) :—

	£	s.	d.	
On Debentures	5	5	8	"
On Debenture Stock	4	0	0	"

Interest paid to Loan Commissioners :—

	£	s.	d.	
Rate of Interest	4	0	0	"

This railway, together with the Cork and Macroom, the Cork and Kinsale Junction, and the West Cork, connect the southern and western part of the county with the city and harbour of Cork.

The district of country which may be considered to be accommodated by the line embraces an area of 65,891 acres, with a population of 106,711 persons.

THE LINE.

The line from Carrigeens near Cork to Bandon was constructed under an Act of 1845, and the extension to the present station in the city of Cork under an Act of 1847. 8 & 9 Vict. c. 122. 10 & 11 Vict. c. 134.

The following table shews the dates when the works were authorised, and the several portions of the line sanctioned for traffic :—

Date of Act.	Length sanctioned by Board of Trade, with Date of Sanction.			
	From	To	Distance.	Date.
			Miles.	
21 July 1845	Bandon	Ballinhassig	10	30 July 1849.
21 July 1845	Ballinhassig	Carrigeens	10	6 Dec. 1851.
9 July 1847	Carrigeens	Cork		

Relations of the Cork and Bandon with other Railway Companies.

The lines in connexion with the Cork and Bandon Railway are stated in the following table :—

Name of Railway Company.	Point of Junction.	Page of Report.
Lines worked and maintained.		
The Cork and Kinsale Junction	13½ miles from Cork	83
Other completed Lines.		
The Cork and Macroom Direct	Ballyphehane Junction	84
The West Cork	Bandon	131

The Cork and Kinsale Junction Railway.

This line may be considered a branch of the Cork and Bandon line, and is worked by that Company.

The Cork and Macroom Direct Railway.

This Company works over the Cork and Bandon line from Ballyphehane Junction to the Cork station.

The West Cork Railway.

This line connects Dunmanway with the Cork and Bandon line at Bandon.

* Paid by deferred dividend warrants.

21. THE CORK AND KINSALE JUNCTION RAILWAY.

From Innishannon Junction to Kinsale.

LENGTH OF LINE.

	Single.	Double.	Total.
	Miles.	Miles.	Miles.
Innishannon Junction to Kinsale - - - - - -	10½	—	10½

This line is worked by the Cork and Bandon Company.

CAPITAL.

Capital authorized :—

	£
Shares - - - - - -	85,000
Borrowing Powers - - - -	28,200
Total - - - - -	£113,200

Financial position on the 30th of June 1867, as ascertained by the Commission :—
Capital raised by the Company :—

	£
Ordinary Shares - - - -	20,630
Preference Shares - - - -	6,530
Debentures - - - -	21,600
Total Capital - - -	£48,760

Floating liabilities, less floating assets - - - £46,103

Net revenue of each of the last three years, from Company's accounts :—

	£
1864–65 - - - -	1,368
1865–66* - - - -	1,638
1866–67* - - - -	1,784
Average of three years - - -	£1,597

Dividend on Ordinary Shares :—

1864–65, 1865–66, 1866–67 - - Nil.

Dividend on Preference Shares :—
Average of the three years ended the 30th of June 1867, Nil.

Interest (average rate on the 30th of June 1867) :—
On Debentures - - - 5*l.* 14*s.* 6*d.* per cent.

A receiver was appointed by the Irish Court of Chancery on the 21st of March 1866.
This line connects the port of Kinsale with the Cork and Bandon line.
The district of country which may be considered to be accommodated by the line embraces an area of 65,642 acres, with a population of 20,157 persons.

THE LINE.

The line was constructed under an Act of 1859.

Date of Act.	Length certified by Board of Trade, with Date of Sanction.			
	From	To	Distance.	Date.
			Miles.	
19 April 1859 -	Innishannon Junction	Kinsale - - -	11	27 June 1863.

* No published accounts after the 30th of June 1865; the remaining half-years' net revenues are taken from the amount ascertained by the Commission.

RELATIONS OF THE CORK AND KINSALE JUNCTION WITH OTHER RAILWAY COMPANIES:—

Name of Railway Company.	Point of Junction.	Page of Report.
The Cork and Bandon	10½ miles from Cork	80

The Cork and Bandon Railway.

This Company works and maintains the Cork and Kinsale Junction Railway for 30 per cent. of the gross traffic.

A Bill is being promoted in the present session for authorising the sale or lease of the line to the Cork and Bandon Company.

---

33. THE CORK, BLACKROCK, AND PASSAGE RAILWAY.

CORK to PASSAGE.

LENGTH OF LINE.

	Single.	Double.	Total.
	Miles.	Miles.	Miles.
CORK to PASSAGE	6½	—	6½

CAPITAL.

	£
Capital authorised:—	
Shares	130,000
Borrowing Powers	43,330
Total	£173,330

Financial position on the 30th of April 1867, as ascertained by the Commission:—

Capital raised by the Company:	£
Ordinary Shares	118,340
Debentures	38,450
Loan Commissioners	3,324
Total Capital	£160,114

Cr. Floating assets, less floating liabilities - £3,721

Net revenue of each of the last three years, from Company's accounts:—

	£
1864-65	3,767
1865-66	4,401
1866-67	3,467
Average for three years	£3,878

Dividend on Ordinary Shares:—

	£	s.	d.	
1864-65	2	0	0	per cent.
1865-66	2	0	0	"
1866-67	1	5	0	"

Interest (average rate on the 30th of April 1867):—
On Debentures - 5*l.* 5*s.* 5*d.* per cent.

Interest paid to Loan Commissioners:—
Rate of interest - 4*l.* 0*s.* 0*d.* per cent.

This railway connects the town of Passage and the suburb of Blackrock with the city of Cork.

The district of country which may be considered to be accommodated by the line embraces an area of 90,939 acres, with a population of 89,904 persons.

THE LINE.

The line was constructed under an Act of 1846, upon the site of a line which had been authorized in 1837, but the powers for making which had expired.

Date of Act.	Length sanctioned by Board of Trade, with Date of Sanction.			
	From	To	Distance.	Date
			Miles.	
16 July 1846 -	Cork - - - -	Passage	6	21 May 1850.

---

34. THE CORK AND MACROOM DIRECT RAILWAY.

From Junction near Cork with Cork and Bandon line to Macroom.

LENGTH OF LINE.

	Single	Double	Total.
	Miles.	Miles.	Miles
BALLYPHEHANE JUNCTION to MACROOM	23¼		23¼

CAPITAL.

Capital authorised :—

	£
Shares - - - - - -	120,000
Borrowing Powers - - - -	40,000
Total - - -	£160,000

Financial position on the 30th of June 1867, as ascertained by the Commission:—

Capital raised by the Company :

	£
Ordinary Shares - - - - -	69,096
Debentures - - - - -	37,350
Total Capital - -	£106,446

Floating liabilities, less floating assets - - - - £45,331

Net revenue since the opening of the line, as returned by the Company :—

	£
From the 12th of May to the 30th of June 1866 -	835
1866–67 - - - - - - -	4,031
Average for period since line opened -	£4,346

Dividend on Ordinary Shares :—

1866–67 - - - - - - 2*l.* 0*s.* 0*d.* per cent.

Interest (average rate on the 30th of June 1867) :— £ *s.* *d.*

On Debentures - - - - - 5 10 10 per cent.

This railway connects the town of Macroom with the city and port of Cork. The district of country which may be considered to be accommodated by the line embraces an area of 226,672 acres, with a population of 124,849 persons.

THE LINE

The line was constructed under an Act of 1861.

Date of Act.	Length sanctioned by Board of Trade, with Date of Sanction.			
	From	To	Distance.	Date.
			Miles.	
1 August 1861 -	Ballyphehane Junction with the Cork and Bandon line.	Macroom - -	24	12 May 1866.

RELATIONS OF THE CORK AND MACROOM DIRECT WITH OTHER RAILWAY COMPANIES.

Name of Railway Company.	Point of Junction.	Page of Report.
The Cork and Bandon -	- Ballyphehane Junction -	80

The Cork and Bandon Railway.

The Cork and Macroom Company is authorised to work over the Cork and Bandon Line, between Ballyphehane Junction and Cork, and to use the station at Cork. The Board of Trade is empowered to compel the Cork and Bandon Company to lay down an additional line of rails between these points, at the expense of the Cork and Macroom Company. Power is also given for traffic arrangements with the Cork and Bandon Company.

---

35. THE DUBLIN AND BELFAST JUNCTION RAILWAY.

DROGHEDA to PORTADOWN.

LENGTH OF LINE.

MAIN LINE.	Single	Double	Total
	Miles.	Miles.	Miles.
DROGHEDA to PORTADOWN - - - - -	—	55½	55½
Total number of miles owned by the Company - -	—	55½	55½
LINE WORKED AND MAINTAINED BY THE COMPANY.			
The BANBRIDGE JUNCTION (from Scarva to Banbridge) - - -	6¾	—	6¾
Total mileage worked and maintained by the Company - -	6¾	55½	62¼

Length of main line - - - - 55½ miles.
Length of line worked and maintained but not owned by the Company - - - 6¾ "
Total mileage worked and maintained - - 62¼ miles.

CAPITAL.

Capital authorized :—	£
Shares - - - - - -	873,500
Borrowing Powers - - - - -	291,160
Total - - - -	£1,164,660

Financial position on the 30th of June 1867, as ascertained by the Commission :—

Capital raised by the Company :	£
Ordinary Shares - - - -	873,500
Debentures - - - - -	227,510
Debenture Stock - - - -	4,645
Total Capital - - -	£1,105,655

Cr. Floating assets, less floating liabilities - - - £5,589

Net revenue of each of the last three years, as returned by the Company :—

	£
1864–65 - - - - -	48,170
1865–66 - - - - -	45,652
1866–67 - - - - -	45,464
Average of the three years - -	£46,429

Dividend on Ordinary Shares :—	£	s.	d.	
1864–65 - - - -	3	10	0	per cent.
1865–66 - - - -	4	5	0	"
1866–67 - - - -	4	0	0	"
Interest (average rate on the 30th of June 1867) :—				
On Debentures - - - -	4	15	3	"
On Debenture Stock - - 4*l.* and	4	5	0	"

This railway connects the Dublin and Drogheda with the Ulster and the Irish North Western lines, and forms the main route from Dublin to Belfast and to the North of Ireland.

The district of country which may be considered to be accommodated by the line embraces an area of 298,511 acres, with a population of 153,379 persons.

THE LINE.

This line was authorised by an Act of 1845. The works progressed very slowly, and by an Act of 1850 an extension of seven years was given to complete them, and the Company received advances from the Public Works Loan Commissioners to the extent of 75,000*l.*, at 5 per cent., which after the 20th of December 1850 was reduced to 4 per cent. per annum.

The following table shows the dates when the works were authorized, and the several portions of the line opened for traffic :—

Length sanctioned by Board of Trade, with Date of Sanction.

The Banbridge Junction Railway.

This line is leased by the Dublin and Belfast Junction Company for 91 years from the 20th of September 1857 at a rent of 2,000*l.* a year.

The Dublin and Drogheda Railway.

The Dublin and Belfast Junction Company use the station of the Dublin and Drogheda Company at Drogheda, at a rent of 1,000*l.* a year.

The Irish North Western Railway.

The Dublin and Belfast Junction has an identity of interest with the Irish North Western Company in the traffic to places between Dundalk and Omagh, but has a competing interest with that Company for traffic to places between Omagh and Londonderry, as such traffic can be brought to it at Portadown, by the Portadown, Dungannon, and Omagh Railway.

The Newry and Armagh Railway.

The line of this Company crosses the Dublin and Belfast Junction line at Goragh Wood Junction, giving a route to Armagh of 18 miles, the route from the same point to Armagh by the Dublin and Belfast Junction and Ulster Railways viâ Portadown being 29¼ miles.

The Ulster Railway.

The Dublin and Belfast Junction Company use the Ulster Company's station at Portadown at a rent of 675*l.* a year.
The present agreement is for three years, from the 1st of July 1865.

---

36. THE BANBRIDGE JUNCTION RAILWAY.

BANBRIDGE to SCARVA.

LENGTH OF LINE.

	Single	Double	Total
	Miles.	Miles.	Miles.
BANBRIDGE to SCARVA -	6¾	—	6¾

The line is worked and maintained by the Dublin and Belfast Junction Company.

CAPITAL.

	£
Capital authorized :—	
Shares - - - - -	60,000
Borrowing Powers - - -	20,000
Total - - - - -	£80,000

Financial position on the 30th of June 1867, as ascertained by the Commission :—

	£
Capital raised by the Company :	
Ordinary Shares - - - -	22,128
Preference Shares - - - -	17,800
Debentures - - - - -	17,250
Total Capital - - - -	£57,178

Floating liabilities, less floating assets - - -	£184

Net revenue of each of the last three years, as returned by the Company:—

	£
1864–65 - - - - - -	2,000
1865–66 - - - - - -	2,000
1866–67 - - - - - -	2,000
Average for three years - - -	£2,000

Dividend on Ordinary Shares:—

1864–65 - - - - -	No dividend.
1865–66 - - - - -	2*l*. 10*s*. 0*d*. per cent.
1866–67 - - - - -	No dividend.

Dividend on Preference Shares:—

Average of three years ended the 30th of June 1867, 5*l*. 0*s*. 0*d*. per cent.

Interest (average rate payable at the 30th of June 1867):—

On Debentures - - - - - 4*l*. 10*s*. 11*d*. per cent.

This railway connects Banbridge with the Dublin and Belfast Junction line at Scarva. The district of country which may be considered to be accommodated by the line embraces an area of 25,768 acres, with a population of 10,754 persons.

THE LINE.

The line was made under an Act of 1853, the time for completing the works having been extended in 1856 when the name of the Company was changed from the Banbridge, Newry, Dublin, and Belfast Junction Company to that of Banbridge Junction Company.

Date of Act.	Length sanctioned by Board of Trade, with Date of Sanction.			
	From	To	Distance.	Date.
			Miles	
20 August 1853 -	Banbridge - -	Scarva - -	7	7 February 1859.

Relations of the Banbridge Junction with other Railway Companies.

The lines in connexion with the Banbridge Junction are stated in the following table:—

Name of Railway Company.	Point of Junction.	Page of Report.
Completed lines.		
The Dublin and Belfast Junction - - -	Scarva Junction - - - -	43
The Banbridge, Lisburn, and Belfast - -	Banbridge - - - -	132

The Dublin and Belfast Junction Railway.

The Banbridge Junction Railway is leased to this Company under the Act of 1857; for 21 years, from the 20th of September 1857, at a rent of 2,000*l*. a year.

The Banbridge, Lisburn, and Belfast Railway.

This line connects the Banbridge Junction with the Ulster Railway at Knockmore Junction.

37. THE DUBLIN AND DROGHEDA RAILWAY.

Dublin to Drogheda, with branches to Howth and Oldcastle.

LENGTH OF LINE.

MAIN LINE.	Single	Double.	Total
	Miles.	Miles.	Miles.
Dublin to Drogheda - - - - -	—	31¾	31¾
BRANCHES.			
(a.) The Howth Branch (from Howth Junction to Howth) - -	3½	—	3½
(b.) The Oldcastle Branch (from Drogheda to Oldcastle) - -	39½	—	39½
Total number of miles owned by the Company - -	43	31¾	74¾

Length of main line - - - - - 31¾ miles.
Length of branches - - - - - - 43 „
Total length of main line and branches - - - 74¾ miles.

CAPITAL.

Capital authorised :—

	£
Shares - - - - - -	953,000
Borrowing Powers - - - -	317,333
Total - - - -	£1,270,333

Financial position on the 30th of June 1867, as ascertained by the Commission :—

Capital raised by the Company :—

	£
Ordinary shares - - - - -	644,800
Preference shares - - - -	155,775
Guaranteed 4 per cent. stock, perpetual -	94,225
Debentures - - - - -	250,498
Debenture Stock - - - - -	43,722
Loan Commissioners - - - -	2,670
Total Capital - - -	£1,191,690

Floating liabilities, less floating assets - - - £12,920

Net revenue of each of the last three years, as returned by the Company :—

	£
1864–65 - - - - - - -	54,573
1865–66 - - - - - - -	55,003
1866–67 - - - - - - -	56,255
Average of three years - -	£55,277

Dividend on Ordinary Shares :—

	£	s.	d.	
1864–65 - - - -	4	5	0	per cent.
1865–66 - - - -	4	15	0	„
1866–67 - - - -	4	12	6	„

Dividend on Preference Shares :—

Average of three years ended the 30th of June 1867 - 4 12 6 per cent.

Interest on guaranteed 4 per cent. Perpetual Stock :—

Average of three years ended the 30th of June 1867 - 4 0 0 per cent.

M 4

Interest (average rate on the 30th of June 1867):—
On Debentures - - - - - - 4 10 3 per cent.
On Debenture Stock - - - - - 4 0 0 "

Interest paid to Loan Commissioners:—
Rate of Interest - - - - 4*l.* 0*s.* 0*d.* per cent.

The district of the country which may be considered to be accommodated by the line embraces an area of 472,893 acres, with a population of 162,875 persons.

THE MAIN LINE.

Dublin to Drogheda.

(31¾ miles, double line.)

The main line was commenced under an Act of 1836, but the works proceeded slowly, and in 1840, before one-half of the capital was paid up, the Company obtained power to borrow, from the Public Works Loan Commissioners, the sum of 156,000*l.*, with priority over all other mortgages and securities. The share capital of the Company at the same time was reduced, two years extension was granted to purchase lands, and five years to complete the line. The Company received from the Public Works Loan Commissioners 156,000*l.* between the 16th of December 1842 and the 28th of February 1848.

Date of Act.	Length sanctioned by Board of Trade, with Date of Sanction.			
	From	To	Distance.	Date.
			Miles.	
13 Aug. 1836 -	- Dublin -	- Drogheda -	- 32	June 1844.

THE BRANCHES.

(*a.*) *The Howth Branch.*

Howth Junction to Howth Harbour.

(3½ miles, single line.)

This Branch was made under an Act of 1845, and the following table shows when the works were authorized and the several portions sanctioned for traffic:—

Date of Act.	Length sanctioned by Board of Trade, with Date of Sanction.			
	From	To	Distance.	Date.
			Miles.	
21 July 1845 -	- Howth Junction -	First Terminus -	[illegible]	30 July 1846.
" "	First Terminus -	Second Terminus -	[illegible]	May 1847.

(*b.*) *The Oldcastle Branch.*

Drogheda to Oldcastle.

(39¼ miles, single line.)

The portion of this branch from Drogheda to Navan was granted to the Dublin and Belfast Junction Company; the right of making it was purchased by the Dublin and Drogheda Company under the provisions of an Act of 1847, and the works were executed by the latter Company.

From Navan to Kells was made under an Act of 1847, and from Kells to Oldcastle under an Act of 1850.

The following table shows the dates when the works were authorised and the several portions of the branch sanctioned for traffic :— Dublin and Drogheda Railway.

Date of Act.	Length sanctioned by Board of Trade, with Date of Sanction.			
	From	To	Distance.	Date.
			Miles.	
21 July 1845	Drogheda	Navan	17	Dec. 1849.
9 July 1847	Navan	Kells	9½	5 July 1853.
3 July 1860	Kells	Oldcastle	12½	14 March 1863.

RELATIONS OF THE DUBLIN AND DROGHEDA WITH OTHER RAILWAY COMPANIES.

The lines in connexion with the Dublin and Drogheda Railway are stated in the following table :—

Name of Railway.	Point of Junction.	Page of Report.
Completed Lines.		
The Dublin and Belfast Junction	Drogheda	65
The Dublin and Meath	Navan	66
Lines authorised but not commenced.		
The Dublin Trunk Connecting	Two points near Amiens Street Terminus, Dublin.	60
The Navan and Kingscourt	Navan	49

The Dublin and Belfast Junction Railway.

The Dublin and Belfast Junction Railway forms the connecting link between the main line of the Dublin and Drogheda and the principal railways in the north and north-west of Ireland. In 1847 Parliamentary powers were obtained to enable the Dublin and Drogheda, the Dublin and Belfast Junction, the Dundalk and Enniskillen (now the Irish North-western), and the Ulster companies, or any of them, to amalgamate, but these powers have not been exercised. 10 & 11 Vict. c. [illegible]

The Dublin and Belfast Junction Company uses the station of the Dublin and Drogheda Company at Drogheda at a rent of 1,000*l.* a year.

The Dublin and Meath Railway.

This line connects Navan with the Midland Great Western line at Clonsilla Junction.

The Dublin and Meath Company uses the portion of the line between Navan and Kells and the Kells station of the Dublin and Drogheda Company, paying a rent of 219*l.* 15*s.* a year, and tolls as agreed for the traffic.

The Dublin Trunk Connecting.

This line, if made, would connect the Dublin and Drogheda with the Dublin and Kingstown, the Midland Great Western, and the Great Southern and Western Railways.

The Navan and Kingscourt Railway.

This line, when made, will form a continuation of the Dublin and Meath Railway for 19 miles into a portion of country not directly supplied with railway accommodation.

Dublin and Meath Railway.

38. THE DUBLIN AND MEATH RAILWAY.

Clonsilla Junction to Navan, with Branch to Athboy.

LENGTH OF LINK.

	Single.	Double.	Total.
MAIN LINK.	Miles.	Miles.	Miles.
Clonsilla Junction to Navan - - - -	23¼	—	23¼
BRANCH.			
(a.) The Athboy Branch (from Kilmessan Junction to Athboy) - -	12¼	—	12¼
Total number of Miles owned by the Company - - -	35½	—	35½

Length of main line - - - - 23¼ } miles.
Length of branch - - - - 12¼ }
Total length of main line and branch - - 35½ miles.

CAPITAL.

Capital authorized :—

	£
Shares - - - - -	390,000
Borrowing Powers - - -	115,000
	£505,000

Financial position on the 30th of June, 1867, as ascertained by the Commission :—

Capital raised by the Company :—

	£
Ordinary shares - - - -	133,155
Preference shares - - - -	183,460
Debentures - - - -	101,494
Loan Commissioners - - -	13,500
Total capital - - -	£431,609

Floating liabilities, less floating assets - - - £50,953

Net revenue of each of the last three years, as returned by the Company :—

	£
1864–65 - - - - -	4,784
1865–66 - - - - -	5,519
1866–67 - - - - -	3,844
Average of three years -	£4,716

Dividend on Ordinary Shares :—
1864–65 }
1865–66 } - - - - - - Nil.
1866–67 }

Dividend on Preference Shares :—
Average of three years, ended the 30th of June 1867 Nil.

Interest, average rate on the 30th of June 1867 :—
On Debentures - - - - - 5*l.* 0*s.* 0*d.* per cent.

Interest paid to Loan Commissioners :—
Rate of Interest - - - - - 5*l.* 0*s.* 0*d.* per cent.

This Company connects a large part of the county of Meath with Dublin.

The district of country which may be considered to be accommodated by the line embraces an area of 215,731 acres, with a population of 348,298 persons.

(a.) *The Athboy Branch.*

The branch was constructed under the Act of 1858.

Date of Act.	Length sanctioned by Board of Trade, with Date of Sanction.			
	From	To	Distance.	Date.
[illegible] July 1858 - -	Kilmessan Junction -	Athboy - - -	Miles. 12	[illegible] February 1864.

The Relations of the Dublin and Meath with other Railway Companies.

The lines in connexion with the Dublin and Meath are stated in the following table :—

Name of Railway Company	Point of Junction.	Page of Report
Completed Lines.		
The Midland Great Western - - - -	Clonsilla Junction - - -	119
The Dublin and Drogheda - - - -	Navan - - - - -	[illegible]
Line authorised but not commenced.		
The Navan and Kingscourt - - - -	Navan - - - - -	[illegible]

The Midland Great Western Railway.

The traffic of the Dublin and Meath Company runs on the Midland Great Western line between Clonsilla and Dublin. The terms are fixed by an award of July 1861, modified by a subsequent agreement with the Midland Great Western Company.

The Dublin and Drogheda Railway.

The Dublin and Meath Company uses the part of the Oldcastle Branch of the Dublin and Drogheda line between Navan and Kells and the Kells Station, paying a rent of 219*l.* 18*s.* a year for the station, with tolls for the traffic as agreed.

The Navan and Kingscourt Railway.

This Railway will be a continuation of the Dublin and Meath line into a district of country not hitherto supplied with railway accommodation.

Dublin, Wicklow, and Wexford Railway.

39. THE DUBLIN, WICKLOW, AND WEXFORD RAILWAY.

From Dublin to Enniscorthy, with branches to Dalkey, Wicklow, and Shillelagh, and extension commenced but not completed, from Enniscorthy to Wexford, and branch authorized but not commenced between Ranelagh and Merrion.

LENGTH OF LINE.

	Single.	Double.	Total.
MAIN LINE.	Miles.	Miles.	Miles.
Dublin to Enniscorthy - - - - - - -	64¾	13	77¾
BRANCHES.			
(a.) The Shanganagh and Dalkey Branch (from Shanganagh Junction to Dalkey).	4	–	4
(b.) The Wicklow Branch (from Wicklow Junction to Wicklow) - -	17	–	17
(c.) The Shillelagh Branch (from Shillelagh Junction to Shillelagh) -		–	
Total number of miles owned by the Company - -	85¾	13	98¾
OTHER LINE WORKED BY THE COMPANY.			
Dublin and Kingstown (from Dublin to Dalkey, including connecting line to passenger pier).	3	5	8
Total mileage worked - -	88¾	18	106¾
EXTENSION COMMENCED BUT NOT COMPLETED.			
(d.) The Wexford Extension (from Enniscorthy to Wexford) - -	15	–	15
BRANCH AUTHORIZED BUT NOT COMMENCED.			
(e.) The Kingstown connecting Branch (from Ranelagh to Merrion) -	2	–	2
Total mileage authorized - -	105¾	18	123¾

Length of main line - - - - 77¾ miles.
Length of branches - - - - 21 „

Total length of main line and branches - 98¾ miles.

Length of railway worked and maintained but not owned by the Company - - 8 „

Total mileage worked - - - 106¾ „

Length of extension commenced but not completed - - - - - 15 „

Length of branch authorized but not commenced 2 „

Total mileage authorized - - - 123¾ „

CAPITAL.

	£
Capital authorized:—	
Shares - - - - -	1,460,000
Borrowing Powers - - - - -	450,932
Total - - - -	£1,910,932

Financial position on the 30th of June 1867, as ascertained by the Commission:—

	£
Capital raised by the Company:	
Ordinary Shares - - - -	510,050
Preference Shares - - - -	705,030
Debentures - - - -	234,581
Loan Commissioners - - - -	219,324
Total Capital - - -	£1,668,985
Floating liabilities, less floating assets - - -	£138,267

Dublin, Wicklow, and Wexford Railway.

Net revenue of each of the last three years, as returned by the Company:—

	£
1864-65 - - - - -	59,979
1865-66 - - - - -	71,785
1866-67 - - - - -	64,635
Average of the three years - -	£65,464

Dividend on Ordinary Shares:—

1864-65 - - - -	4*l.* 10*s.* 0*d.*	per cent.
1865-66 - - - -	4*l.* 0*s.* 0*d.*	"
1866-67 - - - -	Nil.	

Dividend on Preference Shares:—

Average of three years ended the 30th of June 1867, 5*l.* 6*s.* 8*d.* per cent.

Interest (average on the 30th of June 1867):—

On Debentures - - - 4*l.* 16*s.* 11*d.* per cent.

Interest paid to Loan Commissioners:—

Rate of Interest - - - 4*l.* 16*s.* 8*d.* per cent.

This Company was incorporated in 1846 as the Waterford, Wexford, Wicklow, and Dublin Railway Company; in 1851 its name was changed to the Dublin and Wicklow Railway Company, and in 1860 to the Dublin, Wicklow, and Wexford Railway Company.

The original plan was a very extensive one for connecting Waterford with Wexford, Carlow, Kingstown, and Dublin.

In 1848 the South Wales Railway Company agreed to subscribe for 250,000*l.* with a right to appoint a majority of the directors of the Waterford, Wicklow, and Wexford and Dublin Company. 11,200 original 20*l.* shares, or 224,000*l.*, were allotted to that Company, who paid upon them 38,000*l.*; in January 1859 the South Wales Company sold their shares for 10,000*l.*

In 1851 all the provisions for making the portion of the railway south of Wicklow were repealed.

The district of country which may be considered to be accommodated by the line embraces an area of 896,658 acres, with a population of 370,209 persons.

THE MAIN LINE.

Dublin to Enniscorthy.

(77½ miles; 19 double line and 58½ single line.)

The main line from Dublin to Dundrum was partly made by the Dublin, Dundrum, and Rathfarnham Railway Company, afterwards called the Dublin and Bray Company, under an Act of 1846. The Dublin and Bray Company was unable to complete the works, although the time was extended in 1851, and it was ultimately finished by the Dublin, Wicklow, and Wexford Company, with which the Dublin and Bray Company was incorporated. (9 & 10 Vict. c. [illegible]. 14 & 15 Vict. c. 107. 20 & 21 Vict. c. [illegible].)

The main line from Dundrum to Wicklow was made under the Company's original Act of 1846, the time for completing it having been extended in 1851 to the 24th of July 1865. (9 & 10 Vict. c. [illegible]. 14 & 15 Vict. c. [illegible].)

The extension from the old to the new terminus in Dublin was made under the Act of 1857, the extension from Wicklow to Gorey under that of 1859, and the extension from Gorey to Enniscorthy under that of 1860. (20 & 21 Vict. c. [illegible]. 22 & 23 Vict. c. [illegible]. 23 & 24 Vict. c. [illegible].)

The following table shews the dates when the works were authorised, and the several portions of the line sanctioned for traffic:—

(a.) *The Shanganagh and Dalkey Branch.*

Dalkey to Shanganagh Junction.

(4 miles, single line.)

In 1846 the Dublin and Kingstown Company was authorized to make this continuation of the Dalkey Branch, but under an Act of the same session the Dublin, Wicklow, and Wexford Company purchased the Dublin and Kingstown Company's rights and powers, and it has since completed the Railway.

Date of Act.	Length sanctioned by Board of Trade, with Date of Sanction.			
	From	To	Distance.	Date.
16 July 1846 - -	Dalkey - - -	Shanganagh Junction	Miles. 4	4 July 1854.

(b.) *The Wicklow Branch.*

Wicklow Junction to Wicklow.

(½ a mile, single line.)

This branch, connecting the town and harbour of Wicklow with the main line, was made under the Company's original Act, with certain deviations authorised in 1851.

Date of Act.	Length sanctioned by Board of Trade, with Date of Sanction.			
	From	To	Distance.	Date.
16 July 1846 - -	Wicklow Junction -	Wicklow - -	Miles. ½	20 Oct. 1855.

(c.) *The Shillelagh Branch.*

Shillelagh Junction to Shillelagh.

(16½ miles; single line.)

This branch was made under an Act of 1863, and plans have been lodged in the present session of Parliament for a station at Shillelagh.

Date of Act.	Length sanctioned by Board of Trade, with Date of Sanction.			
	From	To	Distance.	Date.
22 June 1863 - -	Shillelagh Junction -	Shillelagh - -	Miles. 16½	14 May 1865.

EXTENSION COMMENCED BUT NOT COMPLETED.

(d.) *The Wexford Extension.*

Enniscorthy to Wexford.

(15 miles.)

The extension was authorized in 1864, and was partly made; the time for the compulsory purchase of land for the rest of the branch expired in June 1867, but the Company has applied in its Bill of the present session for revival of its power and extension of time.

BRANCH AUTHORISED BUT NOT COMMENCED.

(a.) *The Kingstown connecting Branch.*

Ranelagh to Merrion.

(2 miles.)

This branch, when made, will connect the Dublin, Wicklow, and Wexford line, at Ranelagh, with the Dublin and Kingstown line near Merrion, and will thus give Kingstown traffic access to the Harcourt Street Station, and to the authorised central station of the Dublin and Rathmines, &c. line, and if the Dublin and Rathmines, &c., and Dublin Metropolitan Junction lines be made, it will form a connexion also with the Great Southern and Western line. It was authorized in 1865, and the time for compulsory purchase of land will expire in July 1868. No part of the land has been taken, but the Company has applied in its Bill of the present session for an extension of time for the purchase of the land and for completing the works.

RELATIONS OF THE DUBLIN, WICKLOW, AND WEXFORD WITH OTHER RAILWAY COMPANIES.

The lines in connexion with the Dublin, Wicklow, and Wexford Railway are stated in the following table:—

Name of Railway.	Point of Junction.	Page of Report.
Line worked.		
The Dublin and Kingstown - -	Dalkey - - - -	99
Lines authorised but not commenced.		
The Dublin Metropolitan Junction -	Harcourt Street Station - -	43
The Waterford and Wexford - -	Wexford - - - - -	46
The Waterford, New Ross, and Wexford	Ballyhoge Junction - - -	47
The Bray and Enniskerry - -	Bray - - - - -	49

The Dublin and Kingstown Railway.

The Dublin, Wicklow, and Wexford, under powers in their original Act, have leased the Dublin and Kingstown line. The particulars of the leases and agreements between the two companies are herein-after noticed (p. 100).

The Dublin Metropolitan Junction Railway.

This line, when made, will connect the main line of the Dublin, Wicklow, and Wexford Company with the authorized Dublin and Rathmines line, and with the central station in Dublin, and will also connect it with the Great Southern and Western line.

The Waterford and Wexford Railway.

This line when made will connect the Wexford Extension of the Dublin, Wicklow, and Wexford Company, with Ballyhack Ferry, opposite proposed Waterford and Passage line.

The Waterford, New Ross, and Wexford Railway.

The Ballyhoge Branch of this line, if made, would connect the Wexford Extension of the Dublin, Wicklow, and Wexford line with the Waterford, New Ross, and Wexford authorized line at Ballywilliam.

The Bray and Enniskerry Railway.

The Dublin, Wicklow, and Wexford Railway is empowered to subscribe 15,000*l.* to this undertaking.

	Single.	Double.	Total.
MAIN LINE.	Miles.	Miles.	Miles.
Dublin to Kingstown	—	6	6
BRANCH.			
(a.) The Dalkey Branch (from Kingstown to Dalkey) including connecting line to Carlisle pier.	2¼	—	2¼
Total number of miles owned by the Company	2¼	6	8¼

Length of main line - - - - - 6 miles.
Length of branch - - - - - - 2¼ "
Total length of main line and branch - - - 8¼ miles.

The line is leased to, and maintained and worked by, the Dublin, Wicklow, and Wexford Company.

CAPITAL.

Capital authorised:—

	£
Shares	350,000
Borrowing Powers	110,000
Total	£460,000

Financial position on the 31st of August, 1867, as ascertained by the Commission:—

Capital raised by the Company:—

	£
Ordinary shares	350,000
Debenture Stock	70,000
Total capital	£420,000

Cr. Floating assets, less floating liabilities - - - £7,935

Net revenue of each of the last three years from Company's accounts:—

	£
1865	32,233
1866	36,759
1867	34,765
Average of three years	£34,586

Dividend on Ordinary Shares:—

	£	s.	d.	
1865	9	0	0	per cent.
1866	10	0	0	"
1867	9	5	0	"

Interest (average rate on the 30th of June 1867):—

On Debenture Stock - - - - 4*l.* 0*s.* 0*d.* per cent.

This was the first passenger railway authorised in Ireland which was carried to a successful issue. The Company applied for its first Act in 1830, but so distrustful was Parliament of railway enterprise before the Liverpool and Manchester Railway was completed, that the Bill was thrown out, and it was not until the next session, 1831, that it was passed.

The line for six miles, cost upwards of 60,000*l.* per mile, and like the earlier lines in England, was at first laid down with stone blocks, since replaced by wooden sleepers.

The gauge of the line at first was 4 feet 8½ inches, but upon the line being leased to the Dublin, Wicklow, and Wexford Company it was altered, at the cost of that Company, to the uniform gauge of 5 feet 3 inches, established for Ireland.

The district of country which may be considered to be accommodated by the line embraces an area of 6,312 acres, with a population of 312,142 persons.

THE MAIN LINE.

Dublin and Kingstown Railway.

The main line, as far as the western pier of Kingstown Harbour, was made under the Act of 1831. The extension to the present terminus under that of 1834. The Company received loans from the Commissioners of Public Works in Ireland of 75,000*l.* in 1833, and of 37,200*l.* in 1836. 1 & 2 Wm. 4. c. 69. 4 & 5 Wm. 4. c. 67.

The following table shows the dates when the works were authorized, and the several portions of the line opened for traffic:—

Date of Act.	Date of opening of Line.*			
	From	To	Distance.	Date.
			Miles.	
6 September 1831 -	Dublin - -	Western Pier, Kingstown.	5½	17 December 1834.
22 May 1834 - -	Western Pier, Kingstown.	Present Terminus, Kingstown.	½	May 1837.

(a.) *The Dalkey Branch.*

This branch was made by the Dublin, Wicklow, and Wexford Company under the Act of 1846, the Dublin and Kingstown Company having transferred their powers of making it to that Company in 1847. The Dublin and Kingstown Company at the same time transferred to them a lease from the Harbour Commissioners of Kingstown of the site of the branch railway to the old terminus at Dalkey, which was worked on the atmospheric principle. The Dublin, Wicklow, and Wexford Company afterwards obtained a new lease from the Harbour Commissioners for a long term, and in 1856 leased the entire branch, as far as the present terminus at Dalkey, to the Dublin and Kingstown Company, at a nominal rent for 99 years, from the 25th of March 1856. By an Act of 1866, the lease for 99 years was converted into a lease for 980 years, subject to be reduced to the original term of 99 years at the election of the Dublin, Wicklow, and Wexford Company, if a competing line of railway or tramway should be established between Dublin and Kingstown. The branch is included in the sub-lease of the entire line by the Dublin and Kingstown Company to the Dublin, Wicklow, and Wexford Company. 9 & 10 Vic. c. 2[illegible].

Date of Act.	Length sanctioned by Board of Trade, with Date of Sanction.			
	From	To	Distance.	Date.
			Miles.	
16 July 1846 - -	Kingstown - -	Dalkey - -	2	10 October 1855.

RELATIONS OF THE DUBLIN AND KINGSTOWN WITH OTHER RAILWAY COMPANIES.

The lines in connexion with the Dublin and Kingstown, are stated in the following table:—

Name of Railway Company.	Place of Junction.	Page of Report.
Completed Line.		
The Dublin, Wicklow, and Wexford - -	Dalkey -	94
Line commenced but not completed.		
The Dublin Trunk Connecting - - -	Near Westland Row Terminus in Dublin.	60
Line authorized but not commenced.		
The Kingstown Connecting Branch, of the Dublin, Wicklow, and Wexford.	Near Merrion - - -	94

* This line was not sanctioned by the Board of Trade, having been opened before the formation of the Railway Department.

Dublin and Kingstown Railway.

The Dublin, Wicklow, and Wexford Railway.

In 1856 this Company took a lease of the entire Dublin and Kingstown line, for 35 years, at a rent of 32,000*l.* subject to be increased under certain contingencies. In 1859, the lease was modified, and in 1866 it was extended to 980 years, and the rent increased to 36,000*l.* subject to the contingency of the parties being restored to their original position if a competing line of railway or tramway was established between Dublin and Kingstown.

The changes made in 1866 in the lease arose from the Dublin, Wicklow, and Wexford Company obtaining authority to construct the Kingstown Connecting Branch (from the Kingstown line near Merrion, to the Wicklow line near Harcourt Street Station), which was expected to divert part of the Dublin and Kingstown traffic.

The Dublin Trunk Connecting Railway.

This railway, if made, would connect the Dublin and Kingstown with the Dublin and Drogheda, Midland Great Western, and Great Southern and Western Railways.

Great Southern and Western Railway.

41. THE GREAT SOUTHERN AND WESTERN RAILWAY.

DUBLIN to CORK, with branches to Kilkenny, Athlone, Parsonstown, Birdhill, Fermoy, Tralee, Youghal, and Queenstown.

LENGTH OF LINE.

	Single.	Double.	Total.
MAIN LINE.	Miles.	Miles.	Miles.
DUBLIN to CORK - - - - - - -	—	165¾	165¾
BRANCHES.			
(*a.*) THE KILKENNY BRANCH (from Cherryville Junction to Lavistown Junction) -	25	23¼	48¼
(*b.*) THE ATHLONE BRANCH (from Portarlington to Athlone) - - -	39	—	39
(*c.*) THE PARSONSTOWN BRANCH (from the Roscrea Junction to Parsonstown) -	23¼	—	23¼
(*d.*) THE BIRDHILL BRANCH (from Roscrea to Birdhill) - - -	31¾	—	31¾
(*e.*) THE FERMOY BRANCH (from Mallow to Fermoy) - - -	16¾	—	16¾
(*f.*) THE TRALEE BRANCH (from Mallow to Tralee) - - - -	62	—	62
(*g.*) THE YOUGHAL BRANCH (from Cork to Youghal) - - -	25¼	1¼	26½
(*h.*) THE QUEENSTOWN BRANCH (from the Queenstown Junction to Queenstown)	5¾	—	5¾
Total number of miles owned by the Company - -	228⅝	190¼	418⅞
LINE WORKED BY THE COMPANY.			
CORK AND LIMERICK DIRECT (from Charleville to Foynes Junction) -	17½	—	17½
Total mileage worked by the Company - -	245⅝	190¼	436

Length of main line - - - - 165¾ miles.
Length of branches - - - - 253⅛ "
Total length of main line and branches - 418⅞ miles.
Length of railway worked but not owned by the Company - - - - 17½ "
Total mileage worked and maintained - 436 "

CAPITAL.

Capital authorised :—	£
Shares - - - - -	5,709,940
Borrowing Powers - - - - -	630,965
Total - - - -	£6,340,905

Great Southern and Western Railway.

Financial position on the 30th of June, 1867, as ascertained by the Commission:—

Capital raised by the Company:—

	£
Ordinary Shares - - - - -	4,107,980
Preference Shares - - - - -	1,329,100
Debentures - - - - - -	484,672
Debenture Stock - - - - -	500
Loan Commissioners - - - - -	77,597
Total Capital - -	£5,999,849

Floating liabilities, less floating assets - - - £82,386

Net revenue of each of the last three years, as returned by the Company:—

1865 - - - - - - -	246,829*l.*
1866 - - - - - - -	260,886*l.*
1867 - - - - - - -	272,294*l.*
Average of three years - -	263,669*l.*

Dividend on Ordinary Shares:—

1864–65 - - - - -	4*l.* 10*s.* 0*d.* per cent.
1865–66 - - - - -	5*l.* 0*s.* 0*d.* „
1866–67 - - - - -	4*l.* 15*s.* 0*d.* „

Dividend on Preference Shares:—

Average of the three years ended the 30th of June 1867, 4*l.* 0*s.* 0*d.* per cent.

Interest (average on the 30th of June 1867):—

On Debentures - - - -	4*l.* 8*s.* 1*d.* per cent.
On Debenture Stock - - - -	4*l.* 0*s.* 0*d.* per cent.
Interest paid to Loan Commissioners - -	4*l.* 0*s.* 0*d.* per cent.

The Great Southern and Western Railway is the largest railway system in Ireland, representing in length about one-fourth of the whole of the Irish railways, and in revenue 28 per cent. of their total receipts. The district of the country which may be considered to be accommodated by the line embraces an area of 4,030,119 acres, with a population of 1,293,824 persons.

THE MAIN LINE.

Dublin to Cork.

(165½ miles, double line.)

The main line from the Kingsbridge terminus in Dublin to Thurles was constructed under the Company's first Act, which was passed in 1844. The extension from Thurles to Cork under an Act of 1845, and the extension at Cork to the present terminus under an Act of 1846.

7 & 8 Vict. c. 100.
8 & 9 Vict. c. 84.
9 & 10 Vict. c. 194.

The works of the line were rapidly executed after the Acts of Parliament were obtained, and the following table shows the dates when the works were authorised and the several portions of the line sanctioned for traffic:—

Date of Act.	Length sanctioned by Board of Trade, with Date of Sanction.			
	From	To	Distance.	Date.
			Miles.	
6 Aug. 1844 - -	Dublin - -	Monasterevin -	23½	July 1846.
	Monasterevin -	Maryborough -	20	June 1847.
	Maryborough -	Ballybrophy -	17	Aug. 1847.
	Ballybrophy -	Thurles - -	19	Feb. 1848.
21 July 1845 - -	Thurles - -	Ballykisteen -	20	5 July 1848.
	Ballykisteen -	Mallow - -	37½	6 Aug. 1849.
	Mallow - -	Kilbarry - -	19	25 Oct. 1849.
26 July 1846 - -	Kilbarry - -	Quay at Cork -	1½	21 Nov. 1855.

BRANCHES.

(a.) *The Kilkenny Branch.*

Kildare Junction to Kilkenny.

(48½ miles; 25 miles single, 23½ double.)

This branch from Kildare Junction to Carlow was constructed by the Great Southern and Western Company under its first Act of 1844.

A line from Dublin to Kilkenny by Carlow had been sanctioned as early as 1837, and its construction entrusted to the Great Leinster and Munster Company, but that Company, although it obtained renewed powers in 1841, was unable to carry out the project.

The extension from Carlow to the junction with the Waterford and Kilkenny line near Kilkenny was constructed by the Irish South Eastern Company under the powers of an Act of 1846, and was worked independently by that Company until 1863, when it was incorporated with the Great Southern and Western Company.

The following table shows the dates when the works were authorized, and the several portions of the branch sanctioned for traffic:—

Date of Act.	Length sanctioned by Board of Trade, with Date of Sanction.			
	From	To	Distance.	Date.
			Miles.	
6 August 1844 - -	Near Monasterevin -	Carlow - -	23½	July 1846.
16 July 1846 - -	Carlow - -	Bagenalstown -	10	24 July 1848.
" "	Bagenalstown -	Junction with Waterford and Kilkenny.	13½	December 1850.
" "	Junction with Waterford and Kilkenny.	Kilkenny - -	1½	Not stated.

(b.) *The Athlone Branch.*

Portarlington to Athlone.

(39 miles, single line.)

This branch from Portarlington to Tullamore was constructed under an Act of 1847, the powers conferred by which were revived in 1852. The extension to Athlone was made under an Act of 1857.

The following table shows the dates when the works were authorized, and the several portions of the branch sanctioned for traffic:—

Date of Act.	Length sanctioned by Board of Trade, with Date of Sanction.			
	From	To	Distance.	Date.
			Miles.	
2 July 1847 - -	Portarlington -	Tullamore -	15½	3 October 1854.
27 July 1857 - -	Tullamore - -	Athlone -	24	5 October 1859.

(c.) *The Parsonstown Branch.*

Roscrea Junction to Parsonstown.

(22½ miles, single line.)

This branch was authorized in 1853 to be made by a separate Company, with power to amalgamate with or sell to the Great Southern and Western Company. In 1855 the authority to make the line under the above powers was transferred to the Great Southern and Western Company, who completed it. Great Southern and Western Railway.

The following table shows the dates when the works were authorized, and the several portions of the branch sanctioned for traffic:—

Date of Act.	Length sanctioned by Board of Trade, with Date of Sanction.			
	From	To	Distance.	Date.
			Miles.	
4 Aug. 1853 - -	Roscrea Junction -	Roscrea - -	10	19 October 1857.
" " - -	Roscrea - -	Parsonstown -	12	2 March 1858.

(*d.*) *The Birdhill Branch.*

Roscrea to Birdhill.

(32½ miles, single line.)

This branch was made under an Act of 1861, and the following table shows the dates when the works were authorized, and the several portions sanctioned for traffic:— 24 & 25 Vict. c. 161.

Date of Act.	Length sanctioned by Board of Trade, with Date of Sanction.			
	From	To	Distance.	Date.
			Miles.	
11 July 1861 -	Roscrea - - - -	Nenagh - - - -	19½	1 Oct. 1863.
" " -	Nenagh - - - -	Birdhill - - - -	13	21 Mar. 1864.

(*e.*) *The Fermoy Branch.*

Mallow to Fermoy.

(16¾ miles, single line.)

This line was constructed under the authority of an Act of Parliament obtained by an independent Company in 1854; but in 1857 the Company was dissolved and its powers were transferred to the Great Southern and Western. 17 & 18 Vict. c. 160. 20 & 21 Vict. c. 82.

Date of Act.	Length sanctioned by Board of Trade, with Date of Sanction.			
	From	To	Distance	Date.
			Miles.	
27 July 1857 -	Mallow - - - -	Fermoy - - - -	17	17 May 1860.

(*f.*) *The Tralee Branch.*

Mallow to Killarney and Tralee.

(69 miles, single line.)

The portion of this branch from Mallow to Killarney (39 miles) was made under an Act obtained by the Killarney Junction Company in 1846. 9 & 10 Vict. c. 280.

The works proceeded slowly until 1851, when an Act was passed to sanction a re-arrangement of the capital, and to enable the Company to borrow money on the security of baronies in the counties of Cork and Kerry. In 1854 the Killarney Junction Company was incorporated with the Great Southern and Western Railway, and power was given to release the baronies from their guarantee.

Great Southern and Western Railway.

The portion of this branch from Killarney to Tralee (22 miles) was made under an Act of 1853, obtained by the Tralee and Killarney Company.

In 1857 the Company was authorised to exercise the whole of their borrowing powers before their share capital had been fully subscribed, and a loan of 60,000*l.* was granted by Government for the purposes of the undertaking.

16 & 17 Vict. c. 168.
20 & 21 Vict. c. 17.
22 Vict. c. 16.

In 1859 the Company was incorporated with the Great Southern and Western Company, and the time for the completion of the line was extended.

The following table shows the dates when the works were authorised, and the several portions of the branch sanctioned for traffic :—

Date of Act.	Length sanctioned by Board of Trade, with Date of Sanction.			
	From	To	Distance.	Date.
			Miles.	
16 July 1846 - -	Mallow - -	Freemount - -	22¼	22 May 1853.
" - -	Headford - -	Killarney - -	7	17 June 1853.
" - -	Freemount - -	Headford - -	4	15 July 1853.
15 Aug. 1853 - -	Killarney - -	Tralee - -	22	18 July 1859.

(*g*.) *The Youghal Branch.*

Cork to Youghal.

(26¾ miles ; 1¼ double line, and 25½ single line.)

10 & 11 Vict. c. 101.
19 & 20 Vict. c. 52.
29 & 30 Vict. c. 134.
29 & 30 Vict. c. 344.

This branch was constructed under an Act of 1846 In 1866 the affairs of the Company were wound up and the Company dissolved, and in the same year the Great Southern and Western were authorised to purchase the line for 310,000*l.* of the paid-up stock of that Company.

The following table shows the dates when the works were authorised, and the several portions of the branch line sanctioned for traffic :—

Date of Act.	Length sanctioned by Board of Trade, with Date of Sanction.			
	From	To	Distance.	Date.
			Miles.	
—— 1846 - -	Dunkettle - -	Midleton - -	9	15 November 1859.
" - -	Midleton - -	Killeagh - -	7	7 March 1860.
" - -	Killeagh - -	Youghal - -	6½	24 May 1860.
" - -	Tivoli - -	Dunkettle - -	2	8 October 1861.
23 June 1856 -	Bruin Lodge -	Tivoli - -	1¼	2 January 1862.

(*h*). *The Queenstown Branch.*

Queenstown Junction to Queenstown.

(5¾ miles, single line.)

This branch was constructed under the Act of 1855.

Date of Act.	Length sanctioned by Board of Trade, with Date of Sanction.			
	From	To	Distance.	Date.
			Miles.	
8 July 1855 - -	Queenstown Junction	Queenstown - -	3¾	12 March 1862.

Relations of the Great Southern and Western with other Railway and Canal Companies.

The lines in connexion with the Great Southern and Western are stated in the following table:—

Name of Railway Company.	Points of Junction.	Page of Report.
Lines worked by the Company.		
The Cork and Limerick Direct - - -	Charleville Junction - - -	105
Completed Lines.		
The Limerick and Castleconnell - -	Birdhill - - - - - -	142
The Midland Great Western - - -	Athlone and Clara - - - -	116
The Waterford and Kilkenny - - -	Kilkenny Branch near Kilkenny - -	108
The Kilkenny Junction - - -	Kilkenny and Maryborough - - -	108
The Waterford and Limerick - - -	Limerick Junction - - - -	140
Lines commenced but not completed.		
The Dublin Trunk - - - -	Kingsbridge Terminus - - -	60
The Midland Counties and Shannon Junction -	Clara - - - - -	63
The Parsonstown and Portumna Bridge -	Parsonstown - - - -	65
The Southern of Ireland - - -	Thurles - - - - -	66
The Waterford, New Ross, and Wexford -	Bagenalstown - - - -	67
Lines authorized but not commenced.		
The Central of Ireland - - -	Maryborough and Geashill - - -	45
The Dublin Metropolitan - - -	Kingsbridge Terminus - - -	49
The Waterford, Lismore, and Fermoy - -	Fermoy - - - - -	51

The Cork and Limerick Direct Railway.

This line connects Limerick (53¼ miles distant) and the intervening districts with the port of Cork. The line is worked by the Great Southern and Western at 40 per cent. of its gross receipts.

The Limerick and Castleconnell (with Killaloe Extension) Railway.

This line connects the Birdhill Branch of the Great Southern and Western Railway with Limerick. The distance from Limerick to Roscrea Junction by Birdhill is 57¼ miles, and the distance by the Limerick Junction of the Waterford and Limerick line is 61¼ miles.

The Midland Great Western Railway.

The route by this line from Athlone to Dublin is 78½ miles; that by the Great Southern and Western is 80¾ miles. The route from Clara to Dublin by the Midland Great Western line is 69 miles, and by the Great Southern and Western 65 miles. Competition by the two companies between Athlone and Dublin is regulated by the Great Southern and Western Railway (Athlone Extension) Act, 1857, s. 15.

The Waterford and Kilkenny Railway.

This line connects the Great Southern and Western line with Waterford and the south part of Kilkenny.

The Kilkenny Junction Railway.

This is a continuation of the Waterford and Kilkenny line to Maryborough, where it joins the Great Southern and Western.

The Waterford and Limerick Railway.

The portion of this line between Limerick and Limerick Junction was originally part of the only direct connexion between Limerick and Dublin. The Great Southern and Western Company had powers to make this portion of the line in case the Waterford and Limerick Company failed to do so, and has running powers over it which it does not exercise. The Birdhill Branch now gives the Great Southern and Western line a

Great Southern and Western Railway.

shorter route from Dublin to Limerick, whereby a larger portion of their own line is utilized, but the Limerick and Castleconnell line being worked by the Limerick and Waterford Company, the time of the trains by Birdhill is so fixed that it takes an hour less time to go by Limerick Junction than by Birdhill.

The Dublin Trunk Connecting Railway.

This line includes amongst its objects that of connecting the Great Southern and Western with the Kingstown line and with the harbour of Dublin.

The Midland Counties and Shannon Junction Railway.

This line will join the Great Southern and Western at Clara, and will connect it with the Shannon and form part of a route from the Shannon to Dublin.

The Parsonstown and Portumna Bridge Railway.

This line will continue the Parsonstown Branch to the Shannon at Portumna Bridge. The Great Southern and Western Company has authority to subscribe 13,000*l.* to this undertaking, and has done so to the extent of 1,000*l.*

The Southern Railway.

This line, from Clonmel to Thurles, will give the traffic from Clonmel and part of South Tipperary a much shorter route to Dublin, by cutting off the angle formed by the Limerick Junction.

The Waterford, New Ross, and Wexford Railway.

This Company has purchased the Bagenalstown and Wexford line which, until it was closed in 1863, had been worked by the Great Southern and Western Company.

The Central Ireland Railways.

This line will run from Maryborough to Mullingar. It is a continuation of the Kilkenny Junction Railway, and it will join the Great Southern and Western Line at Maryborough, and cross the Athlone Branch at Geashill.

The Dublin Metropolitan Junction Railway.

This line, when made, will connect the Great Southern and Western Railway with the central station in Dublin on the authorized Dublin and Rathmines, &c. line, and also by the authorized Kingstown connecting branch of the Dublin and Wicklow, &c. with the Kingstown line.

The Waterford, Lismore, and Fermoy Railway.

This line will join the Great Southern and Western Railway at Fermoy. The Company has power to make working arrangements with the Great Southern and Western Company.

Cork and Limerick Direct Railway.

43. THE CORK AND LIMERICK DIRECT RAILWAY.

From the GREAT SOUTHERN AND WESTERN LINE near Charleville to the LIMERICK AND FOYNES LINE near Patrick's Well.

LENGTH OF LINE.

	Single.	Double.	Total.
	Miles.		Miles.
CHARLEVILLE JUNCTION to PATRICK'S WELL JUNCTION . . .	17½	—	17½

The line is worked and maintained by the Great Southern and Western Company.

Cork and Limerick Direct Railway.

CAPITAL.

Capital authorised :—

	£
Shares - - - - - -	105,000
Borrowing Powers - - - -	33,000
Total - - - -	£138,000

Financial position on the 30th of June, as ascertained by the Commission :—

Capital raised by the Company :—

	£
Ordinary Shares - - - - -	71,375
Preference Shares - - - -	11,782
Debentures - - - - -	33,000
Total Capital - - -	£116,157

Floating liabilities, less floating assets - - - £3,796

Net revenue of each of the last three years, as returned by the Company :—

	£
1864–65 - - - - -	3,539
1865–66 - - - - -	4,243
1866–67 - - - - -	4,900
Average for three years - -	£4,229

Dividend on Ordinary Shares :—

1864–65 - - - -	1*l.* 15*s.* 0*d.* per cent.
1865–66 - - - -	2*l.* 5*s.* 0*d.* ,,
1866–67 - - - -	3*l.* 0*s.* 0*d.* ,,

Dividend on Preference Shares - - - 5*l.* 0*s.* 0*d.* per cent.

Interest (average rate on the 30th of June 1867) on Debentures 6*l.* 5*s.* 1*d.* per cent.

This railway establishes direct communication between Cork and Limerick.

The district of country which may be considered to be accommodated by the line embraces an area of 19,024 acres, with a population of 73,082 persons.

THE LINE.

Date of Act.	Length sanctioned by Board of Trade, with Date of Sanction.			
	From	To	Distance	Date.
			Miles.	
6 July 1860 - -	Charleville Junction	Patrick's Well Junction.	10¾	28 July 1862.
" " -	Branch into Limerick	- - -	½	20 April 1862.

Relations of the Cork and Limerick Direct with other Railway Companies.

The lines in connexion with the Cork and Limerick Direct Railway are stated in the following table :—

Name of Railway Company.	Point of Junction.	Page of Report.
The Great Southern and Western - -	Near Charleville - - -	100
The Limerick and Foynes - - -	Foynes Junction and Limerick -	146
The Waterford and Limerick - -	Limerick - - - -	140

The Great Southern and Western Railway.

The Great Southern and Western Company works the Cork and Limerick Direct line for 40 per cent. of the gross receipts.

The Limerick and Foynes Railway.

The Cork and Limerick Direct Company pays the Limerick and Foynes Company 1,400*l.* a year for the use of its line from Patrick's Well Junction to Limerick.

The Waterford and Limerick Railway.

The Cork and Limerick Direct Company pays a rent of 432*l.* 10*s.* a year for the use of the Limerick terminus of the Waterford and Limerick Railway.

---

43. THE IRISH NORTH-WESTERN RAILWAY.

DUNDALK to ENNISKILLEN, with branches to Cootehill, and from Clones to Cavan.

LENGTH OF LINE.

	Single.	Double.	Total.
MAIN LINE.	Miles.	Miles.	Miles.
DUNDALK to ENNISKILLEN - - - -	63	—	63
BRANCHES.			
(a.) THE COOTEHILL BRANCH (from Shantonagh Junction to Cootehill) -	8	—	8
(b.) THE CLONES AND CAVAN BRANCH (from Clones to Cavan) - -	15¼	—	15¼
Total number of miles owned by the Company - - -	86¼	—	86¼
LINES WORKED BY THE COMPANY.			
THE ENNISKILLEN, BUNDORAN, AND SLIGO - - - - -	35¼	—	35¼
THE FINN VALLEY - - - - - - -	13¼	—	13¼
THE LONDONDERRY AND ENNISKILLEN - - - - -	50¾	9½	60
Total number of miles worked - - - - -	185½	9½	195

Length of main line - - - - 63 miles.
Length of branches - - - - 23¼ „
Total length of main line and branches - 86¼ miles.
Length of railways worked and maintained by the Company - - - - } 108¾ „
Total mileage worked - - - 195

CAPITAL.

	£
Capital authorized :—	
Shares - - - - - -	900,000
Borrowing Powers - - - - -	300,000
Total - - - -	£1,200,000

Financial position on the 30th of June 1867, as ascertained by the Commission :

	£
Capital raised by the Company :—	
Ordinary Shares - - - - -	171,420
Special Clones and Cavan Shares - -	27,887
Preference Shares - - - - -	807,307
Debentures - - - - -	169,616
Debenture Stock - - - - -	57,316
Loan Commissioners - - - - -	82,398
Total Capital - - -	£998,006

Floating liabilities, less floating assets - - - £15,836

Irish North-Western Railway.

Net revenue of each of the last three years, as returned by the Company:—

		£
1864-65	- - - - - -	15,183
1865-66	- - - - - -	16,033
1866-67	- - - - - -	21,210
	Average for three years - -	£17,475

Dividend on Ordinary Shares:—

1864-65, 1865-66, 1866-67 - - Nil.

Dividend on Preference Shares:—

Average of three years, ended the 30th of June 1867 - Nil.

Interest (average rate payable at the 30th of June 1867):—

On Debentures - - - 5*l.* 9*s.* 8*d.* per cent.

On Debenture Stock - - 5*l.* 0*s.* 0*d.* "

Interest paid to Loan Commissioners:—

Rate of Interest - - - 4*l.* 0*s.* 0*d.* per cent.

This railway connects the town of Enniskillen and the Londonderry and Enniskillen line with the Dublin and Belfast Junction line at Dundalk, with the Ulster line at Clones, and with the Midland Great Western line at Cavan.

The district of country which may be considered to be accommodated by the line embraces an area of 725,280 acres, with a population of 255,180 persons.

THE MAIN LINE.

Dundalk to Enniskillen.

(63 miles, single line.)

The main line to Castleblaney was constructed under the Act of 1845, and to Ballybay under the same Act, the time having been extended in 1850. The line from Ballybay to Enniskillen was constructed under an Act of 1852, the time for the part between Newbliss and Enniskillen having been extended in 1857. 8 & 9 Vict. c. 98. 13 & 14 Vict. c. 78. 15 & 16 Vict. c. 61. 20 & 21 Vict. c. 104.

The following table shows when the works were authorized, and the several portions of the line sanctioned for traffic:—

Date of Act.	Length sanctioned by Board of Trade, with Date of Sanction.			
	From	To	Distance.	Date.
			Miles.	
21 July 1845 -	Dundalk -	Castleblaney -	20	10 February 1849.
" " -	Castleblaney -	Ballybay -	6½	11 August 1854.
1852 -	Ballybay -	Newbliss -	10	16 August 1855.
" -	Newbliss -	Lisnaskea -	16½	7 July 1858.
" -	Lisnaskea -	Lisbellaw -	6	16 August 1858.
" -	Lisbellaw -	Enniskillen -	4½	15 February 1859.

BRANCHES.

(a.) *The Cootehill Branch.*

Shantonagh Junction to Cootehill.

(8 miles, single line.)

This branch, part of the original Cavan branch of the Company, was constructed under an Act of 1853. 16 & 17 Vict. c. 164.

Date of Act.	Length sanctioned by Board of Trade, with Date of Sanction.			
	From	To	Distance.	Date.
			Miles.	
8 July 1853 -	Shantonagh Junction	Cootehill -	7½	18 October 1860.

Irish North Western Railway.

(h.) *The Clones and Cavan Branch.*

Clones to Cavan.

(15½ miles, single line.)

22 & 23 Vict. c. 11.

This branch was constructed under an Act of 1859, under the name of Clones and Cavan Extension, and the Ulster Company subscribed 27,887*l.* to the undertaking.

Special accounts are kept for this branch and it is managed by special board meetings, at which a director appointed by the Ulster Company can attend.

Date of Act.	Length sanctioned by Board of Trade, with Date of Sanction.			
	From	To	Distance.	Date.
1 August 1859 -	Clones	Cavan	Miles. 15	29 March 1862.

Relations of the Irish North Western with other Railway Companies.

The lines in connexion with the Irish North Western are stated in the following table:—

Name of Railway Company.	Point of Junction.	Page of Report.
Lines worked by the Irish North Western.		
The Londonderry and Enniskillen - - -	Enniskillen - - - - -	114
The Enniskillen, Bundoran, and Sligo - -	Bundoran Junction - - -	111
The Finn Valley - - - - - -	Strabane - - - - -	112
Other completed Lines.		
The Dublin and Belfast Junction - - -	Dundalk - - - - - -	85
The Ulster - - - - - - -	Clones - - - - - -	130
The Midland Great Western - - - -	Cavan - - - - - -	118
Line authorized but not commenced.		
The Dundalk and Greenore - - - - -	Dundalk - - - - -	47

The Londonderry and Enniskillen Railway.

The Irish North Western Company has leased this line in perpetuity at a minimum rent of 26,000*l.* for 35 years, subject to be raised to a maximum of 33,000*l.* a year.

The Enniskillen, Bundoran, and Sligo Railway.

The Irish North Western Company works this line for 2*s.* per train mile.

The Finn Valley Railway.

The Irish North Western Company works this line for 35 per cent. of the gross receipts, the Finn Valley Company paying land charges, and a rent for the use of Strabane station of 375*l.* per annum.

The Dublin and Belfast Junction Railway.

Under Parliamentary authority this Company subscribed 30,000*l.* for ordinary capital and 20,000*l.* for third-class preference shares in the Clones and Cavan Extension. The Dublin and Drogheda Company subscribing a like amount.

The Ulster Railway.

This Company subscribed, under the Act of 1859, 30,000*l.* for special Clones and Cavan Extension shares, and has entered into agreements with the Irish North Western Company for the use of the Omagh station of the Portadown, Dungannon, and Omagh Railway, leased to the Ulster Company.

The Midland Great Western Railway.

The Cavan branch of this line joins the Clones and Cavan branch of the Irish North Western line at Cavan.

The Dundalk and Greenore Railway.

By an Act of 1867 the Irish North Western Company is authorised to make traffic arrangements with the Dundalk and Greenore Company.

---

44. THE ENNISKILLEN, BUNDORAN, AND SLIGO RAILWAY.

From the LONDONDERRY AND ENNISKILLEN LINE to BUNDORAN, with authorised Extension to SLIGO.

LENGTH OF LINE.

	Single	Double	Total
	Miles.	Miles.	Miles.
BUNDORAN JUNCTION to BUNDORAN - - - - - -	35¼	—	35¼
Total completed and owned - - -	35¼	—	35¼
AUTHORIZED EXTENSION.			
(a) The SLIGO EXTENSION (from Bundoran to Sligo) - - - -	—	—	23
Total number of miles authorised - - - - -	—	—	58¼

Length of line - - - - 35¼ miles.
Length of extension authorised - - - 23 "
Total mileage authorised - - 58¼ miles.

The line is worked and maintained by the Irish North Western Company.

CAPITAL.

Capital authorised:—

	£
Shares - - - - - -	450,000
Borrowing Powers - - - -	149,900
Total - - -	£599,900

Financial position on the 30th of September 1867, as ascertained by the Commission:—
Capital raised by the Company:—

	£
Ordinary Shares - - - -	45,714
Preference Shares - - - -	100,000
Debentures - - - -	85,400
Total Capital - - -	£231,114

Floating liabilities, less floating assets - - - £108,411

Net revenue since the opening of the line, from Company's accounts:—

	£
1865–66 (from 15th June 1866) - - -	499
1866–67 - - - - - -	1,015
Average - - - -	£1,962

Dividend on Ordinary Shares - - - - - - Nil.
Dividend on Preference Shares:— Nil.

Interest (average rate payable at the 30th of June 1867):—
On Debentures - - - - - 5*l.* 0*s.* 0*d.* per cent.

The line connects Bundoran (a sea bathing place), and a portion of the county of Donegal, with the Irish North Western system of railways, near Enniskillen.

The district of country which may be considered to be accommodated by the line embraces an area of 314,858 acres, with a population of 73,900 persons.

THE LINE.

The line to Bundoran was authorised in 1861.

Date of Act.	Length sanctioned by Board of Trade, with Date of Sanction.			
	From	To	Distance.	Date.
11 July 1861 - -	Bundoran Junction -	Bundoran - -	Miles 35½	28 March 1866.

(a.) *The Sligo Extension.*

Bundoran to Sligo (23 miles).

This extension was authorised in 1862; but no land has been taken nor any capital expended on the works. In 1865 the time for completing the works was extended to the 19th of June 1868.

RELATIONS OF THE ENNISKILLEN, BUNDORAN, AND SLIGO WITH OTHER RAILWAY COMPANIES.

The lines in connexion with the Enniskillen, Bundoran, and Sligo are stated in the following table:—

Name of Railway Company.	Point of Junction.	Page of Report.
Completed Lines.		
The Londonderry and Enniskillen (worked by the Irish North Western).	Bundoran Junction -	114
The Midland Great Western - - - -	Sligo - - - -	118

The Londonderry and Enniskillen Railway (worked by the Irish North Western Railway Company).

The Enniskillen, Bundoran, and Sligo Railway joins the Londonderry and Enniskillen line about ten miles from Enniskillen. The Irish North Western Company works and maintains the line for 2s. per train mile.

The Midland Great Western Railway.

The Sligo Extension of the Enniskillen, Bundoran, and Sligo Railway will, if completed, join the Sligo branch of the Midland Great Western Railway at Sligo.

Capital authorised :—	£
Shares - - - - -	60,000
Borrowing Powers - - -	20,000
Total - - - - - -	£80,000

Financial position on the 30th of June 1867, as ascertained by the Commission :—

Capital raised by the Company :—	£
Ordinary Shares - - - - -	47,705
Preference Shares - - - -	2,120
Loan Commissioners - - - -	20,000
Total Capital - - - -	£69,825
Floating liabilities, less floating assets - - - -	£7,058

Net revenue of each of the last three years, as returned by the Company :—

	£
1864-65 - - - - - -	2,025
1865-66 - - - - - -	1,940
1866-67 - - - - - -	2,086
Average for three years - - -	£2,017

Dividend on Ordinary Shares :—

1864-65 1865-66 1866-67 } - -	Nil.

Dividend on Preference Shares :—
Average of three years ended the 30th of June 1867 - 5*l.* 0*s.* 0*d.* per cent.

Interest paid to Loan Commissioners :—
Rate of interest - - - - - 5*l.* 0*s.* 0*d.* per cent.

This line connects Stranorlar and part of the county of Donegal with the Londonderry and Enniskillen line at Strabane.

The district of country which may be considered to be accommodated by the line embraces an area of 198,376 acres, with a population of 70,839 persons.

THE LINE.

The line was authorised in 1860.

Date of Act.	Length sanctioned by Board of Trade with Date of Sanction.			
	From	To	Distance	Date.
15 May 1860 - -	Strabane - -	Stranorlar - -	Miles 13	20 August 1863.

RELATIONS OF THE FINN VALLEY WITH OTHER RAILWAY COMPANIES.

Name of Railway Company	Point of Junction.	Page of Report
The Londonderry and Enniskillen (leased to the Irish North Western).	Strabane - - - - -	114

The Irish North Western Railway.

Under an agreement of the 25th of June 1862 the Irish North Western Company works the Finn Valley line for 10 years, from the 1st of November 1863, for 35 per cent. of the gross receipts, the Finn Valley Company paying all rates, rents, taxes, and land charges, and 375*l.* per annum for the use of Strabane station.

—	Single.	Double.	Total.
MAIN LINE.	Miles.	Miles.	Miles.
Londonderry to Enniskillen - - - - - - -	49¼	9¾	59
BRANCH (WORKED BY HORSE-POWER).			
(a.) The Fintona Branch - - - - - - - (From Fintona Junction to Fintona).	1	—	1
Total number of miles worked and maintained by the Company	50¼	9¾	60

Length of main line - - - - 59 miles.
Length of branch - - - - 1 "
Total number of miles worked and maintained - 60 miles.

This line is leased to the Irish North Western Company.

CAPITAL.

Capital authorized :—

	£
Shares - - - - - -	455,000
Borrowing Powers - - - -	150,000
Total - - - -	£605,000

Financial position on the 30th June 1867, as ascertained by the Commission :—

Capital raised by the Company :—

	£
Ordinary Shares - - - -	129,400
Preference Shares - - - -	325,600
Debentures - - - - -	76,000
Debenture Stock - - - -	46,070
Loan Commissioners - - - -	17,059
Total Capital - - -	£594,129

Floating liabilities, less floating assets - - - £70,185

Net revenue of each of the last three years, as returned by the Company :—

	£
1864–65 - - - - - - -	24,664
1865–66 - - - - - - -	25,223
1866–67 - - - - - - -	25,097
Average for three years - -	£24,995

Dividend on Ordinary Shares :—

1864–65 }
1865–66 } - - - Nil.
1866–67 }

Dividend on Preference Shares :—

Average of three years ended the 30th of June 1867, 3*l.* 9*s.* 9*d.* per cent. (including payment on account of arrears of preference dividends).

Interest (average rate payable at the 30th of June 1867) :—

On Debentures - - - - 5*l.* 2*s.* 0*d.* per cent.

On Debenture Stock - - - - { 4*l.* 5*s.* 0*d.* per cent. / 4*l.* 10*s.* 0*d.* per cent. / 5*l.* 0*s.* 0*d.* per cent. }

Interest paid to Loan Commissioners :—

Rate of Interest - - - 4*l.* 0*s.* 0*d.* per cent.

This railway connects the towns of Enniskillen, Omagh, and Strabane with the city and port of Londonderry, and forms part of the route from Londonderry to Dublin. Londonderry and Enniskillen Railway.

The district of country which may be considered to be accommodated by the line embraces an area of 577,528 acres, with a population of 158,908 persons.

THE MAIN LINE.

Londonderry to Enniskillen.

(49½ miles single line, and 9¾ double line.)

The main line from Londonderry to Strabane was constructed under an Act of 1845, from Strabane to Omagh under an Act of 1850, and from Omagh to Enniskillen under an Act of 1852. 8 & 9 Vict. c. 99. 13 Vict. c. 14. 15 Vict. c. xl.

The following table shows the dates when the works were sanctioned, and the several portions of the line were opened for traffic:—

Date of Act.	Length sanctioned by Board of Trade, with Date of Sanction.			
	From	To	Distance.	Date.
			Miles.	
21 July 1845	Londonderry	Strabane	14	March 1847.
3 August 1846	Old Terminus near Londonderry.	New Terminus in Londonderry.	¾	18 April 1850.
31 May 1850	Strabane	Newtown Stewart	9½	9 February 1852.
Do.	Newtown Stewart	Omagh	9½	13 September 1852.
28 May 1852	Omagh	Fintona Junction	6¼	15 June 1853.
Do.	Fintona Junction	Dromore Road	5¾	16 January 1854.
Do.	Dromore Road	Enniskillen	13¼	31 July 1854.

(a.) *The Fintona Branch.*

Fintona Junction to Fintona.

(1 mile, single line.)

This branch was constructed under an Act of 1854, and is worked by horse-power. 17 & 18 Vict. c. 185.

Date of Act.	Length sanctioned by Board of Trade, with Date of Sanction.			
	From	To	Distance.	Date.
			Miles.	
3rd July 1854	Fintona Junction	Fintona	1	Not stated.

RELATIONS OF THE LONDONDERRY AND ENNISKILLEN WITH OTHER RAILWAY COMPANIES.

The lines in connexion with the Londonderry and Enniskillen are stated in the following table:—

Name of Railway Company.	Point of Junction.	Page of Report.
The Irish North Western	Enniskillen	108
The Enniskillen, Bundoran, and Sligo	Bundoran Junction	111
The Portadown, Dungannon, and Omagh (leased to the Ulster Company).	Omagh	184
The Finn Valley	Strabane	112

The Irish North Western Railway.

The Irish North Western Company work and maintain the Londonderry and Enniskillen line under a perpetual lease renewable every thirty-five years for a minimum rent of 20,000l. a year, subject to be increased, on certain contingencies, to a maximum of 23,000l. a year.

Londonderry and Enniskillen Railway.

The Enniskillen, Bundoran, and Sligo Railway.

This line joins the Londonderry and Enniskillen railway near Lowtherstown.

The Portadown, Dungannon, and Omagh Railway (leased to the Ulster Company).

This railway joins the Londonderry and Enniskillen line at Omagh. The use of the Omagh station of the Omagh Market branch and of the station of the Portadown, Dungannon, and Omagh Railway, is arranged between the Ulster and the Irish North Western Companies.

The Finn Valley Railway.

This line connects Stranorlar and part of the county of Donegal with the Londonderry and Enniskillen line at Strabane.

Londonderry and Lough Swilly Railway.

47. THE LONDONDERRY AND LOUGH SWILLY RAILWAY.

LONDONDERRY to BUNCRANA, with branch to Farland.

LENGTH OF LINE.

	Single.	Double.	Total.
	Miles.	Miles.	Miles.
MAIN LINE.			
LONDONDERRY to BUNCRANA - - - -	12¼		12¼
BRANCH.			
(a.) THE FARLAND BRANCH (from Junction with Main Line to Farland) -	2¼	—	2¼
Total number of miles owned by the Company -	14½	—	14½

Length of main line - - - - -	12¼ miles.
Length of branch - - - - -	2¼ „
Total length of main line and branch - -	14½ miles.

CAPITAL.

	£
Capital authorized :—	
Shares - - - - - - -	105,000
Borrowing Powers - - - - -	26,200
Total - - - -	£131,200

Financial position on the 30th June 1867, as ascertained by the Commission :—

	£
Capital raised by the Company :—	
Ordinary Shares - - - - -	34,459
Debentures - - - - -	6,600
Loan Commissioners - - - -	13,000
Total capital - - - -	£54,059
Floating liabilities, less floating assets - - -	£53,509

Net revenue of each of the last three years, as returned by the Company :—

	£
1864-65 - - - - - -	158
1865-66 - - - - - -	1,116
1866-67 - - - - - -	1,148
Average of three years - -	£807

Dividend on Ordinary Shares :—

1864–65 } 1865–66 } 1866–67 }	- - - - -	Nil.

Interest (average rate on the 30th of June 1867):—

On Debentures	- - - -	6l. per cent.

Loan Commissioners:—

Rate of Interest	- - -	5l. per cent.

This railway connects Buncrana and a portion of the county of Donegal with the city of Londonderry.

The powers for making a more convenient station at Londonderry have expired, but the Port and Harbour Commissioners are making a tramway along the quays to connect the different railways having termini in Londonderry, which, when completed, will facilitate the interchange of traffic between them.

The district of country which may be considered to be accommodated by the line embraces an area of 207,839 acres, with a population of 69,258 persons.

THE MAIN LINE.

The main line, as far as the junction with the Farland Branch, was constructed under an Act of 1853, certain deviations having been authorized by an Act of 1859, it was completed under an Act of 1861.

The following table shows the dates when the works were authorized and the several portions of the line sanctioned for traffic:—

Date of Act.	Length sanctioned by Board of Trade, with Date of Sanction.			
	From	To	Distance.	Date.
			Miles	
26 June 1853 -	- Londonderry -	Junction with Farland Branch.	6¼	12 Nov. 1863.
22 July 1861 -	- Junction with Farland Branch.	Buncrana - -	6	9 Sept. 1864.

(a.) *The Farland Branch.*

From Junction with Main Line to Farland.

(2¼ miles, single line.)

This branch was constructed under the Act of 1853, with the deviations authorized by the Act of 1859.

Date of Act.	Length sanctioned by Board of Trade, with Date of Sanction.			
	From	To	Distance.	Date.
			Miles.	
26 June 1853 -	Junction with Main Line. Trains ceased to run since July 1866.	Farland - -	2¼	12 Nov. 1863.

Relations of the Londonderry and Lough Swilly with other Railway Companies.

Name of Railway Company.	Point of Junction.	Page of Report.
The Letterkenny - - - -	Near Farland - - - -	

The authorized Letterkenny line will be an extension of the Farland Branch of the Londonderry and Lough Swilly to Letterkenny, in the county of Donegal.

Midland Great Western Railway.

48. THE MIDLAND GREAT WESTERN RAILWAY.

DUBLIN to GALWAY, with branches to North Wall Quay, Dublin, Sligo, Cavan, and Clara.

LENGTH OF LINE.

	Single.	Double.	Total.
MAIN LINE.	Miles.	Miles.	Miles.
DUBLIN to GALWAY - - - - -	29¼	97¼	126½
BRANCHES.			
(a.) The LIFFEY BRANCH (from Liffey Junction to North Wall Quay, Dublin)	–	3	3
(b.) The SLIGO BRANCH (from Mullingar to Sligo) - - - -	68¾	15¾	84½
(c.) The CAVAN BRANCH (from Cavan Junction to Cavan) - - -	25	-	25
(d.) The CLARA BRANCH (from near Streamstown to Clara) - - -	7½	–	7½
Total number of miles owned by the Company - -	131	115½	246½
OTHER LINES WORKED AND MAINTAINED BY THE COMPANY :—			
The ATHENRY and TUAM (from Athenry to Tuam) - - -	15½	–	15½
The GREAT NORTHERN and WESTERN (from Athlone to Westport) -	82½	–	82½
Total mileage worked and maintained by the Company - -	229	115½	344½

Length of main line - - - - -	126½ miles.
Length of branches - - - - -	120 „
Total length of main line and branches -	246½ miles.
Length of railway worked and maintained but not owned by the Company - -	98 „
Total mileage worked and maintained -	344½ miles.

CAPITAL.

Capital authorized :—	£
Shares - - - - -	2,750,000
Borrowing Powers - - - -	1,286,076
Total - - -	4,036,076

Financial position on the 30th of June 1867, as ascertained by the Commission :—

Capital raised by the Company :—	£
Ordinary Shares - - - - -	2,157,175
Preference Shares - - - -	180,572
Debentures - - - - -	698,311
Royal Canal Mortgage - - - -	135,861
Loan Commissioners - - - -	448,016
Total Capital - - -	£3,620,435

Floating liabilities, less floating assets - - - -	£31,442

Net revenue of each of the last three years, as returned by the Company :—

	£
1864–5 - - - - - -	110,333
1865–6 - - - - - -	120,421
1866–7 - - - - - -	120,880
Average of three years - -	£117,211

Dividends on Ordinary Shares :—

1864–65 - - - - -	2*l.* 2*s.* 6*d.* per cent.
1865–66 - - - - -	2*l.* 10*s.* 0*d.* „
1866–67 - - - - -	2*l.* 10*s.* 0*d.* „

Dividend on Preference Shares:— Midland Great Western Railway.

Average of three years ending the 30th of June 1867, 5*l.* per cent.

Interest (average rate on the 30th of June 1867):—

On Debentures - - -	- 4*l.* 9*s.* 4*d.* per cent.
Loan Commissioners - -	- 3*l.* 10*s.* 0*d.* per cent.

The district of the country which may be considered to be accommodated by the line embraces an area of 2,818,273 acres, with a population of 981,328 persons.

The Midland Great Western Company under its first Act purchased the Royal Canal, and a considerable portion of the railway between Dublin and Mullingar was constructed on land acquired by that purchase. The Railway Company became responsible to keep the canal open for traffic at the Parliamentary rates of toll. Further particulars are given in the part of the Report relating to canals (p. 163).

THE MAIN LINE.

Dublin to Galway.

(126¾ miles; 29¼ single line, 97½ double line.)

The main line from Dublin to Mullingar was authorised by an Act of 1845; from Mullingar to Athlone by an Act of 1846; and from Athlone to Galway by an Act of 1847, certain deviations having been sanctioned in 1847 and 1848. 8 & 9 Vict. c. 119. 9 & 10 Vict. c. [illegible]

The completion of the line from Mullingar to Galway was accelerated by an Act of 1849, which enabled the Company, with the approval of the Commissioners of Public Works, to enter at once upon possession of lands required for the railway on delivering a certificate of value to the persons entitled to receive it. The satisfactory operation of this Act contributed to the passing of the general measure in 1851 (Railways, Ireland, Act, 1851), which has so much facilitated the making of railways in Ireland. 10 & 11 Vict. c. [illegible] 11 & 12 Vict. c. [illegible] 14 & 15 Vict. c. [illegible]

Under the Act of 1849 the Company was enabled to obtain loans from the Public Works Loan Commissioners to the extent of 500,000*l.* at 3½ per cent. to be charged in half-yearly sums of 1*l.* 15*s.* per cent. on a local tax on the lands and premises liable to county cess in the county of Galway, the county of the town of Galway, and in the baronies of Moycarne and Athlone in the county of Roscommon. The profits of this portion of the line to go in reductions of the tax, and if the profits exceed 3½ per cent. in any half year they are to be carried to the next half year. The Company was under the obligation to pay off each advance at the rate of 1½ per cent. per annum, commencing at the end of 10 years from the date of its being made. The Company received advances from the Public Works Loan Commissioners amounting in all to 500,000*l.* at various dates between the 25th of October 1849 and the 29th of April 1852. 12 & 13 Vict. c. [illegible]

By an Act of 1854 the sum, on which the interest was chargeable on local taxes was fixed at 470,000*l.* By an Act of 1865, an arrangement was made between the Company and the inhabitants of the districts liable to the local tax, by which all arrears of charge on the local taxes should be paid up, and all liability for interest should cease on the 28th of October 1870. 17 & 18 Vict. c. [illegible] (Pub.) 28 & 29 Vict. c. [illegible]

The following table shows the dates when the works were authorised, and the several portions of the line sanctioned for traffic:—

Date of Act.	Length sanctioned by Board of Trade, with Date of Sanction.			
	From	To	Distance.	Date.
21 July 1845 - -	Dublin - -	Enfield -	26½	June 1847.
" " - -	Enfield - -	Hill of Down -	9½	October 1847.
" " - -	Hill of Down -	Mullingar - -	14½	27 Sept. 1848.
16 July 1846 - -	Mullingar - -	Athlone - -	28	31 July 1851.
9 July 1847 - -	Athlone - -	Galway - -	48½	31 July 1851.

THE BRANCHES.

(a.) *The Liffey Branch.*

Liffey Junction to North Wall Quay, Dublin.

(3 miles, double line.)

This branch was made under an Act of 1859. Powers to make it had been obtained in 1846; but they were not exercised.

Date of Act.	Length sanctioned by Board of Trade, with Date of Sanction.			
	From	To	Distance.	Date.
1 August 1859 -	Liffey Junction -	North Wall Quay, Dublin.	Miles. 3	9 Sept. 1864.

(b.) *The Sligo Branch.*

Mullingar to Sligo.

(84¼ miles; 16¼ double line, 68¼ single line.)

The portion of this branch between Mullingar and Longford was included in the Company's first Act of 1845.

In 1848 the time for purchasing lands and completing the works was extended by the Railway Commissioners, and in 1850 a further extension of time was granted by Parliament. In 1852 deviations from the original line were sanctioned.

In 1857 the remaining portion of the Sligo Branch, from Longford to the town of Sligo, was sanctioned, with certain small connecting lines to Knockmuldowney Mills and to the Ballast Quay at Sligo.

The following table shows the dates when the works were authorised, and the several portions of the branch sanctioned for traffic:—

Date of Act.	Length sanctioned by Board of Trade, with Date of Sanction.			
	From	To	Distance.	Date.
21 July 1845 -	Mullingar -	Longford -	Miles. 26	8 Nov. 1855.
27 July 1857 -	Boyle -	Sligo -	23	1 Nov. 1862.
" " -	Carrick -	Boyle -	9¼	7 Nov. 1862.
" " -	Longford -	Carrick -	21½	17 Nov. 1862.
" " -	Old Terminus, Sligo -	New Terminus, Sligo		Not sanctioned.

(c.) *The Cavan Branch.*

From Cavan Junction to Cavan.

(25 miles, single line.)

This branch was made under an Act of 1852. It connects the Midland Great Western Railway, through the Cavan branch of the Irish North Western, with the railway systems of the North of Ireland.

Date of Act.	Length sanctioned by Board of Trade, with Date of Sanction.			
	From	To	Distance.	Date.
30 June 1852 -	Junction with the Sligo Branch.	Cavan -	Miles. 25	2 July 1856.

Midland Great Western Railway.

(d.) *The Clara Branch.*

From near Streamstown to Clara Junction.

(7½ miles, single line.)

This branch was made under an Act of 1857; it joins the Great Southern and Western line at Clara, and is noticed in the part of the report on that Company (p. 105). 20 & 21 Vict. c. 115.

Date of Act.	Length sanctioned by Board of Trade, with Date of Sanction.			
	From	To	Distance.	Date.
10 August 1857	Streamstown	Clara	Miles 7½	24 Feb. 1863.

Relations of the Midland Great Western Railway Company with other Companies.

The lines in connexion with the Midland Great Western are:—

Name of Railway.	Place of Junction.	Page of Report.
Lines worked by the Midland Great Western.		
The Athenry and Tuam	Athenry	182
The Great Northern and Western	Athlone	184
Other completed Lines.		
The Dublin and Meath	Clonsilla	87
The Irish North Western	Cavan	108
The Great Southern and Western	Clara and Athlone	100
Lines commenced but not completed.		
The Athenry and Ennis	Athenry	54
The Dublin Trunk Connecting	Two points near Broadstone Terminus and one with the Liffey Branch.	60
Lines authorized but not commenced.		
The Sligo and Ballaghaderreen	Near Boyle	60
The Central of Ireland	Mullingar	48
The Sligo Extension of the Enniskillen, Bundoran and Sligo.	Sligo	111

The Athenry and Tuam Railway.

This line connects the town of Tuam and a portion of the county of Galway with the Midland Great Western line at Athenry, and is leased at 4,000*l.* a year to the Midland Great Western Company, which works and maintains it.

The Great Northern and Western Railway.

This line connects the counties of Roscommon and Mayo with the Midland Great Western line at Athlone, and is worked and maintained by the Midland Great Western Company, for 1*s.* 6¾*d.* per train mile, between Athlone and Castlereagh; and for 2*s.* per train mile between Castlereagh and Westport.

Under authority of Acts of 1858, 1859, and 1861, the Midland Great Western Railway contributed 113,850*l.* to the Great Northern and Western Railway. 21 & 22 Vict. c. 94. 22 & 23 Vict. c. 98. 24 Vict. c. 47.

The Dublin and Meath Railway.

This line joins the Midland Great Western line at Clonsilla Junction, 7½ miles from Dublin, from which place the traffic of the Dublin and Meath Railway for Dublin runs on the Midland Great Western line.

The terms are fixed by an award dated the 29th of July 1861, modified by a subsequent agreement between the Companies.

The Irish North-Western Railway.

The Clones and Cavan branch of the Irish North-Western Company forms a junction with the Cavan branch of the Midland Great Western at Cavan, and connects the Midland Great Western with the railways in the north and north-west of Ireland.

The Great Southern and Western Railway.

The junctions of this line at Athlone and Clara are described in the part of the report on the Great Southern and Western Company.

The Athenry and Ennis Railway.

This line, when completed, will establish a continuous railway communication from Athenry, *viâ* Limerick, to Cork and Waterford.

The Dublin Trunk Connecting Railway.

This line, if made, will connect the Midland Great Western Railway with the Great Southern and Western, the Dublin and Drogheda, and the Dublin and Kingstown Railways.

The Sligo and Ballaghaderreen Railway.

This line will form an extension of the Midland Great Western system.

The Central of Ireland Railway.

This line will form an extension of the Kilkenny Junction to Mullingar.

The Enniskillen, Bundoran, and Sligo Railway.

This line is complete as far as Bundoran. If extended to Sligo, it would establish a continuous railway communication from Sligo, *viâ* Enniskillen and Dundalk, to Dublin.

The London and North-Western Railway.

The London and North-Western Railway Company, under an Act of 1861, has constructed premises for steamboat traffic adjoining the Liffey terminus, which are connected by a branch railway with the Midland Great Western.

---

49. THE ATHENRY AND TUAM RAILWAY.

LENGTH OF LINE.

	Single.	Double.	Total.
	Miles.	Miles.	Miles.
ATHENRY to TUAM	15½	—	15½

The line is worked and maintained by the Midland Great Western Company.

CAPITAL.

	£
Capital authorized:—	
Shares	90,000
Borrowing Powers	30,000
Total	£120,000

Financial position on the 29th of September 1867, as ascertained by the Commission :— Athenry and Tuam Railway.

Capital raised by the Company :—

	£
Ordinary Shares - - - -	61,018
Loan Commissioners - - - -	30,000
Total Capital - - -	£91,018

Cr. Floating assets, less floating liabilities - - - £600

Net revenue of each of the last three years, as returned by the Company :—

	£
1865 - - - - - -	3,757
1866 - - - - - -	3,757
1867 - - - - - -	3,455
Average for the three years - -	£3,656

Dividend on Ordinary Shares :—

1865 - - - - -	3*l.* per cent.
1866 - - - - -	3*l.* ,,
1867 - - - - -	3*l.* ,,

Interest paid to Loan Commissioners :—

Rate of Interest - - - - 5*l.* per cent.

This railway connects the town of Tuam with Galway and Dublin.

The district of country which may be considered to be accommodated by the line embraces an area of 263,979 acres, with a population of 57,864 persons.

THE LINE.

The line was constructed under an Act of 1858. 21 & 22 Vict. c. 115.

Date of Act.	Length sanctioned by Board of Trade, with Date of Sanction.			
	From	To	Distance.	Date.
22 July 1858 - -	Athenry - -	Tuam - -	Miles. 15¼	23 Sept. 1860.

Relations of the Athenry and Tuam with other Railway Companies.

Name of Railway Company.	Point of Junction.	Page of Report.
The Midland Great Western - -	Athenry - - - -	118

The Midland Great Western Railway.

In 1859 the Athenry and Tuam Company entered into an agreement with the Midland Great Western Company to lease the line to them for 10 years from the completion of the railway, at 4,000*l.* a year.

The Athenry and Tuam Company undertook, during the continuance of the lease, not to extend its line beyond Tuam towards Castlebar, Westport, or Ballina, or to promote any similar extensions by any other Company or persons.

This agreement was confirmed by statute in 1860, and the Companies were empowered to enter into a lease for 10 years. They were further empowered, with the sanction of the Board of Trade, to enter into a renewed lease for a further period not exceeding 10 years. Power was also given for the sale of the railway to the Midland Great Western Company. 23 & 24 Vict. c. 1[illegible].

50. THE GREAT NORTHERN AND WESTERN OF IRELAND RAILWAY.

Athlone to Manulla Junction, near Castlebar, and thence to Westport and Ballina.

LENGTH OF LINE.

	Single.	Double.	Total.
MAIN LINE.	Miles.		Miles.
Athlone to Westport - - - - - - - -	69¾	—	69¾
Total completed and working - - - - -	69¾	—	69¾
BRANCH COMMENCED BUT NOT COMPLETED.			
(a.) The Foxford Branch (from Manulla Junction to Foxford) - -	—	—	11¼
EXTENSION AUTHORIZED BUT NOT COMMENCED.			
(b.) The Ballina Branch Extension (from Foxford to Ballina) -	—	—	9½
(c.) The Westport Quay Extension (from Westport to Westport Quay) -	—	—	1½
Total mileage authorized - - - - - - -	—	—	106¼

Length of main line - - - - - 69¾ miles.
Length of branch, commenced but not completed - - 11¼ "
Length of extensions, authorized but not commenced - 11 "
Total length of main line, branch, and extensions authorized - - - - - - - 106¼ miles.

The line is worked and maintained by the Midland Great Western Company.

CAPITAL.

Capital authorized:—

	£
Shares - - - - - -	554,000
Borrowing Powers - - - -	184,000
Total - - -	£738,000

Financial position on the 30th of June 1867, as ascertained by the Commission:—

Capital raised by the Company:—

	£
Ordinary Shares - - - -	261,690
Shares held by Midland Great Western Company	113,316
Preference Shares - - - -	51,960
Loan Commissioners - - - -	134,000
Total Capital - - -	£561,200

Floating liabilities, less floating assets - - - £67,003

Net revenue of each of the last three years, as returned by the Company:—

	£
1864–65 - - - - - -	14,780
1865–66 - - - - - -	19,575
1866–67 - - - - - -	22,438
Average for three years - -	£18,931

Dividend on Ordinary Shares:—

	£	s.	d.	
1864–65 - - - - -	2	7	6	per cent.
1865–66 - - - - -	3	5	0	"
1866–67 - - - - -	1	12	6*	"

Dividend on Shares held by Midland Great Western Company:—

	£	s.	d.	
1864–65 - - - - -	2	14	8	per cent.
1865–66 - - - - -	3	6	11	"
1866–67 - - - - -	1	14	8	"

* Though the balance of net revenue for the second half year of 1866–67 was sufficient for a dividend at the rate of 3l. 10s. per cent., no dividend was declared, but the sum was retained for the purpose of paying liabilities. If it had been declared it would make the average dividend for 1866–67, 3l. 7s. 6d. per cent.

Dividend on Preference Shares :—
Average of three years ended the 30th of June 1867 - 5*l.* 0*s.* 2*d.* per cent.
Interest paid to Loan Commissioners :—
Rate of Interest - - - - - 4*l.* 3*s.* 1*d.* „ Great Northern and Western Railway.

This railway connects Westport and Castlebar, and generally the counties of Mayo and Roscommon, with the Midland Great Western and the Great Southern and Western Railway systems.

The district of country which may be considered to be accommodated by the line embraces an area of 1,251,014 acres, with a population of 296,237 persons.

THE MAIN LINE.

The main line as far as Castlereagh was constructed under an Act of Parliament passed in 1857; from Castlereagh to Castlebar under an Act passed in 1859, and from Castlebar to Westport under an Act passed in 1861. 20 & 21 Vict. c. 91.

The following table shows the dates when the works were authorised, and the several portions of the line sanctioned for traffic :—

Date of Act.	Length sanctioned by Board of Trade, and Date of Sanction.			
	From	To	Distance.	Date.
			Miles.	
27 July 1857 - -	Athlone - -	Roscommon - -	18	10 Feb. 1860.
	Roscommon - -	Castlereagh - -	16 1/2	11 Nov. 1860.
1 Aug. 1859 - -	Castlereagh - -	Ballyhaunis - -	11	24 Aug. 1861.
	Ballyhaunis - -	Claremorris - -	11	7 May 1862.
	Claremorris - -	Castlebar - -	14	19 Nov. 1862.
12 June 1861 - -	Castlebar - -	Westport - -	11	23 Jan. 1866.

Branch commenced but not completed.

(*a.*) *The Foxford Branch.*

Manulla Junction to Foxford.

(11 1/2 miles.)

The line from Manulla Junction to Ballina has been completed to Foxford, with the exception of a bridge at that place, but it is not yet opened for traffic.

This line was originally authorised in 1862, but by a subsequent Act, passed in 1866, the time for completion of the works was extended to the 16th of July 1869, after which period the Company is liable to a penalty of 50*l.* per day until the branch shall be opened for traffic. 25 & 26 Vict. c. 207. 29 & 30 Vict. c. 237.

Extensions authorised but not commenced.

(*b.*) *The Ballina Extension.*

From Foxford to Ballina.

(9 3/4 miles.)

The Company has now applied to the Board of Trade for leave to abandon the portions of this line not yet commenced between Foxford and Ballina.

(*c.*) *The Westport Quay Extension.*

From Westport to Westport Quay.

(1 1/2 mile.)

This is part of the line authorised by the Act of 1861, but by a subsequent Act, passed in 1866, the time for its completion was extended to the 1st of July 1868, after which date the Company is liable to a penalty of 50*l.* per day until the completion of the line. 24 & 25 Vict. c. 67. 29 & 30 Vict. c. 237.

The Company has now applied to the Board of Trade for leave to abandon this extension.

RELATIONS OF THE GREAT NORTHERN AND WESTERN OF IRELAND WITH OTHER RAILWAY COMPANIES.

Name of Railway Company.	Point of Junction.	Page of Report.
The Midland Great Western - - -	Athlone - - - -	118

The Midland Great Western Railway.

By provisions of the Acts passed in 1857, 1859, and 1861 the Great Northern and Western Company acquired powers to use the Athlone station of the Midland Great Western Railway Company, and also, with the approval of the Board of Trade, in case the Midland Great Western Company should at any time cease to work the Great Northern and Western Railway, to use that portion of the Midland Great Western Railway lying between the junctions of that line with the Great Northern and Western and with the Great Southern and Western Companies.

The Great Northern and Western is worked and maintained by the Midland Great Western Company under the following agreements, entered into (under Parliamentary powers) with that Company:—Agreement, dated the 1st of August 1859, to work and maintain that portion of the line between Athlone and Castlereagh for 10 years, at 1*s.* 6½*d.* per train mile, and under a subsequent agreement to work and maintain the portion between Castlereagh and Westport, until the same period, at 2*s.* per train mile.

The Midland Great Western Company hold shares in the Great Northern and Western Company to the amount of 113,850*l.* which they are restrained from selling so long as the above-mentioned agreement of the 1st of August 1859 remains in force.

---

31. THE NEWRY AND ARMAGH RAILWAY.

From NEWRY to ARMAGH.

LENGTH OF LINE.*

—	Single.	Double.	Total.
NEWRY to ARMAGH - - - -	Miles. 21	Miles. —	Miles. 21

CAPITAL.

	£
Capital authorised:—	
Shares - - - - - - -	408,120
Borrowing powers - - - - -	78,000
Total - - - -	£486,120

Financial position on the 30th of June, 1867, as ascertained by the Commission:—

	£
Capital raised by the Company:—	
Ordinary Shares - - - - -	46,965†
Preference Shares - - - - -	101,116
Debentures - - - - -	78,000
Total capital - - -	£226,081
Floating liabilities, less floating assets - - -	£277,252

* The Company is also joint proprietor with the Newry and Warrenpoint Company, of the town of Newry connecting line, three-quarters of a mile in length between the two lines in Newry.

† The shares were reduced to one-third the original amount by the Act of 1857.

Net revenue of each of the last three years, as returned by the Company:—

	£
1864–65 - - - - - - -	1,069
1865–66 - - - - - - -	2,288
1866–67 - - - - - - -	4,121
Average of three years - - -	2,490

Dividend on Ordinary Shares:—

1864–65, 1865–66, 1866–67 - - Nil.

Interest on Debentures:—

Dividend on Preference Shares - - Nil.

(Average rate on the 30th of July 1867*) - 3*l.* per cent.

This railway connects the city of Armagh with the town and port of Newry. It also connects the town of Newry and the Newry and Warrenpoint line with the Dublin and Belfast Junction line at Goragh Wood Junction.

The district of country which may be considered to be accommodated by this line embraces an area of 100,635 acres, with a population of 54,801 persons.

THE LINE.

The line from Newry to Goragh Wood Junction was constructed under an Act of 1845, the time for completing the works having been extended in 1847. From Goragh Wood Junction to Armagh under an Act of 1857. The name of the Company was altered in 1857 from the Newry and Enniskillen to the Newry and Armagh Company after the powers for completing the line to Enniskillen had expired. The short connecting line between the two lines at Newry was made under an Act of 1859.

A receiver has been appointed by the Irish Court of Chancery, and a Bill is being promoted by creditors in the present session for authorising the sale of the line by the English Court of Chancery, and for the dissolution of the Company.

The following table shews when the works were authorised and the several portions of the line sanctioned for traffic:—

Date of Act	Length sanctioned by Board of Trade, with Date of Sanction.			
	From	To	Distance.	Date.
			Miles.	
22 July 1845 - -	Edward Street Station, Newry	Goragh Wood	3¼	7 January 1854.
4 August 1853 -	Albert Basin, Newry	The Junction with the Town of Newry Connecting Line.	½	8 August 1864.
17 August 1857 -	Goragh Wood -	Near Armagh -	17	10 August 1864.
" " -	Near Armagh -	Ulster Terminus -	¼	9 February 1865.

RELATIONS OF THE NEWRY AND ARMAGH WITH OTHER RAILWAY COMPANIES.

The Companies in connexion with the Newry and Armagh Railway are stated in the following table:—

Name of Railway Company.	Point of Junction.	Page of Report
Completed Lines.		
The Newry, Warrenpoint, and Rostrevor -	Newry - - - -	188
The Dublin and Belfast Junction - -	Goragh Wood Junction - -	65
The Ulster - - - - -	Armagh - - - -	150
Line commenced but not completed.		
The Newry and Greenore - - -	Newry - - - -	64

* The shares were reduced to one-third the original amount by the Act of 1857.

The Newry, Warrenpoint, and Rostrevor Railway.

The town of Newry connecting line, from near the old terminus of the Newry and Warrenpoint line to near the Edward Street station of the Newry and Armagh line, is the joint property of both companies and is managed by a joint committee.

The Dublin and Belfast Junction Railway.

This line forms a junction with the Newry and Armagh Railway at Goragh Wood, and provision is made by the Act of 1857 for the junction being maintained.

The Ulster Railway.

The Newry and Armagh Company has a right under the Act of 1859 to use the Armagh station of the Ulster Company, upon conditions to be settled by the Board of Trade. It pays a rent of 634*l.* per annum for use of Armagh station and a portion of the line, and 100*l.* for services at the junction.

The Newry and Greenore Railway.

This line will connect the Newry and Armagh Railway with the projected pier at Greenore. Traffic arrangements between the Companies are authorized.

---

59. THE NEWRY, WARRENPOINT, AND ROSTREVOR RAILWAY

(with the Town of Newry Connecting Line).

NEWRY to WARRENPOINT.

LENGTH OF LINE.

—	Single.	Double.	Total.
	Miles.	Miles.	Miles.
NEWRY to WARRENPOINT - - - - - - -	6¼	—	6¼
Total owned by the Newry, Warrenpoint, and Rostrevor Company -	6¼	—	6¼
(a.) THE TOWN OF NEWRY CONNECTING LINE (from the line to the old terminus of Newry, Warrenpoint, and Rostrevor Railway to the Albert Basin line of the Newry and Armagh Railway).	¼	—	¼
Total joint property of Newry, Warrenpoint, and Rostrevor and Newry and Armagh Companies.	¼	—	¼

CAPITAL.

	£
Capital authorized :—	
Shares - - - - - -	120,000
Borrowing Powers - - - -	39,933
Total - - - -	£159,933

Financial position on the 30th of June 1867, as ascertained by the Commission :—

	£
Capital raised by the Company :—	
Ordinary Shares - - - -	99,910
Preference Shares - - - -	20,000
Debentures - - - -	31,300
Loan Commissioners - - - -	8,400
Total Capital - - -	£159,610

Floating liabilities, less floating assets - - - - £3979

Newry, Warrenpoint, and Rostrevor Railway.

Net revenue of each of the last three years, as returned by the Company:—

	£
1864–65 - - - - - -	3,108
1865–66 - - - - - -	2,271
1866–67 - - - - - -	3,467
Average of three years - -	£2,948

Dividend on Ordinary Shares:—
1864–65, 1865–66, 1866–67 - - - - Nil.

Dividend on Preference Shares:—
Average of three years ended the 30th of June 1867 - Nil.

Interest (average rate on the 30th of June 1867):—
On Debentures - - - - 4*l.* 19*s.* 6*d.* per cent.
Interest to Loan Commissioners - - - 5*l.* per cent.

This line connects Warrenpoint (a sea-bathing place and steamboat harbour) with Newry.

The district of country which may be considered to be accommodated by the line embraces an area of 89,440 acres, with a population of 37,264 persons.

THE LINE.

The original line between Newry and Warrenpoint was constructed under an Act of 1846. The extension at Newry to the Dublin Bridge terminus and Warrenpoint basin were made under an Act of 1857. The extension from the Dublin Bridge terminus to the Newry and Armagh Railway was made under the Act of 1857, the time being extended by an Act of 1860. 9 & 10 Vict. c. 344. 20 & 21 Vict. c. 41. 23 Vict. c. 27.

Date of Act.	Length sanctioned by Board of Trade, with Date of Sanction.			
	From	To	Distance.	Date.
27 July 1846 - -	Warrenpoint -	Newry - -	Miles. 4½	24 May 1849.

(a.) The Town of Newry Connecting Line.

From the line to the old terminus of the Newry, Warrenpoint, and Rostrevor Railway to the Albert Basin line of the Newry and Armagh Railway.

(¾ mile, single line.)

This line was made by the Newry, Warrenpoint, and Rostrevor Company under the Act of 1857, but is the joint property of that Company and the Newry and Armagh Company.

The following table shows the dates when the works were authorised and the several portions of the line sanctioned for traffic:—

Date of Act.	Length sanctioned by Board of Trade, with Date of Sanction.			
	From	To	Distance.	Date.
27 July 1857 - -	Old Terminus, Newry	Dublin Bridge Station	Miles. 1¼*	22 April 1861.
27 July 1857 - -	Dublin Bridge Station	Junction with Armagh Railway.		20 August 1861.

* This includes a portion of the Newry and Armagh Railway sanctioned for passenger traffic.

Newry, Warrenpoint, and Rostrevor Railway.

RELATIONS OF THE NEWRY, WARRENPOINT, AND ROSTREVOR WITH OTHER RAILWAY COMPANIES.

Name of Railway Company.	Point of Junction.	Page of Report.
The Newry and Armagh - - -	Newry - - - -	128

The Newry and Armagh Railway.

Under the Act of 1860 the Newry and Armagh Company contributed half the cost of the Newry Connecting line, upon which the Dublin Bridge station, used by both Companies, is situated. The town of Newry Connecting Line is managed by a committee of both Companies.

Ulster Railway.

53. THE ULSTER RAILWAY.

BELFAST to CLONES.

LENGTH OF LINE.

—	Single.	Double.	Total.
MAIN LINE.	Miles.	Miles.	Miles.
BELFAST to CLONES - - - - - - -	16	48½	64½
Total number of miles owned by the Company - -	16	48½	64½
LINES WORKED BY THE COMPANY.			
The BANBRIDGE, LISBURN, and BELFAST (from Banbridge to Knockmore Junction, near Lisburn).	15	—	15
The PORTADOWN, DUNGANNON, and OMAGH (from Portadown to Omagh) -	41	—	41
Total mileage worked and maintained by the Company -	72	48½	120½

Length of main line - - - - - - 64½ miles.
Length of railway worked but not owned by the Company 56 "
Total mileage worked and maintained by the Company 120½ miles

CAPITAL.

Capital authorized:

	£
Shares - - - - - -	1,300,000
Borrowing Powers - - - - -	309,000
Total - - - - -	£1,609,000

Financial position on the 30th of June 1867, as ascertained by the Commission:—

Capital raised by the Company:—

	£
Ordinary Shares - - - - -	1,000,000
Preference Shares - - - - -	89,235
Debentures - - - - -	233,885
Debenture Stock - - - - -	53,185
Total Capital - - - -	£1,376,305

Floating liabilities, less floating assets - - - £27,551

Net revenue of each of the last three years, from Company's accounts:—

	£
1864-65 - - - - - - -	56,510
1865-66 - - - - - - -	61,536
1866-67 - - - - - - -	58,578
Average of three years - - -	£58,874

	£	s.	d.	
Dividend on Ordinary Shares :—				
1864–65 - - - - -	4	5	0	per cent.
1865–66 - - - - -	4	0	0	"
1866–67 - - - - -	4	0	0	"
Dividend on Preference Shares - - - -	4	10	0	per cent.
Interest (average rate on the 30th of June 1867):—				
On Debentures - - - -	4	6	1	per cent.
On Debenture Stock - - - -	4	0	0	"

This railway connects the counties of Monaghan and Armagh, and parts of Down and Tyrone with the town and port of Belfast, and from Belfast to Portadown it forms part of the direct route between Belfast and Dublin.

The district of country which may be considered to be accommodated by the line embraces an area of 369,699 acres, with a population of 310,796 persons.

THE LINE.

The line from Belfast to Portadown was constructed under an Act of 1836; from Portadown to Armagh under an Act of 1845 (the powers for making this portion given in the Act of 1836 having been allowed to expire); from Armagh to Monaghan under an Act of 1855; and from Monaghan to Clones under an Act of 1859.

The line from Belfast to Portadown was at first laid down on a gauge of six feet two inches, according to the recommendation in the Report of the Irish Railway Commissioners of 1838, but was altered to the gauge of five feet three inches, which had been adopted by the Dublin and Drogheda Company, and afterwards established by Statute as the general gauge for Ireland. Part of the cost of this alteration of gauge was borne by the Dublin and Drogheda and Dublin and Belfast Junction Railway Companies.

The following table shows the dates when the works were authorised and the several portions of the line sanctioned for traffic :—

Date of Act.	Length sanctioned by Board of Trade, with Date of Sanction.			
	From	To	Distance.	Date.
			Miles.	
19 May 1836 - -	Belfast - -	Lisburn - -	7½	Opened in 1839.*
" " -	Lisburn - -	Portadown - -	17¾	13 October 1841.
21 July 1845 - -	Portadown - -	Armagh - -	11	January 1848.
15 June 1855 - -	Armagh - -	Monaghan - -	16	June 1858.
1 August 1859 - -	Monaghan - -	Clones - -	12	21 February 1863.

RELATIONS OF THE ULSTER WITH OTHER RAILWAY COMPANIES.

The lines in connexion with the Ulster Company are stated in the following table :—

Name of Railway Company.	Point of Junction.	Page of Report.
Lines worked by the Ulster.		
The Banbridge, Lisburn, and Belfast - -	Knockmore Junction - -	160
The Portadown, Dungannon, and Omagh Junction.	Portadown - -	164
Other completed Lines.		
The Dublin and Belfast Junction - -	Portadown - -	85
The Irish North Western - - -	Clones - - -	108
The Newry and Armagh - - -	Armagh - - -	185
Lines commenced but not completed.		
The Belfast Central - - - -	Near the Terminus and Goods Station of the Ulster Railway in Belfast.	57

* Opened in 1839 before the Railway Department of the Board of Trade was constituted.

The Banbridge, Lisburn, and Belfast Railway.

This railway connects Banbridge and part of the county of Down with the Ulster Railway.

The Portadown, Dungannon, and Omagh Junction Railway.

This railway connects Omagh and Dungannon and parts of the counties of Armagh and Tyrone with the Ulster Railway.

The Dublin and Belfast Junction Railway.

This railway forms part of the main route between Dublin and the North of Ireland; there are statutable powers authorising an amalgamation between it, the Ulster, the Dublin and Drogheda, and the Irish North Western Companies, which have never been exercised.

This Company uses the Portadown station of the Ulster Company under an agreement of the 1st of July 1865 for three years, at a rent of 675*l.* a year.

The Irish North Western Railway.

The Clones and Cavan branch of this Company connects the Ulster line with the Midland Great Western line at Cavan. The Ulster Company under an Act of 1859 subscribed 27,687*l.* to this branch.

The Newry and Armagh Railway.

This Company uses the Armagh station of the Ulster Company, and the line between that station and the junction, paying a rent of 634*l.* for use of Armagh station and portion of line, and 100*l.* for services at the junction.

The Belfast Central Railway.

This line, when completed, will be connected with the Ulster Railway near the terminus at Belfast; the Ulster Company has running powers over it to the proposed central station, upon terms to be settled by arbitration.

---

54. THE BANBRIDGE, LISBURN, AND BELFAST RAILWAY.

BANBRIDGE to KNOCKMORE JUNCTION near Lisburn.

LENGTH OF LINE.

	Single.	Double.	Total.
	Miles.		Miles.
BANBRIDGE to KNOCKMORE JUNCTION	15	—	15

The line is worked and maintained by the Ulster Company.

CAPITAL.

Capital authorised :—	£
Shares	150,000
Borrowing Powers	49,000
Total	£199,000

Financial position on the 30th of June 1867, as ascertained by the Commission :— Banbridge, Lisburn, and Belfast Railway.

	£
Capital raised by the Company :—	
Ordinary Shares - - - - -	87,969
Preference Shares - - - - -	34,826
Debentures - - - - -	49,000
Total Capital - -	£171,795
Floating liabilities, less floating assets - -	£25,548

Net revenue of each of the last three years, as returned by the Company :—

	£
1864–65 - - - - - -	1,836
1865–66 - - - - - -	2,330
1866–67 - - - - - -	2,922
Average for three years - -	£2,363

Dividend on Ordinary Shares :—

1864–65, 1865–66, 1866–67 - - - - - Nil.

Dividend on Preference Shares :—

Average of three years ended the 30th of June 1867 - Nil.

Interest on Debentures - - - 5*l.* 1*s.* 3*d.* per cent.

This railway connects Banbridge with Belfast. The district of country which may be considered to be accommodated by the line embraces an area of 72,536 acres, with a population of 47,439 persons.

The line was constructed under an Act of 1858, with certain deviations authorised in 1860. 21 Vict. c. 36. 23 Vict. c. 6.

Date of Act.	Length sanctioned by Board of Trade, with Date of Sanction.			
	From	To	Distance.	Date.
			Miles.	
14 June 1858 -	Banbridge -	Knockmore Junction	13	13 July 1863.

RELATIONS OF THE BANBRIDGE, LISBURN, AND BELFAST, WITH OTHER RAILWAY COMPANIES.

The lines in connexion with the Banbridge, Lisburn, and Belfast Railway are stated in the following table :—

Name of Railway Company.	Point of Junction.	Page of Report.
Completed Lines.		
The Ulster - - - -	Knockmore Junction - -	160
The Banbridge Junction - -	Banbridge - - -	87
Lines Commenced but not Completed.		
The Banbridge Extension - -	Banbridge - - -	59

The Ulster Railway.

The Ulster Company subscribed 25,000*l.* to the Banbridge, Lisburn, and Belfast Company, under a Parliamentary provision that 4 per cent. interest on that amount should be a first charge against the Company.

Under an Act of 1868 the Ulster Company have power to lease the line for 21 years, upon the following scale. When the receipts for a half year amount to any sum not exceeding 3,000*l.*, 60 per cent. of receipts is paid to the Ulster Company for working 31 & 32 Vict. c. 103.

expenses, when receipts are 7,000*l.* and upwards only 45 per cent. is paid. For the intervening amounts the scale is, for 4,000*l.* 64 per cent., for 5,000*l.* 56 per cent., for 6,000*l.* 48 per cent., and for 6,500*l.* 46 per cent.

The Banbridge Junction Railway.

This is a short line of connexion between the Banbridge, Lisburn, and Belfast and the Dublin and Belfast Junction Railways.

The Banbridge Extension Railway.

The powers for completing the works of this line have expired.

---

55. THE PORTADOWN, DUNGANNON, AND OMAGH JUNCTION RAILWAY.

PORTADOWN to OMAGH.

LENGTH OF LINE.

—	Single.	Double.	Total.
	Miles.	Miles.	Miles.
Portadown to Omagh	41	—	41

This line is leased to and worked by the Ulster Company.

CAPITAL.

Capital authorized:—

	£
Shares	395,775
Borrowing Powers	131,885
Total	£527,160

Financial position on the 30th of June 1867, as ascertained by the Commission:—

Capital raised by the Company:—

	£
Ordinary Shares	250,808
1st Preference Shares, 6 per cent. cumulative and redeemable	66,775
2nd Preference Shares, 4½ per cent. redeemable	48,032
Debentures	107,817
Loan Commissioners	16,768
Total capital	£490,200

Floating liabilities, less floating assets — £1,139

Net revenue of each of the last three years, as returned by the Company:—

	£
1864–65	10,500
1865–66	10,500
1866–67	10,500
Average of three years	£10,500

Dividend on Ordinary Shares:—

1864–65, 1865–66, 1866–67	Nil.

Dividend on 1st Preference Shares:—

Average of three years ended the 30th of June 1867 - 6*l.* per cent.

Dividend on 2nd Preference Shares:—

Average of two years ended the 30th of June 1867 - 1*l.* 1*s.* 7*d.* per cent.

Interest on Debentures:—

Average rate on the 30th of June 1867 - - 4*l.* 10*s.* 10*d.* per cent.

Interest paid to Loan Commissioners:—

Rate of interest - - - - - - 4*l.* per cent.

This railway gives to the towns of Dungannon and Omagh, and a large part of the county of Tyrone, railway communication with the Ulster and the Dublin and Belfast Junction systems of railways. It also establishes a more direct route from the Londonderry and Enniskillen line at Omagh, to Belfast and to Dublin.

The district of country which may be considered to be accommodated by the line embraces an area of 273,071 acres, with a population of 114,177 persons.

THE LINE.

The line from Portadown to Dungannon was constructed under an Act of 1847, the time for completing the works having been first extended by order of the Railway Commissioners in 1848, and afterwards by an Act of 1853. The line was completed to Omagh under an Act of 1857.

The following table shows the dates when the works were authorized, and the several portions of the line sanctioned for traffic:—

Date of Act.	Length sanctioned by Board of Trade, with Date of Sanction.			
	From	To	Distance.	Date.
			Miles.	
9 July 1847 - -	Portadown - -	Dungannon - -	13¼	18 April 1858.
10 August 1857 -	Dungannon - -	Omagh - - -	27¼	23 Aug. 1861.

RELATIONS OF THE PORTADOWN, DUNGANNON, AND OMAGH WITH OTHER RAILWAY COMPANIES.

The lines in connexion with the Portadown, Dungannon, and Omagh Junction Railway are stated in the following table:—

Name of Railway Company.	Point of Junction.	Page of Report.
The Londonderry and Enniskillen - -	Omagh - - - -	114
The Ulster - - - - -	Portadown - - - -	130
The Dublin and Belfast Junction - -	Portadown - - - -	83

The Londonderry and Enniskillen Railway (worked by the Irish North Western Railway).

The Londonderry and Enniskillen Railway Company, under the Act of 1860, made a joint station at Omagh, and by an award dated the 12th of October 1861, the Portadown, Dungannon, and Omagh Junction Company pays to the Irish North-Western Company, who work the traffic of the Londonderry and Enniskillen line, 2½ per cent. per annum on the total cost of the Omagh station and offices.

The Ulster Railway.

The Portadown, Dungannon, and Omagh Junction Railway is leased to the Ulster Company for 999 years, from the 27th of February 1861, subject to a power reserved to the Board of Trade to determine the lease. The rent varies from a minimum of 10,500*l.* a year, according to the traffic receipts.

The Dublin and Belfast Junction Railway.

The Portadown, Dungannon, and Omagh Junction Railway joins the Ulster Railway at the same point as the Dublin and Belfast Junction line, at Portadown.

Waterford and Kilkenny Railway.

56. THE WATERFORD AND KILKENNY RAILWAY.

Waterford to Kilkenny.

LENGTH OF LINE.

	Single.	Double.	Total.
	Miles.	Miles.	Miles.
MAIN LINE.			
Waterford to Kilkenny* - - - - -	29	—	29
Total number of miles owned by the Company - - -	29	—	29
LINE WORKED BY THE COMPANY.			
The Kilkenny Junction (from Kilkenny to Abbeyleix) - - -	19	—	19
Total mileage worked and maintained by the Company -	48	—	48

Length of main line - - - - 29 miles.
Length of railway worked but not owned by the Company 19 „

Total mileage worked and maintained by the Company. 48 „

CAPITAL.

Capital authorised:—

	£
Shares† - - - - - -	450,000
Borrowing Powers† - - - -	149,000
Total - - - -	£599,000

Financial position on the 29th September 1867, as ascertained by the Commission:—

Capital raised by the Company:—

	£
Ordinary Shares - - - - -	250,000
Preference Shares - - - - -	195,885
Debentures - - - - - -	29,046
Debenture Stock - - - - -	61,331
Loan Commissioners - - - - -	56,658
Total Capital - - -	£593,920

Floating liabilities, less floating assets - - - £157,521

Net revenue of each of the last three years, as returned by the Company:—

	£
1864–65 - - - - - -	10,764
1865–66 - - - - - -	11,327
1866–67 - - - - - -	11,212
Average of three years - -	£11,101

Dividend on Ordinary Shares:—

1864–65, 1865–66, 1866–67 - Nil.

Dividend on Preference Shares:—

Average of three years ended the 29th of Sept. 1867, 1l. 7s. 6d. per cent.

Interest (average rate on the 29th of Sept. 1867):—

On Debentures - - - 5l. 12s. 6d. per cent.
On Debenture Stock - - 5l. per cent.
To Loan Commissioners - - 3l. 18s. 9d. per cent.

---

* The Waterford and Kilkenny Company runs its carriages over 1½ miles of the Waterford and Limerick line.

† In addition to this there are powers for raising 110,000l. in shares and 36,600l. in loans for the Central Ireland Railways, promoted by this and the Kilkenny Junction Company.

Waterford and Kilkenny Railway.

This line connects the city of Kilkenny, the Kilkenny Junction line, and the Kilkenny branch of the Great Southern and Western line with the city of Waterford.

The district of country which may be considered to be accommodated by the line embraces an area of 252,161 acres, with a population of 121,388 persons.

THE LINE.

This railway was constructed under an Act of 1845, certain deviations having been authorized and an extension of line granted in 1846.

It was originally intended to construct the line with wooden rails upon the principle of Prosser's Patent Guide Wheel system, but by the Act of 1850 it was provided that the railway should be constructed with iron rails on the ordinary principle.

The following table shews the dates when the works were authorized, and the several portions of the line sanctioned for traffic:—

Date of Act.	Length sanctioned by Board of Trade, with Date of Sanction			
	From	To	Distance.	Date.
			Miles.	
21 July 1845	Kilkenny	Thomastown	11	12 May 1848.
" "	Thomastown	Jerpoint	1½	29 May 1850.
" "	Jerpoint	Fiddown	16	15 May 1852.
" "	Fiddown	Junction with Waterford and Limerick.	¾	7 Sept. 1854.

Relations of the Waterford and Kilkenny with other Railway Companies.

The lines in connexion with the Waterford and Kilkenny are stated in the following table:—

Name of Railway Company.	Point of Junction.	Page of Report.
Lines worked by the Waterford and Kilkenny Company.		
The Kilkenny Junction	Kilkenny	158
Other Completed Lines.		
The Waterford and Limerick	Waterford	140
The Great Southern and Western	New Kilkenny	160

The Kilkenny Junction Railway.

This line is worked by the Waterford and Kilkenny Company under an agreement of the 31st of October 1865, for five years, determinable on twelve months' notice, for two shillings per train mile for three or more trains daily, and terminal charges for the use of Kilkenny station of the Waterford and Kilkenny Company.

The Waterford and Limerick Railway.

The arrangements between the Waterford and Kilkenny Company and the Waterford and Limerick Company as to the use of the part of the Waterford terminus and line of the latter Company are at present referred to an arbitrator appointed by the Board of Trade.

The Great Southern and Western Railway.

The Kilkenny branch of this railway meets the Waterford and Kilkenny line about two miles from Kilkenny, and runs parallel to it into the Kilkenny station, part of which the Great Southern and Western Company have purchased on a lease in perpetuity from the Waterford and Kilkenny Company at a nominal rent.

57. THE KILKENNY JUNCTION RAILWAY.

KILKENNY to ABBEYLEIX.

LENGTH OF LINE.

	Single.	Double.	Total.
MAIN LINE.	Miles.	Miles.	Miles.
Kilkenny to Abbeyleix - - - - - - -	19	—	19
Total mileage completed and working - - - -	19	—	19
EXTENSION NOT OPEN TILL AFTER 1ST OF MAY 1867.			
(a.) The Maryborough extension from Abbeyleix to Maryborough - -	9½	—	9½
Total mileage authorized - - - - -	—	—	28½

Length of main line - - - - 19 miles.
Length of authorized extension - - - 9½ „

Total mileage authorized - - - 28½ „

The line is worked and maintained by the Waterford and Kilkenny Company.

CAPITAL.

Capital authorized:—

	£
Shares - - - - - -	274,000*
Borrowing Powers - - - - -	90,600*
Total - - - -	£364,600

Financial position on the 1st of May 1867, as ascertained by the Commission:—

Capital raised by the Company:—

	£
Ordinary Shares - - - - -	50,575
Preference Shares - - - - -	40,880
Debentures - - - - - -	65,958
Total Capital - - - -	£157,413

Floating liabilities, less floating assets - - £120,132

Net revenue of each of the last three years, from Company's accounts:—

1864–65, 1865–66, 1866–67 - - - - - - Nil.

No dividend declared.

Interest on Debentures, 5*l.* 0*s.* 0*d.* per cent.

The district of country which may be considered to be accommodated by the line embraces an area of 230,434 miles, with a population of 58,232 persons.

THE MAIN LINE.

The line from Kilkenny to Abbeyleix was constructed under an Act of 1860.

A railway from Kilkenny to the Great Southern and Western line was authorized in 1846, but the powers were allowed to expire. In 1860 the line was proposed to join

* In addition to this there are powers for raising 110,000*l.* in shares and 36,600*l.* in loans for the Central Ireland Railways promoted by this and by the Waterford and Kilkenny Company.

the Great Southern and Western line at Mountrath, but this was abandoned for the Maryborough route in 1861. Kilkenny Junction Railway.

Date of Act.	Length sanctioned by Board of Trade with date of sanction.			
	From	To	Distance	Date.
			Miles.	
23 July 1860	Kilkenny	Abbeyleix	19	11 Feb. 1864

EXTENSION NOT OPEN TILL AFTER THE 1ST OF MAY 1867.

(a.) *The Maryborough Extension.*

Abbeyleix to Maryborough. (9½ miles.)

The extension to Maryborough was authorised in 1861. It was not sanctioned for traffic until the 15th of May 1867, and therefore no returns of traffic have been made under the Treasury Minute.

RELATIONS OF THE KILKENNY JUNCTION WITH OTHER RAILWAY COMPANIES.

The lines which are in connexion with the Kilkenny Junction, are stated in the following table:—

Name of Railway Company.	Point of Junction.	Page of Report.
Completed Lines.		
The Waterford and Kilkenny	Kilkenny	139
The Great Southern and Western	Maryborough and Kilkenny	100
Lines authorised but not commenced.		
The Central Ireland	Maryborough	13

The Waterford and Kilkenny Railway.

This Company holds 8,750*l.* stock of the Kilkenny Junction Company, and works the traffic under an agreement for five years from 31st Oct. 1865, at 2*s.* per train mile and terminal charges if three trains run daily, or 2*s.* 4*d.* per mile if less than three trains are run. 28 & 29 Vict. c. 158.

The Great Southern and Western Railway.

The Kilkenny Junction Railway joins the Great Southern and Western line close to the Maryborough station of the Company.

The Kilkenny Junction Company has recently instituted law proceedings to compel the Great Southern and Western Company to afford facilities for through traffic.

The Central Ireland.

This line is a continuation of the Kilkenny Junction line from Maryborough to Mullingar, and is promoted by the Kilkenny Junction and Waterford and Kilkenny Companies.

58. THE WATERFORD AND LIMERICK RAILWAY.

WATERFORD to LIMERICK.

LENGTH OF LINE.

	Single.	Double.	Total.
	Miles.	Miles.	Miles.
MAIN LINE.			
WATERFORD to LIMERICK - - - -	33¾	43½	77¼
Total number of miles owned by the Company -	33¾	43½	77¼
LINES WORKED AND MAINTAINED BY THE COMPANY.			
The LIMERICK AND CASTLECONNELL, with KILLALOE EXTENSION (from Killonan Junction to Killaloe).	13	—	13
The LIMERICK AND ENNIS (from Limerick to Ennis) - - -	24	—	24
The LIMERICK AND FOYNES (from Limerick to Foynes) - -	25½	¼	25¾
The RATHKEALE AND NEWCASTLE (Co. LIMERICK), (from Ballingrane Junction to Newcastle).	10	—	10
Total number of miles worked by the Company - -	105½	44¼	150¼

Length of main line - - - - - 77¼ miles.
Length of line worked and maintained, but not owned by the Company - - - - - 73¼ „
Total mileage worked and maintained by the Company - 150¼ miles.

CAPITAL.

Capital authorized :—

	£
Shares - -	1,000,000
Borrowing Powers - - - -	328,100
Total - - - -	£1,328,100

Financial position on the 30th of June 1867, as ascertained by the Commission :—

Capital raised by the Company :—

	£
Ordinary Shares - - - -	801,513
Preference Shares - - - -	128,150
Debentures - - - -	251,165
Debenture Stock - - - -	16,000
Loan Commissioners - - - -	54,801
Total Capital - - -	£1,251,629

Floating liabilities, less floating assets - - - - £77,686

Net revenue of each of the last three years, as returned by the Company :—

	£
1864-65 - - - -	38,715
1865-66 - - - -	41,705
1866-67 - - - -	41,795
Average of three years -	£40,738

Dividend on Ordinary Shares :—

1864-65 - - -	15s. per cent.
1865-66 - - -	15s. „
1866-67 - - -	15s. „

Dividend on Preference Shares :—
Average of three years ended the 30th of June 1867, 4l. 17s. 9d. per cent.

Interest (average rate on the 30th of June 1867) :—

On Debentures	- - - -	4*l.* 17*s.* 3*d.* per cent.
On Debenture Stock	- -	4*l.* 0*s.* 0*d.* " 4*l.* 5*s.* 0*d.* " 4*l.* 7*s.* 6*d.* " 4*l.* 10*s.* 0*d.* "

Interest paid to Loan Commissioners :—

Rate of Interest	- - - -	3*l.* 10*s.* 0*d.* per cent.

This railway connects the city of Limerick with the city and port of Waterford with Clonmel and a portion of the counties of Waterford and Tipperary, and with the Great Southern and Western line at the Limerick Junction.

The district of country which may be considered to be accommodated by the line embraces an area of 778,397 acres, with a population of 272,898 persons.

THE LINE.

The line was constructed under an Act of 1845, subject to certain deviations authorised in 1847 and in 1851, when an extension of time was also granted. The extension from the old to the new terminus at Waterford was constructed under an Act of 1860.

The following table shows the dates when the works were authorised and the several portions of the line sanctioned for traffic :—

Date of Act	Length sanctioned by Board of Trade, with Date of Opening.			
	From	To	Distance.	Date.
			Miles	
21 July 1845 - -	Limerick - -	Tipperary - -	25	9 May 1848.
" " - -	Tipperary - -	Clonmel - - -	24	30 April 1852.
" " - -	Clonmel - - -	Fiddown - - -	16½	15 April 1853.
" " - -	Fiddown - - -	Dunkitt - - -	9	23 Aug. 1853.
" " - -	Dunkitt - - -	Waterford - -	1½	7 Sept. 1854.
23 July 1860 - -	Old Terminus, Waterford.	Present Terminus -	½	15 Aug. 1864.

RELATIONS OF THE WATERFORD AND LIMERICK WITH OTHER RAILWAY COMPANIES.

The lines in connexion with the Waterford and Limerick are stated in the following table :—

Name of Railway Company.	Point of Junction.	Page of Report.
Lines worked by the Waterford and Limerick.		
The Limerick and Ennis - - -	Limerick - - - - -	145
The Limerick and Foynes - - -	Limerick - - - - -	148
The Limerick and Castleconnell (with Killaloe Extension)	Limerick - - - -	143
The Rathkeale and Newcastle - -	By working the Limerick and Foynes line.	148
Other completed lines.		
The Waterford and Kilkenny - -	Waterford - - - - -	155
The Great Southern and Western - -	Limerick Junction - - -	160
The Cork and Limerick Direct - -	By the use of part of the Limerick and Foynes line.	105
Line commenced but not completed.		
The Southern - - - - -	Clonmel - -	65
Line authorized but not commenced.		
The Clonmel, Lismore, and Dungarvan -	Clonmel -	14

The Limerick and Ennis Railway.

The Waterford and Limerick Company works and maintains this line for 20 years, from the 23rd of April 1861, for 45 per cent. of gross receipts and 250*l.* a year rent for the use of the Limerick station. The agreement was confirmed by an Act of 1862.

The Limerick and Foynes Railway.

The Waterford and Limerick Company works and maintains this line for 3,700l. a year, and has subscribed 17,500l. to the line. A Bill is being promoted in the present session for confirming the purchase of 6,850l. preference shares in this line.

The Limerick and Castleconnell (with Killaloe Extension) Railway.

The Waterford and Limerick Company has subscribed 5,000l. to this line, and works and maintains it under an agreement of the 20th of July 1860, for six years, ending 28th March 1868, for 1s. 11d. per train mile, if three trains run, and 2s. 3d. if two trains run.

The Rathkeale and Newcastle Railway.

The Waterford and Limerick Company works and maintains this line for 2s. 3d. per train mile, subject to modifications, and has subscribed 5,000l. to it.

The Waterford and Kilkenny Railway.

This Company uses part of the old terminus at Waterford, and a portion of the line of the Waterford and Limerick Company, and the terms of user and rights of the Company are referred at present to an arbitrator, appointed by the Board of Trade.

The Great Southern and Western Railway.

The Great Southern and Western Company has a right under the Act of 1845 to use the portion of the Waterford and Limerick line between the Limerick junction and Limerick.

The Cork and Limerick Direct Railway.

This Company uses the Limerick terminus of the Waterford and Limerick Company, at a rent of 432l. 10s. a year.

The Southern Railway.

This line will join the Waterford and Limerick Railway at the Clonmel station, the Company has power to use that station, and to enter into working agreements with the Waterford and Limerick Company, and to have traffic forwarded over that line to the junction with the Clonmel, Lismore, and Dungarvan Company.

The Clonmel, Lismore, and Dungarvan Railway.

The Waterford and Limerick Company has power to make working agreements with the Clonmel, Lismore, and Dungarvan Company.

The Athenry and Ennis Junction Railway.

The Waterford and Limerick Company has subscribed 4,000l. to this line, which is a continuation of the Limerick and Ennis line (worked by the Waterford and Limerick Company).

	Single.	Double.	Total.
	Miles.	Miles.	Miles.
Killonan Junction to Killaloe	18	—	18
Total number of miles owned by the Company	18	—	18
AUTHORIZED EXTENSION.			
(a) The Shannon Extension (from Killaloe to the Shannon)	—	—	⅞
Total mileage authorized	—	—	18⅞

Length of main line - - - - 18 miles.
Length of authorized extension - - ⅞
Total mileage authorized - - 18⅞ miles.

The line is worked and maintained by the Waterford and Limerick Company.

CAPITAL.

Capital authorized:—

	£
Shares	69,500
Borrowing Powers	23,333
Total	£92,833

Financial position on the 30th of June 1867, as ascertained by the Commission:

Capital raised by the Company:—

	£
Ordinary Shares	53,713
Preference Shares	7,780
Debentures	20,333
Total Capital	£81,826

Floating liabilities, less floating assets - - - £8,549

Net Revenue of each of the last three years, as returned by the Company:—

	£
1864–65	369
1865–66	578
1866–67	649
Average for three years	532

Dividend on Ordinary Shares:—

1864–65, 1865–66, 1866–67 - - - Nil.

Limerick and Castleconnell Railway. The line connects Limerick with Killaloe. The Extension will reach the deep water of the Shannon immediately beyond that place.

It also connects the Birdhill branch of the Great Southern and Western line with Limerick.

The district of country which may be considered to be accommodated by the line embraces an area of 159,136 acres, with a population of 74,437 persons.

THE LINE.

16 & 17 Vict. c. [illegible]. 21 & 22 Vict. c. [illegible]. The line from Killonan Junction to Castleconnell was constructed under an Act of 1853, and the extension to Killaloe under an Act of 1858.

The following table shews the dates when the works were authorized, and the several portions of the line sanctioned for traffic:—

Date of Act.	Length sanctioned by Board of Trade, with Date of Sanction.			
	From	To	Distance.	Date.
			Miles.	
20 June 1853	Killonan Junction	Castleconnell	[illegible]	8 Sept. 1858.
2 Aug. 1858	Castleconnell	Birdhill	[illegible]	1 May 1860.
" "	Birdhill	Killaloe	[illegible]	23 March 1862.

(a.) *The Shannon Extension.*

(From Killaloe to the Shannon.)

(¾ miles.)

29 & 30 Vict. c. [illegible]. This extension was authorized in 1866, but is not yet completed.

RELATIONS OF THE LIMERICK AND CASTLECONNELL WITH OTHER RAILWAY COMPANIES.

The lines in connexion with the Limerick and Castleconnell are stated in the following table:—

Name of Railway Company.	Point of Junction.	Page of Report.
The Waterford and Limerick	Killonan Junction	140
The Great Southern and Western	Birdhill Junction	100

The Waterford and Limerick Railway.

This Company has subscribed 5,000*l.* to the Limerick and Castleconnell Railway, and works the traffic by agreement, as stated in page 142.

The Great Southern and Western Railway.

The Birdhill branch of this railway joins the Limerick and Castleconnell line near the Birdhill Station; the Great Southern and Western Company holds 11,096*l.* of the capital of the Killaloe Extension.

RELATIONS OF THE LIMERICK AND CASTLECONNELL WITH OTHER COMPANIES WITH RESPECT TO THE TRAFFIC ON THE SHANNON.

The Limerick and Castleconnell Company is authorized to make arrangements for navigating steam or other vessels on the Shannon, and to make traffic arrangements with the Grand Canal Company, the City of Dublin Steam Packet Company, the Great Southern and Western, the Midland Great Western, the Midland Counties and Shannon Junction, the Parsonstown and Portumna Bridge, and the Great Northern and Western Railway Companies.

60. THE LIMERICK AND ENNIS RAILWAY.

Limerick to Ennis.

LENGTH OF LINE.

—	Single.	Double.	Total.
	Miles.	Miles.	Miles.
Limerick to Ennis	24	—	24

This line is worked and maintained by the Waterford and Limerick Company.

CAPITAL.

Capital authorised :-

	£
Shares	150,000
Borrowing Powers	75,000
Total	£225,000

Financial position on the 30th of June 1867, as ascertained by the Commission :—

Capital raised by the Company :—

	£
Ordinary Shares	84,563*
Preference Shares	12,325
Debentures	30,150
Loan Commissioners	29,809
Total Capital	£169,847

Floating liabilities, less floating assets - £25,699

Net revenue of each of the last three years, as returned by the Company :—

	£
1864-65	4,557
1865-66	6,026
1866-67	5,364
Average for three years	£4,979

Dividend on Ordinary Shares :—

1864-65, 1865-66, 1866-67 - Nil.

Dividend on Preference Shares :—

Average of three years ended the 30th of June 1867 Nil.

Interest on Debentures :—

Average rate on the 30th of June 1867 - 5*l.* 15*s.* 1*d.* per cent.

Interest paid to Loan Commissioners :—

Rate of interest - 3*l.* 10*s.* 0*d.* per cent.

This railway connects the town of Ennis and a large part of the county of Clare with the city of Limerick.

The district of country which may be considered to be accommodated by the line embraces an area of 384,559 acres, with a population of 131,362 persons.

* This excludes 7,415*l.* forfeited shares.

THE LINE.

The line was constructed under an Act of 1846, the time for compulsory purchase was extended by a warrant of the Railway Commissioners, and was renewed in 1853. The time for completing the works was also extended, and the name of the company changed from the Limerick, Ennis, and Killaloe Junction Company to the Limerick and Ennis Company.

The following table shows when the works were authorised, and the several portions of the line sanctioned for traffic:—

Date of Act.	Length sanctioned by Board of Trade, with Date of Sanction.			
	From	To	Distance	Date.
			Miles.	
16 July 1846 -	- The River Shannon -	Clare Castle	22	26 Dec. 1858.
" "	- Clare Castle	- Ennis -	1½	29 June 1859.

RELATIONS OF THE LIMERICK AND ENNIS WITH OTHER RAILWAY COMPANIES.

The lines in connexion with the Limerick and Ennis railway are stated in the following table:—

Name of Railway Company.	Point of Junction.	Page of Report.
The Waterford and Limerick - - -	Limerick - - - -	140
Line commenced but not completed.		
The Athenry and Ennis - - -	Ennis - - - - -	13

The Waterford and Limerick Railway.

The Waterford and Limerick Company works and maintains the Limerick and Ennis railway for 20 years from the 22nd of April 1861, for 45 per cent. of gross receipts and 250*l.* a year rent for the use of the Limerick station. The agreement was confirmed by an Act of 1862.

The Athenry and Ennis Railway.

This line is an extension of the Limerick and Ennis line to the Midland Great Western at Athenry. The Athenry and Ennis Company is authorised to use the Ennis station of the Limerick and Ennis Company.

61. THE LIMERICK AND FOYNES RAILWAY.

LIMERICK to FOYNES.

CAPITAL.

Capital authorised :—

	£
Shares	175,000
Borrowing Powers	43,300
Total	£218,300

Financial position on the 30th of June 1867, as ascertained by the Commission :—

Capital raised by the Company :—

	£
Ordinary Shares	97,037
Preference Shares	28,488
Debentures	17,500
Loan Commissioners	25,773
Total Capital	£168,798

Floating liabilities, less floating assets - - - £29,949

Net revenue of each of the last three years, as returned by the Company :—

	£
1864–65	2,415
1865–66	3,161
1866–67	4,046
Average of three years	£3,207

Dividend on Ordinary Shares :—

1864–65, 1865–66, 1866–67 - - Nil.

Dividend on Preference Shares :—

Average of three years ended the 30th of June 1867 - Nil.

Interest on Debentures :—

Average rate on the 30th of June 1867, 5*l.* 15*s.* 1*d.* per cent.

Interest paid to Loan Commissioners :—

Rate of interest* - - - 3*l.* 10*s.* per cent.

This line connects the city of Limerick with the Shannon at Foynes, where it was expected an Atlantic steam station would be established. The Government has spent a considerable sum of money in the construction of piers, but they are only used for summer traffic on the Shannon.

The district of country which may be considered to be accommodated by the line embraces an area of 96,909 acres, with a population of 73,829 persons.

THE LINE.

The line was constructed under an Act of 1853.

The following table shows the dates when the works were authorized, and the several portions of the line sanctioned for traffic :—

Date of Act.	Length sanctioned by Board of Trade, with Date of Sanction.			
	From	To	Distance.	Date.
			Miles.	
4 August 1853	Limerick	Rathkeale	16½	12 July 1856.
" "	Rathkeale	Askeaton	4	15 May 1857.
" "	Askeaton	Foynes	6½	27 April 1858.

* The Government loan has been converted into a fixed annuity for 22 years.

RELATIONS OF THE LIMERICK AND FOYNES WITH OTHER RAILWAY COMPANIES.

The lines in connexion with the Limerick and Foynes are stated in the following table:—

Name of Railway Company.	Point of Junction.	Page of Report.
The Waterford and Limerick - - -	Limerick - - -	140
The Cork and Limerick Direct - - -	Patrick's Well Junction -	106
The Rathkeale and Newcastle - - -	Ballingarrane Junction - -	148

The Waterford and Limerick Railway.

The Waterford and Limerick Company has subscribed 17,500*l*. to the Limerick and Foynes line, and works the traffic under an agreement of the 9th of October 1863 for 3,700*l*. a year, for three trains a day in summer, and two trains a day in winter.

The Cork and Limerick Direct Railway.

The Cork and Limerick Direct Company uses the part of the Limerick and Foynes line between Patrick's Well Junction and Limerick.

The Rathkeale and Newcastle Railway.

The Limerick and Foynes Company is authorised to subscribe 5,000*l*. to the Rathkeale and Newcastle line, and that power has been exercised to the extent of 2,500*l*.

The Great Southern and Western Railway.

The Great Southern and Western Company is authorised to subscribe 15,000*l*. to the Limerick and Foynes line, but that power has not been exercised.

---

62. THE RATHKEALE AND NEWCASTLE (Co. LIMERICK) JUNCTION RAILWAY.

From BALLINGARRANE JUNCTION to NEWCASTLE (Co. Limerick).

LENGTH OF LINE.

	Single.	Double.	Total.
	Miles.	Miles.	Miles.
BALLINGARRANE JUNCTION with the LIMERICK AND FOYNES LINE to NEWCASTLE (Co. Limerick).	10	—	10

This line is worked and maintained by the Waterford and Limerick Company.

CAPITAL.

Capital authorised :—	£
Shares - - - - -	62,000
Borrowing Powers - - -	31,600
Total - - - -	£93,600

Financial position on the 30th of June 1867, as ascertained by the Commission:—

Capital raised by the Company:—	£
Ordinary Shares - - - -	16,514
Preference Shares - - - -	10,050
Loan Commissioners - - - -	16,600
Total Capital - - -	£43,164
Floating liabilities, less floating assets - - -	£29,889

Net revenue, as returned by the Company:—	£
1866-67 (from 1st January to 30th June 1867) - -	282

The line was only opened on the 1st of January 1867. No dividend has yet been paid.

Interest paid to Loan Commissioners, 5*l.* per cent.

This railway connects the towns of Newcastle (co. Limerick) and Rathkeale with the city of Limerick.

The district of country which may be considered to be accommodated by the line embraces an area of 212,460 acres, with a population of 50,088 persons.

THE LINE.

The line was constructed under an Act of 1861.

Date of Act.	Length sanctioned by Board of Trade, with Date of Approval.			
	From	To	Distance.	Date.
			Miles.	
22 July 1861 -	- Ballingrane Junction	Newcastle - -	10	30 October 1866.

RELATIONS OF THE RATHKEALE AND NEWCASTLE WITH OTHER RAILWAY COMPANIES.

The lines in connexion with the Rathkeale and Newcastle Railway are stated in the following table:—

Name of Railway Company.	Point of Junction.	Page of Report.
The Limerick and Foynes (worked by the Waterford and Limerick).	Ballingrane Junction near Rathkeale	146
Line authorized but not commenced.		
The Limerick and North Kerry - -	Newcastle - - -	43

The Limerick and Foynes Railway.

The Limerick and Foynes Company has subscribed 2,500*l.* to the Rathkeale and Newcastle Railway. The Cork and Limerick Direct Company has not subscribed, though authorized to do so.

The Waterford and Limerick Company has subscribed 5,000*l.* to the Rathkeale and Newcastle railway, and has agreed to work the line for 10 years from opening at two shillings and threepence per train mile for two trains a day, with a reduction if more than two trains are run. If the gross receipts reach 5,200*l.* per annum, the line is to be worked for 45 per cent. of that amount; the Waterford and Limerick Company on securing the mortgages and interest on preference shares, and 4 per cent. on ordinary shares, may claim a perpetual lease of the line.

The Limerick and North Kerry Railway.

This is an extension of the Rathkeale and Newcastle line to Listowel in the county of Kerry.

LENGTH OF LINE.

	Single.	Double.	Total.
	Miles.	Miles.	Miles.
WATERFORD to TRAMORE - - - - - - -	7¼	—	7¼

CAPITAL.

Capital authorized :—

	£
Shares - - - - - - -	58,000
Borrowing Powers - - - -	19,350
Total - - - - -	£77,350

Financial position on the 30th of June 1867, as ascertained by the Commission :—

Capital raised by the Company :—

	£
Ordinary shares - - - - - -	48,000
Preference shares - - - - -	10,000
Debentures - - - - -	19,350
Total capital - - - -	£77,350

Floating liabilities, less floating assets - - - £205

Net revenue of each of the last three years, as returned by the Company :—

	£	s.	d.
1864-65 - - - - - -	1,850	0	0
1865-66 - - - - - -	1,686	0	0
1866-67 - - - - - -	2,328	0	0
Average of three years - -	£1,955	0	0

Dividend on Ordinary Shares :—

	£	s.	d.	
1864-65 - - - - -	0	15	0	per cent.
1865-66 - - - - -	1	0	0	"
1866-67 - - - - -	1	5	0	"

Dividend on Preference Shares :—

Average of three years ended the 30th of June 1867, 5*l.* per cent.

Interest (average rate on the 30th of June 1867) :—

On Debentures - - - - 5*l.* 1*s.* 4*d.* per cent.

The railway connects the city of Waterford with the town of Tramore (a bathing place on the sea coast).

The district of country which may be considered to be accommodated by the line embraces an area of 78,655 acres, with a population of 47,056 persons.

THE LINE.

The line was constructed under an Act of 1851, and certain improvements in the terminus at Waterford under an Act of 1857.

Date of Act.	Length sanctioned by Board of Trade, with Date of Sanction.			
	From	To	Distance.	Date.
			Miles.	
24 July 1851 - -	Waterford - -	Tramore - - -	7¼	10 Sept. 1853.

RELATIONS OF THE WATERFORD AND TRAMORE WITH OTHER RAILWAY COMPANIES.

Name of Railway.	Point of Junction.	Page of Report.
Authorized but not constructed.		
The Waterford and Passage - - -	Ballytruckle Junction, about half a mile from Waterford.	59

The Waterford and Passage Railway.

This Railway will join the Waterford and Tramore line about half a mile from Waterford; and the Waterford and Passage Company has power to lay down an additional line of rails into Waterford and to use the station on terms to be settled by arbitration in case of difference.

---

64. THE WEST CORK RAILWAY.

BANDON to DUNMANWAY, with extension to Skibbereen.

LENGTH OF LINE.

—	Single.	Double.	Total.
MAIN LINE.	Miles.	Miles.	Miles.
BANDON to DUNMANWAY - - - - - - - -	17½	—	17½
Total number of miles owned by the Company - - -	17½	—	17½
AUTHORIZED EXTENSION.			
(a.) The SKIBBEREEN EXTENSION (from Dunmanway to Skibbereen) - -	—	—	16
Total number of miles authorized - - - - -	—	—	33½

Length of main line - - - - - 17½ miles.
Length of authorized extension - - - 16 "
Total mileage authorized - - - 33½ miles.

CAPITAL.

Capital authorized :—

	£
Shares - - - - - -	320,000
Borrowing Powers - - - - -	121,600
Total - - - - -	£441,600

Financial position on the 30th of June 1867, as ascertained by the Commission :—

Capital raised by the Company :—

	£
Ordinary Shares - - - - -	66,817
Preference Shares - - - - -	54,420
Debentures - - - - - -	106,500
Total Capital - - - -	£227,737

Floating liabilities, less floating assets - - - - £99,785

Net revenue, as returned by the Company :—

1866–67 - - - - - - - - £946

Part of line opened 12th June 1866.

Dividend on Ordinary Shares:—

1866–1867 - -	- Nil.
Dividend on Preference Shares -	- Nil

Interest on Debentures:—

Average rate on the 30th of June 1867 - 5l. 0s. 9d. per cent.

This line connects the town of Dunmanway and intermediate places with Cork, and will be extended to Skibbereen.

The district of country which may be considered to be accommodated by the line embraces an area of 347,131 acres, with a population of 98,300 persons.

This line connects the town of Dunmanway and part of the county of Cork with the Cork and Bandon Railway. Communication is thus afforded to Cork. The extension from Dunmanway to Skibbereen is partly commenced.

THE LINE.

Bandon to Dunmanway.

(17½ miles, single line.)

The line to Dunmanway was constructed under an Act of 1860, the time for completing the works having been extended in 1863.

Date of Act.	Length sanctioned by Board of Trade, with Date of Sanction.			
	From	To	Distance.	Date.
			Miles.	
28 August 1860 -	Bandon	Dunmanway	17½	30 June 1866.

EXTENSION COMMENCED BUT NOT COMPLETED.

(a.) *The Skibbereen Extension.*

Dunmanway to Skibbereen.

(16 miles.)

This extension was authorized in 1860, the time for completing the works was extended in 1865, and again in 1867 for two years, ending 12th August 1869.

The provision for the baronies contributing in the Act of 1860 does not begin to operate until the line is completed to Skibbereen. The baronial contribution, when payable, is such a sum as will be equal to the deficiency between half the gross receipts and 4½ per cent. on the mortgages not exceeding 66,000l. and limited to 30 years.

The baronial assessment is imposed by the Grand Jury on the annual value of land and premises, and is payable by the occupier, but the tenant has the right to deduct one-half of the poundage rate of such assessment from each 1l. of his rent. Tithe rentcharges are not liable to any deduction.

CANALS AND RIVER NAVIGATIONS.

Canals and River Navigations	Length in Miles			Page
I.—In the Possession of Companies or Leased to Companies by Private Owners.				
Barrow Navigation	—	42[illegible]		154
Upper Boyne Navigation	—	6		155
Grand Canal	[illegible]			156
(a.) The [illegible] Branch	8			
(b.) The Kildare Branch	7			
(c.) The Blackwood Branch	4			
(d.) The Barrow Line Branch	14			
(e.) The Low Town Lateral Branch	1[illegible]			
(f.) The Milltown Supply Branch	[illegible]			
(g.) The Athy Branch	14			
(h.) The Mountmellick Branch	11[illegible]			
(i.) The Edenderry Branch	1			
(k.) The Kilbeggan Branch	[illegible]			
Total Grand Canal	—	16[illegible]		
Lagan Navigation	—	[illegible]		159
Newry Navigation	—	[illegible]		161
River Suir Navigation	—	16½		162
Royal Canal (Midland Great Western Railway Company)	[illegible]			163
(a.) The Broadstone Harbour Branch				
(b.) The Longford Branch	6			
Total Royal Canal	—	[illegible]		
Foyle Navigation (Strabane to River Foyle)	—	1		
Total Mileage in the Possession of Companies			[illegible]	165
II.—Under Local Trustees.				
Ballinamore and Ballyconnell Navigation	—	37[illegible]		165
Lower Bann Navigation	—	[illegible]		167
Upper Bann Navigation	—	[illegible]		168
Lough Corrib Navigation	—	[illegible]		170
Total Mileage under Local Trustees			[illegible]	
III.—Under Public Works Commissioners.				
Lower Boyne Navigation	—	[illegible]		172
Maigue Navigation	—	6		173
Shannon Navigation	[illegible]			174
(a.) The Boyle Branch	9			
(b.) The Strokestown Branch	6			
Total inland part of Shannon	—	[illegible]		
Tyrone Navigation	—	4½		175
Ulster Canal	—	44		177
Total Mileage under Public Works Commissioners			[illegible]	
Total mileage			7[illegible]	

INLAND NAVIGATIONS IN THE POSSESSION OF COMPANIES, OR LEASED TO COMPANIES BY PRIVATE OWNERS.

65. THE BARROW NAVIGATION (COMPANY).

ATHY to SCAR below St. Mullins.

(42¼ miles.)

23 locks.

Summit level, at Athy, 180 feet above Ordnance datum, which is 8 feet below the mean sea level.

CAPITAL.

Financial position as ascertained by the Commission on the 30th of June 1867 :—

	£	s.	d.
Capital raised by the Company :			
Ordinary Shares - - -	60,000	0	0
Cr. Floating assets, less floating liabilities - -	3,014	13	9

Net revenue of each of the last three years, from Company's accounts :—

	£
1864–65 - - - - -	3,846
1865–66 - - - - -	3,269
1866–67 - - - - -	3,100
Average of three years - - -	£3,405

Dividend on Ordinary Shares :—

1864–65 - - -	4*l.* 0*s.* 0*d.* per cent.
1865–66 - - -	4*l.* 10*s.* 0*d.* per cent.
1866–67 - - -	5*l.* 0*s.* 0*d.* per cent.

This navigation connects the Athy branch of the Grand Canal with the tidal part of the river Barrow below St. Mullins and affords water communication to Carlow, Leighlin Bridge, Bagenalstown, Gore's Bridge, and Graiguenamanagh.

The Company acts as the principal carrier on the navigation. It has tug steamers for towing barges from St. Mullins to Waterford, and landing barges at New Ross and Waterford. It has also a carrying trade to Dublin and to the Shannon by means of the Grand Canal.

THE NAVIGATION.

The works were commenced in 1759 by the Commissioners of Inland Navigation in Ireland, and 20,769*l.** of public money was expended. In 1790 the completion of the works was undertaken by the Barrow Navigation Company under the Act which enabled grants of public money to be made to the extent of one-third of the expenditure, and the Company received a grant of 20,000*l.* (Irish) 4 per cent. Government debentures, which produced only 16,597*l.*,† in consideration of its raising a capital of 40,000*l.* (Irish). The Barrow Navigation Company obtained further grants after the Union, under the Act setting apart 500,000*l.* for the completion of inland navigations in Ireland.

RELATIONS OF THE BARROW NAVIGATION WITH OTHER NAVIGATIONS.

Name of Navigation.	Point of Junction.	Page of Report.
The Grand Canal - - - -	Athy - - - -	156

RAILWAY COMPANIES COMPETING WITH THE BARROW NAVIGATION FOR THE CARRIAGE OF GOODS.

Name of Railway Company.	Page of Report.
The Great Southern and Western - - - - -	100
The Waterford and Kilkenny - - - - -	136
The Kilkenny Junction - - - - -	159

* 22,500*l.* Irish. † 17,897*l.* Irish.

The Kilkenny Branch of the Great Southern and Western Railway runs nearly parallel to the Barrow Navigation from Athy to Bagenalstown. There is consequently competition for the goods traffic of this district between the navigation and the Great Southern and Western Railway. The Barrow Navigation. (Company)

The Great Southern and Western and Kilkenny Junction Railways compete also with the navigations for Dublin and Waterford traffic.

66. THE UPPER BOYNE NAVIGATION (COMPANY).

The Upper Boyne Navigation (Company).

NAVAN to CARRICKDEXTER, near Slane.

(6 miles.)

8 locks.

Summit level, at Navan, 50 feet above the Boyne River at Carrickdexter.

CAPITAL.

No information from the Company.

Cost before 1800 - - - - - £34,968*

This navigation joins the Lower Boyne Navigation near Slane, and thus connects the town of Navan and the port of Drogheda.

THE NAVIGATION.

The works were commenced about 1790, under an Act of the Irish Parliament, by the Boyne Navigation Company, which received before 1800 in public grants 9,964l.† 30 Geo. 3. c. 20. (Irish).

RELATIONS OF THE UPPER BOYNE NAVIGATION WITH OTHER NAVIGATIONS.

Name of Navigation.	Point of Junction.	Page of Report.
The Lower Boyne Navigation - - -	Above Carrickdexter Lock (near Slane).	172

The Lower Boyne Navigation.

The Upper Boyne Navigation is an extension of the Lower Boyne Navigation to Navan, and thus completes the water communication between Navan and Drogheda.

RAILWAY COMPANIES COMPETING WITH THE UPPER BOYNE NAVIGATION.

Name of Railway Company.	Page of Report.
The Dublin and Drogheda - - - - - -	89

The Dublin and Drogheda Railway.

The Upper and Lower Boyne Navigations run parallel to the Oldcastle branch of the Dublin and Drogheda Railway between Navan and Drogheda.

* 37,152l. Irish. † 10,800l. Irish.

67. THE GRAND CANAL (COMPANY).

(163¾ miles.)
64 canal locks.
2 ship locks.

From DUBLIN to BALLINASLOE, with branches to the Liffey, Robertstown, Blackwood Reservoir, Monasterevin, St. James's Well, Athy, Mountmellick, Edenderry, and Kilbeggan.

	Length in Miles.	Number of Locks.		
		Single.	Double.	Total.
MAIN NAVIGATION.				
DUBLIN to BALLINASLOE - - - - -	79½	[illegible]	5	[illegible]
BRANCH NAVIGATIONS.				
(a.) The LIFFEY BRANCH (from first mile of Main Navigation to the Liffey, including Ringsend Docks) - - -	3¼	7 / 2	1 (ship locks)	10
(b.) The KILDARE BRANCH (from Sallins to Robertstown) -	7½	5	—	5
(c.) The BLACKWOOD BRANCH (from Bonynge Bridge (24th mile) to Blackwood Reservoir).	4	—	—	—
(d.) The BARROW LINE BRANCH (from Fenton Bridge (26th mile) to Monasterevin).	14	4	2	6
(e.) The LOW TOWN LATERAL BRANCH (from the 23¼ mile on Main Navigation to the 1½ mile on the Barrow Line Navigation.)	1½	—	—	—
(f.) THE MILLTOWN SUPPLY BRANCH (from the 1½ mile on Barrow Line Branch to St. James's Well, near Newbridge).	6½	—	—	—
(g.) The ATHY BRANCH (from Monasterevin to the Barrow Navigation at Athy).	14½	4	—	4
(h.) The MOUNTMELLICK BRANCH (from Monasterevin to Mountmellick).	11½	3	—	3
(i.) The EDENDERRY BRANCH (from Downshire Bridge (37th mile) to Edenderry).	1	—	—	—
(k.) The KILBEGGAN BRANCH (from Camphile Bridge (51½ mile) to Kilbeggan).	8½	—	—	—
Total - - - - -	163¾	58	8	66

Summit level 279 feet above Ordnance datum, and 164 feet above the Shannon at Shannon Harbour.

CAPITAL.

Capital authorized :—

Shares -	{ Amount of new stock created by the conversion of debentures and old stock into shares, under Stat. 11 & 12 Vic. c. 134. } - -	£665,938	14	6
Borrowing Powers - - - -	{ No power to borrow without leave of Lord Lieutenant.			
Total - - - -		£665,938	14	6

Financial position on the 30th of June 1867, as ascertained by the Commission :—

Capital raised by the Company :—

	£	s.	d.
Ordinary Shares - - - - -	665,938	14	6
Cr. Floating assets, less floating liabilities - -	95,440	7	10

Net revenue of each of the last three years, from Company's accounts :—

	£
1864–65 - - - - - - -	17,588
1865–66 - - - - - - -	15,069
1866–67 - - - - - - -	15,625
Average of three years -	£16,094

The Grand Canal (Company).

Dividend on Ordinary Shares :—

	£
1864–65 - - - - - -	2*l.* 10*s.* 0*d.* per cent.
1865–66 - - - - - -	2*l.* 12*s.* 6*d.* per cent.
1866–67 - - - - - -	2*l.* 12*s.* 6*d.* per cent.

This navigation connects the Shannon navigation and the Barrow navigation and the intervening districts with Dublin.

THE NAVIGATION.

The works were commenced about 1755 by the Commissioners of Inland Navigation in Ireland. The first grant of public money for the Grand Canal was made in 1755; further grants were made before 1772, amounting in all to 70,496*l.** In that year the completion of the canal was entrusted to a company. Between 1772 and 1800 the Company received grants of public money, which, after providing for a debt of 2,308*l.*† on the canal before it was transferred to it realized 63,778*l.*‡ In consideration of these grants in 1793 provision was made that as soon as the Barrow and Shannon were completely navigable the toll on corn, meal, malt, and flour brought to Dublin from 10 miles below Athy or 10 miles below Banagher should be reduced from 3*d.* to 1½*d.* per ton per mile. 16,231*l.*§ was given to secure the completion of the Ringsend Docks, with a restriction as to the maximum rate of dock dues.

The main line of the canal from James Street Harbour, Dublin, to its junction with the Barrow Line Branch and the Milltown and Blackwood supply Branches and the Barrow Line Branch to Monasterevin were opened for traffic in 1787.

The Athy Branch was opened in 1798, and the Company obtained a loan of public money to the extent of 27,692*l.*‖

The extension from Lowtown to the Shannon and the Edenderry Branch were opened in 1800.

The Liffey Branch was opened in 1801.

On the application of the Grand Canal Company for assistance, on the grounds that the grant received in 1799 on account of the reduction of the tolls was inadequate, a grant of 138,461*l.*¶ was made, as recommended by Government, and approved by a Committee of the House of Commons in 1813. Regulations were, however, carefully framed to guard against the payment of dividends out of capital, a practice which had previously prevailed, and to establish the Company on such a solvent basis that its effectual management might be secured. The terms were :—

That the Company should raise 46,154*l.*,** to be applied, along with the 138,461*l.*¶ granted in the payment of their debts in such manner as the Lords of the Irish Treasury should approve.

That no dividend should thereafter be made by the Company, except from the clear profits of their canal, after defraying all its expenses and the interest of their debt.

That they should every half-year make out a full statement of their accounts for the preceding six months, verified on the oath of their general accountant, and distribute faithful copies of them ten days at least before each half-yearly meeting to the members of the Company, and to the Lords of the Irish Treasury.

That their colliery should be sold, and the sum it produced be applied, as soon as it could be disposed of at a fair value, to the liquidation of the principal of their debt.

That till the sale took place the income arising from it should be applied to the same purpose, excepting so much (if any) of it as might be necessary to make their increasing income equal to pay the interest of their debt, and the necessary expenses of their navigation.

That they should thereafter raise no further sum of money by way of loan, except with the approbation of the Lords of the Irish Treasury.

That an account should be kept of the amount of all the debt paid by the revenue or by the sale of the colliery, and one-third part of the interest, which would have been payable on that amount, should constitute a sinking fund at compound interest, and be applicable to the reduction of their remaining debt.

And, further, that at all future times the Company should keep 27,692*l.*‖ in Government Securities, to provide for unforeseen demands upon their navigation.

The Kildare Branch was made by the Kildare Canal Company, which received a grant of public money of 2,215*l.*†† in 1789. The Company was wound up, and the Kildare Canal purchased in Chancery by the Grand Canal Company.

---

* 76,[illegible]*l.*, Irish.
† [illegible]*l.*, Irish.
‡ [illegible]*l.*, Irish.
§ 17,[illegible]*l.*, Irish.
‖ 30,000*l.*, Irish.
¶ 150,000*l.*, Irish.
** 50,000*l.*, Irish.
†† [illegible]*l.*, Irish.

The extension of the canal from the Shannon to Ballinasloe, and the Mountmellick and Kilbeggan Branches were subsequently made for the purpose of giving employment to the poor, and 98,524*l.* was advanced to facilitate their execution. The extensions were opened in 1830. In 1844 the repayment of this sum was commuted by statute for 10,000*l.*

By an Act of 1848 the original company called "the Undertakers of the Grand Canal," was reconstituted under the name of the Grand Canal Company, and the several classes of debenture holders were converted into shareholders along with the original shareholders on the following scale:—

The reduced 6*l.* per cent. debentures receiving 4*l.* per cent., being allotted 90*l.* new stock for every 100*l.* of debentures; the reduced 5*l.* per cent. debentures then receiving 3*l.* 6*s.* 8*d.* per cent.—75*l.* new stock for every 100*l.* of debentures; the reduced 4*l.* per cent. debentures then receiving 2*l.* 13*s.* 4*d.*—60*l.* new stock for every 100*l.* of debentures, and the ordinary shareholders in the old company being allotted 9*l.* of new stock for every 100*l.* of old stock.

RELATIONS OF THE GRAND CANAL COMPANY WITH OTHER NAVIGATIONS.

Name of Navigation.	Point of Junction.	Page of Report.
The Shannon Navigation - - -	Shannon Harbour - -	171
The Barrow Navigation - - -	Athy - -	154

The Shannon navigation connects the Grand Canal with a considerable district, and completes the water communication from Dublin to Limerick. The Barrow navigation completes the communication from Dublin to Waterford.

RAILWAY COMPANIES COMPETING WITH THE GRAND CANAL FOR THE CARRIAGE OF GOODS.

Name of Railway Company.	Page of Report.
Completed Lines.	
The Great Southern and Western - - - -	100
The Midland Great Western - - - - -	118
Lines commenced but not completed.	
The Midland Counties and Shannon Junction - - - -	65
The Parsonstown and Portumna Bridge - - - - -	64

The Great Southern and Western Railway competes directly with the Grand Canal from Dublin to Athy and to Tullamore, and indirectly for traffic brought to the Grand Canal by the Barrow navigation and the Shannon. The competition for the Shannon traffic will be increased on the completion of the Parsonstown and Portumna Bridge and the Midland Counties and Shannon Junction Railways. The Midland Great Western Railway competes with the Grand Canal to Ballinasloe.

The passenger traffic on the Grand Canal ceased on the opening of the railway system, but the Canal Company received a remission of its debt to the Government (as already noticed) to the extent of 88,524*l.*

The Grand Canal Company carries goods on its own navigation, and on the Shannon from Athlone to Limerick.

68. THE LAGAN NAVIGATION (COMPANY).

The Lagan Navigation (Company).

LOUGH NEAGH to the Town of BELFAST.

(26¼ miles.)

25 locks.

Summit level 120 feet above Ordnance datum and 72 feet above Lough Neagh.

CAPITAL.

Capital authorized :—
Amount held in certain Debentures in 1843 to be the Joint stock of the Company, viz. :—

	£	s.	d.
Principal - - - -	57,230	15	7
Interest capitalized - - -	22,919	3	4
Total Shares - -	80,149	18	11
Special Debentures - - -	584	16	11
Power to Loan Commissioners to lend -	12,000	0	0
Total - - -	£92,734	15	10

Financial position on the 31st of March 1867, as ascertained by the Commission :—
Capital raised by the Company :—

	£	s.	d.
Ordinary Stock - - -	80,149	18	11
Debentures - - -	584	16	11
Total Capital - -	£80,734	15	10
Cr. Floating assets, less floating liabilities - -	£3,619	10	9

Net revenue of each of the last three years to the 31st of March 1867, from the Company's accounts :—

	£
1864–65 - - - -	1,192
1865–66 - - - -	1,229
1866–67 - - - -	1,183
Average of three years - -	£1,201

Dividend on Ordinary Stock :—

	£	s.	d.	
1864-65 - - - -	1	10	0	per cent.
1865-66 - - - -	1	10	0	"
1866-67 - - - -	1	15	0	"

Interest on Debentures :—
Average rate on the 31st of March 1867 - 5*l.* 0*s.* 0*d.* per cent.

This navigation connects Lough Neagh with the port of Belfast.

THE NAVIGATION.

The works were commenced by the Commissioners of Inland Navigation in Ireland, the expense being defrayed by a local toll on beer, ale, and spirits imposed by an Act of 1753. 27 G. 2. c. 8 (Irish.)

The Lagan Navigation (Company).

11 & 12 G. 3, c. [illegible]

In 1771 the prosecution of the works was handed over to Local Commissioners, who raised money on the security of these local taxes.

In 1779 the creditors who had advanced money were constituted into a Company for undertaking the Lagan Navigation.

In 1814 the Company was continued for 21 years.

11 & 12 G. [illegible]

54 Geo. 3, c. 191.

In 1835 the powers of the original Company expired; but in 1843 the creditors of the original Company were constituted into the present Lagan Navigation Company. These creditors had advanced their money at a time when the navigation was supported by the local taxes already referred to, which were subsequently abolished by Parliament. The Act of Incorporation recited that all the claims of the creditors should be confined to the navigation, and that the navigation and the right of tolls should be accepted by the creditors, subject to a rent of 300*l*. a year to the Queen, in full discharge of their claims. The Act limited the grant of the navigation to the new Company to 31 years, which will expire in 1874, but it contains an express recital that it was so limited for the purpose of more effectually securing the due improvement and maintenance of the navigation, but without being intended to exclude the creditors from thereafter making an application for a further extension of time, if in the meantime they should well conduct themselves in the management of the navigation.

The Lagan Navigation Company does not act as carriers on the canal.

RELATIONS OF THE LAGAN NAVIGATION WITH OTHER NAVIGATIONS.

Name of Navigation.	Point of Junction.	Page of Report.
The Upper Bann Navigation	Lough Neagh	166

The Upper Bann Navigation.

The entrance of the Lagan Navigation into Lough Neagh is in the County Down, and that is within the part of the Lough entrusted for purposes of navigation to the Upper Bann Navigation Trustees. Through this part of the Lough the Lagan Navigation is connected with the Newry Navigation, the Lower Bann Navigation, the Tyrone Canal, and the Ulster Canal.

RAILWAY COMPANIES COMPETING WITH THE LAGAN NAVIGATION COMPANY FOR THE CARRIAGE OF GOODS.

Name of Railway Company.	Page of Report.
The Ulster	130

The Ulster Railway.

The Lagan Navigation runs parallel to the Ulster Railway from Belfast to Moira and in connexion with Lough Neagh, and the Newry and Ulster Canals competes with that Railway as far as Portadown and Clones.

69. THE NEWRY NAVIGATION (COMPANY).

The Newry Navigation (Company)

LOUGH NEAGH to WARRENPOINT.

(35 miles.)

13 canal locks.

1 ship lock.

Summit level - - - - 76 feet above the Ordnance datum.
Do. - - - - 28 feet above Lough Neagh.

CAPITAL.

Capital authorized :—

	£
Shares - - - - - - -	80,000
Borrowing Powers - - - - -	80,000
Total - - - - -	£ 160,000

Financial position on the 5th of April 1867, as ascertained by the Commission :—

Capital raised by the Company :—

	£	s.	d.
Ordinary Shares - - - -	68,495	7	2
Debentures - - - -	10,600	0	0
Loan Commissioners - - -	35,078	4	7
Total Capital - -	£113,173	11	9

Floating liabilities, less floating assets - - £2,428 8 0

Net revenue of each of the last three years :—

	£
1864–65 - - - - - - -	2,872
1865–66 - - - - - - -	4,038
1866–67 - - - - - - -	2,785
Average of the three years - - -	£3,231

Dividend on Ordinary Shares - - - - - Nil.

Interest on Debentures :—

Average rate on the 5th of April 1867 - 5*l.* 0*s.* 0*d.* per cent.

Interest paid to Loan Commissioners :—

Rate of Interest - - - 3*l.* 10*s.* 0*d.* per cent.

The navigation commences at Warrenpoint and ends in Lough Neagh, and by that means connects itself with the Tyrone Canal, the Ulster Canal, Lough Erne, and the Lower Bann navigation. The portion from Warrenpoint to Newry is a ship canal, and the part in the town of Newry is enlarged so as to form a floating harbour. The navigation was commenced for the purpose of supplying Dublin with native coal, but the abundance and cheapness of English sea-borne coal in Dublin has prevented this object being attained.

THE NAVIGATION.

The works were commenced in 1739 by the Commissioners of Inland Navigation in Ireland, under an Act of the Irish Parliament of 1730, and finished from Newry to the River Bann about 1740 and from Newry to Fathom about 1770 entirely at the public expense. In 1787 the navigation was intrusted to a Local Board of Trustees called "the Corporation for promoting and carrying on the Newry Navigation." In 1800 the Local Board was abolished, and the navigation transferred to the Directors General of Inland Navigations in Ireland, and public money to the extent of 21,532*l.** is returned by the Commissioners of Public Works as having been expended between 1800 and 1829.

3 Geo. 2.

27 Geo. 3.

* 23,326*l.* Irish.

In 1829 the navigation, with the right of levying toll, was transferred to the Newry Navigation Company, but the Act of 1829 contained a clause that if the works were not completed within seven years, or the improvement of the canal was wilfully neglected or abandoned by the Company, the Lord Lieutenant of Ireland should have power to terminate the interest of the Company in the navigation, and that it should revert to the Directors General of Inland Navigations for the benefit of the public.

The time for completing the works was extended in the years 1836, 1841, and 1848; the last limit fixed being the 22nd of July 1852.

RELATIONS OF THE NEWRY NAVIGATION WITH OTHER NAVIGATIONS.

Name of Navigation.	Point of Junction.	Page of Report.
The Upper Bann Navigation - -	The entrance of the Upper Bann into Lough Neagh.	168

The Newry Navigation ends at the entrance of the Upper Bann River into Lough Neagh, and the channel through the bar of the Upper Bann, which was made part of the navigation works in the drainage district of the Lough, is placed by the award by the Commissioners of Public Works under the Drainage Acts in charge of the trustees of the Upper Bann Navigation to be kept dredged by them, the expenses being defrayed out of the tolls and local taxation at their disposal.

RAILWAY COMPANIES COMPETING WITH THE NEWRY NAVIGATION COMPANY FOR THE CARRIAGE OF GOODS.

Name of Railway Company.	Page of Report.
The Newry, Warrenpoint, and Rostrevor - - - - -	128
The Newry and Armagh - - - - - - - -	126
The Dublin and Belfast Junction - - - - -	63

This navigation runs parallel to these lines of railway from Warrenpoint to Newry, and from Newry to Portadown.

---

70. THE RIVER SUIR NAVIGATION (COMPANY).

FROM GRANNY FERRY, near WATERFORD, to CARRICK-ON-SUIR.
(16½ miles.)
No locks.

CAPITAL.

Capital authorized :—

	£
Shares - - - - - - -	10,000
Debentures - - - - -	3,400
Total - - - -	£13,400

Financial position on the 30th of April 1868, as ascertained by the Commission :—

Capital raised by the Company :—

	£
Ordinary Shares - - -	8,960
Total Capital -	£8,960
Floating liabilities, less floating assets -	Nil.

Net revenue of each of the last three years, from Company's accounts :—

	£
1863-64 - - - - - -	40
1864-65 - - - - - -	42
1865-66 - - - - - -	47
Average of three years - -	43

Dividend on Ordinary Shares :—

1864 - - - -	8s. 4d. per cent.
1865-66 - - - -	Nil.
1866 - - - -	12s. 6d. per cent.

The dividends are paid irregularly, and the accounts have been taken for three years ended with the last published account. The dividend in 1864 was declared upon the net earnings of three years at 5s. per share (20l.). The dividend in 1866 was upon the net earnings of two years at 5s. per share.

The object of this navigation is to make a short canal near Carrick-on-Suir, to deepen certain shoals in the River Suir between Carrick and Granny Ferry, so as to make it navigable for ships of a large burden up to Carrick. The tolls are levied only on vessels coming from the sea or outward bound. But the traffic is chiefly carried on in barges from Waterford, which are exempt from toll.

THE NAVIGATION.

The works were authorised in 1836. A short cut, 900 yards long, at Carrick-on-Suir, was executed, and about six acres of land reclaimed, producing a rent of about 24l. a year.

RAILWAY COMPANIES COMPETING WITH THE RIVER SUIR NAVIGATION FOR THE CARRIAGE OF GOODS.

Name of Railway Company.	Page of Report.
The Waterford and Limerick - - - - -	160

This railway runs parallel to the navigable part of the River Suir from Clonmel to Waterford; the competition for traffic is chiefly with barges, which pay no toll to the Navigation Company.

---

71. THE ROYAL CANAL.

Belonging to the Midland Great Western Railway Company.

From DUBLIN to CLOONDARA on the SHANNON, with a branch in DUBLIN to the BROADSTONE HARBOUR, and a branch to LONGFORD.

(96½ miles.)

46 canal locks.

1 ship lock.

Summit level, 324 feet above Ordnance datum.

The Royal Canal — Midland Great Western Railway.

LENGTH OF NAVIGATION.

	Miles.	Number of Locks.
THE MAIN NAVIGATION.		
Dublin to Cloondara - - - -	90½	46
BRANCHES.		
(a.) The Broadstone Harbour Branch (in Dublin) -	[illegible]	—
(b.) The Longford Branch (from Killashee to Longford) -	[illegible]	—
Total - -	[illegible]	46

CAPITAL.

The capital forms part of that of the Midland Great Western Railway.
Net revenue of each of the last three years, from the Company's accounts:—

	£
1864–65 - - - - - -	11,439
1865–66 - - - - - -	10,681
1866–67 - - - - - -	9,794
Average of three years - - -	£10,638

This amount forms part of the revenue of the Midland Great Western Railway.
The canal connects Dublin with Mullingar and Longford, and with the Shannon Navigation at Cloondara.

THE NAVIGATION.

The first Royal Canal Company was incorporated in 1789. It received before the year 1800 grants of public money to the extent of 84,000l.,* and from the Union to 1813, further grants of 87,692l.†

The Royal Canal.

On inquiries before Committees of the House of Commons in 1811 and 1813, it appeared that the Company had expended on making 46 miles of the canal from Dublin to Coolnahay 704,877l.,‡ of this 171,692l.§ had been granted as already mentioned. To provide the balance and to pay the dividends and interest which had been paid out of capital to an extent ascertained to exceed 869,231l.,‖ the Company had borrowed upwards of 738,462l.¶ and raised on share capital 276,923l.** In 1810 the Company had a gross income of only 13,668l.†† and a net income after providing for maintenance and establishment charges of only 3,813l.‡‡ to meet an annual charge for interest of 45,806l.§§ Upon the representation of the Committee of 1813 as to the insolvent state of the Company's affairs the charter was forfeited and the property transferred to the Directors-General of Inland Navigation in Ireland, who expended, between 1813 and 1822, 182,871l.‖‖ of public money in completing the canal from the summit level to the Shannon.

In 1818 the holders of debentures issued by the dissolved Royal Canal Company were constituted the shareholders in the new Royal Canal Company.

In 1845 the Royal Canal was purchased by the Midland Great Western Railway Company for the sum of 298,059l., subject to the obligation of maintaining the navigation, and not varying the tolls without the assent of the Lord Lieutenant of Ireland. The Midland Great Western Railway Company does not act as carriers on the canal, having only a few boats used for repairs to the navigation.

* 91,000l., Irish.
† [illegible], Irish.
‡ [illegible], Irish.
§ [illegible], Irish.
‖ [illegible], Irish.
¶ [illegible], Irish.
** [illegible], Irish.
†† [illegible], Irish.
‡‡ [illegible], Irish.
§§ [illegible], Irish.
‖‖ [illegible], Irish.

The Royal Canal.

Midland Great Western Railway.

RELATIONS OF THE ROYAL CANAL WITH OTHER NAVIGATIONS.

Name of Navigation.	Point of Junction.	Page of Report.
The Shannon Navigation - - -	Termonbarry - - -	174

The Royal Canal falls into the Shannon opposite Termonbarry, and connects the part of the Shannon Navigation to the north of that point with Dublin.

RAILWAY COMPANIES COMPETING WITH THE ROYAL CANAL COMPANY FOR THE CARRIAGE OF GOODS.

Name of Railway Company.	Page of Report.
The Midland Great Western of Ireland - - - - - -	118

This railway competes with the Royal Canal for its entire length. The tolls which the railway company can charge, as owner of the canal, to the carriers who use it, are limited, and cannot be increased without the assent of the Lord Lieutenant.

---

72. THE FOYLE NAVIGATION.

The Foyle Navigation. The Strabane Steam Navigation Company.

STRABANE TO RIVER FOYLE.

(4 miles.)

2 locks.

The navigation is the property of the Marquis of Abercorn, and is leased to the Strabane Steam Navigation Company (Limited), for the unexpired part of a term of 25 years, from the 1st of July 1860. The Company having the option to take a further lease for another period of 25 years.

Financial position of the Company on the 31st of March 1867, as ascertained by the Commission :—

	£	s.	d.
Capital raised by the Company - - -	4,186	0	0
Cr. Floating assets, less floating liabilities -	416	15	11

Net revenue of Company for the last three years from the Company's accounts :—

The Foyle Navigation. The Strabane Steam Navigation Company.

	£	s.	d.
1864–5 - - - - -	206	2	6
1865–6 - - - - -	210	6	5
1866–7 - - - - -	223	3	8
Average of three years - -	£213	4	0

Dividend on Ordinary Shares :—

Of the three years - - - - 5*l.* per cent.

Net revenue of the Marquis of Abercorn from tolls :—

	£	s.	d.
1864–65 - - - - -	458	0	1
1865–66 - - - - -	445	4	11
1866–67 - - - - -	449	2	6
Average of three years - -	£450	15	10
Total average net revenue - -	£663	19	10

THE NAVIGATION.

The works were commenced in the last century, the then Marquis of Abercorn receiving, under an Act of 1791, a grant of public money, amounting to 3,818*l.** for one-third of the expenditure of the canal. 31 G. 3. c. 64. (Irish.)

* Appx. 156.

RAILWAY COMPANY COMPETING WITH THE FOYLE NAVIGATION.

Name of Railway Company.	Page of Report.
The Londonderry and Enniskillen Railway - - -	111

The railway runs parallel to the canal and the navigable part of the River Foyle from Strabane to Londonderry.

INLAND NAVIGATIONS UNDER LOCAL TRUSTEES.

Ballinamore and Ballyconnell Navigation (Trustees).

Under the Statutes for promoting the drainage of land and the improvement of navigations and water power in connexion with drainage in Ireland, works for navigation were carried out in the three drainage districts of Ballinamore and Ballyconnell, of Lough Neagh, and of Loughs Corrib, Mask, and Carra. These works were executed by the Drainage Commissioners in Ireland, the expenses being defrayed in part by grants from general taxes, and in part by advances of public money charged on the local taxation of the districts where the navigations are situated.

73. THE BALLINAMORE AND BALLYCONNELL NAVIGATION (TRUSTEES).

The RIVER SHANNON at LEITRIM to UPPER LOUGH ERNE.

(37¾ miles.)

16 locks.

Summit level - - - 69 feet above Lough Erne.
" - - - 82 " the Shannon at Leitrim.

	£	s.	d.
Cost - - - - - -	228,651	10	5

Which was provided as follows:—	£	s.	d.	£	s.	d.
Grant from imperial taxes - - - - - - -				198,651	10	5
Raised by local taxes:—						
Grand jury cess, co. Cavan - -	10,029	12	0			
Grand jury cess, co. Fermanagh -	2,550	18	0			
Grand jury cess, co. Leitrim -	12,720	6	0			
Grand jury cess, co. Roscommon -	4,699	4	0			
				30,000	0	0
Total - - - - - - -				£228,651	10	5

The amount charged to the local taxes was levied in five years from 1860 in ten equal half-yearly instalments on particular townlands in the counties set forth in the award of the Commissioners of Public Works of the 10th of January 1860.

Income and expenditure:—

Income for three years ended the 14th of October 1867:—

	Three Years. £	s.	d.	Average per year. £	s.	d.
Tolls and rents of canal branches - - - - -	68	5	0	22	15	0
Local taxation on land - - - - - -	133	0	0	44	6	8
Total income - - - -	201	5	0	67	1	8

Ballinamore and Ballyconnell Navigation (Trustees).

Expenditure for three years ended the 14th of October 1867:—

—	Three Years.	Average for one year.
	£ s. d.	£ s. d.
For repairs of works, salaries of lock keeper, engineer, and secretary, law and all other expenses*	306 15 7	102 5 2

This navigation connects the southern system of navigations, Shannon, Barrow, Grand Canal, and Royal Canal, with the northern systems of the Ulster, Tyrone, Upper and Lower Bann, Newry, and Lagan navigations.

THE NAVIGATION.

The works were executed by the Commissioners of Public Works under the Irish Drainage Acts between 1846 and 1859. They were commenced on the 30th of June 1846, and the navigations opened for traffic on the 10th of January 1860.

Relations of the Ballinamore and Ballyconnell with other Navigations.

Name of Navigation.	Point of Junction.	Page of Report.
The Shannon Navigation	Leitrim	174
The Ulster Canal	Lough Erne	177

The Ballinamore and Ballyconnell Navigation falls into the Shannon at the town of Leitrim near Carrick-on-Shannon. It falls into Upper Lough Erne near the entrance of the Ulster Canal into that Lough.

Railways competing with the Ballinamore and Ballyconnell Navigation.

Name of Railway Company.	Page of Report.
The Midland Great Western	118
The Irish North-Western	108

---

74. THE LOWER BANN NAVIGATION (TRUSTEES).

Lower Bann Navigation (Trustees).

From the Bridge at Coleraine in the tidal part of the River Bann to that part of Lough Neagh, which is in the counties of Antrim and Londonderry.

Length of Navigation.

In River Bann	31½ miles
In Lough Neagh (from Lower Bann to entrance of Lagan Navigation)	19 „
Length (including usual route across the lough)	50½ „

5 locks.

Summit level 48 feet above Ordnance datum.

* The last account lodged with the Grand Jury of the County of Cavan gives the particulars of the expenditure for half year ending 30 June 1863, showing the Secretary and Engineer's salary 100l. a year; the salaries of seven lock keepers 24l. a year; law costs, 6l. 7s. 6d.; incidental expenses, 10l. 17s.; and expended on maintenance of navigation, 7l. 4s.

75. THE UPPER BANN NAVIGATION (TRUSTEES).

From Blackwater Town on the River Blackwater, through Maghery Cut to that part of Lough Neagh which is in the counties of Armagh, Down, and Tyrone, including the Channel through the Bar of the Upper Bann.

Length of Navigation.

In River Blackwater - - - - - -	11½ miles
In Lough Neagh (from Maghery Cut to entrance of Lagan Navigation) - - - - - - -	10 „
Length (including usual route across lake) -	21½ „

No locks.

Level.

	£	s.	d.
Cost of Upper and Lower Bann Navigation -	104,374	10	4

Which was provided as follows:—

	£	s.	d.	£	s.	d.
Grant from the imperial taxes - - -				67,237	0	4
Raised by local taxes:—						
Grand jury cess, co. Antrim -	15,032	10	4			
„ co. Armagh -	3,018	3	3			
„ co. Down -	63	17	7			
„ co. Londonderry -	12,894	17	8			
„ co. Tyrone -	6,128	1	2			
				37,137	10	0
Total - -				£104,374	10	4

The amount charged on the local taxes was levied by half-yearly instalments in five years from 1859.

Lower Bann Navigation Trust.

Income in each of three years ended the 30th of June 1867:—

	1864–65.			1865–66.			1866–67.		
	£	s.	d.	£	s.	d.	£	s.	d.
Tolls - - - - - - -	90	16	8	[illegible]	4	5	94	0	11
Local taxation on land - - - -	105	0	0	379	19	11	375	0	0
Amount remitted from Petty Sessions - -	1	13	4	1	16	4	—		
Lower Bann Steamboat Company - - -	2	15	10	7	17	10	7	17	10
Half-year's rent at Portglenone - - -	—			—			5	11	0
Total income - - -	200	5	10	471	15	6	[illegible]	9	9

Average of three years, 484l. 17s.

Expenditure in each of three years ended the 30th of June 1867:—

	1864–65.			1865–66.			1866–67.		
	£	s.	d.	£	s.	d.	£	s.	d.
Maintenance and repairs - - - -	151	10	0	94	12	2	169	17	3
Dredging - - - - -	80	17	0	—			—		
Dragging weeds - - - - -	6	9	0	9	6	6	—		
New cut at Antrim - - - -	—			60	15	6	—		
Salaries and incidentals - - - -	250	0	8	317	9	9	317	5	1
Designs - - - - - -	—			—			40	0	0
Total expenditure - - -	487	16	11	482	5	11	[illegible]	0	7

Average of three years, 497l. 0s. 5d.

Upper and Lower Bann Navigation (Trustees).

Upper Bann Navigation Trust.

Income in each of three years ended 1867 :—

	1865.			1866.			1867.		
	£	s.	d.	£	s.	d.	£	s.	d.
Tolls - - - - - - -	63	13	4	64	9	7	64	4	2
Local taxation on land - - - -	600	0	0	400	0	0	1,300	0	0
Sand sold - - - - - -	4	6	0	5	10	0	14	1	10
Total income - - -	667	19	4	470	19	7	1,378	6	0

Average of three years, 805*l.* 14*s.* 11*d.*

Expenditure in each of three years ended 1867 :—

	1865.			1866.			1867.		
	£	s.	d.	£	s.	d.	£	s.	d.
Dredging - - - - - - -	258	8	4	291	10	1	462	8	8
Maintenance and repairs - - - -	67	4	8	80	13	3	57	1	6
Dragging weeds - - - - -	11	10	8	—			—		
Providing wharfs - - - - -	60	0	0	—			82	15	0
New dredging barge - - - -	—			77	7	8	—		
New steam dredger, 1st instalment - -	—			280	18	5	—		
Do. 2nd do. - -	—			—			350	5	3
Salaries and incidentals - - - -	135	14	1	143	11	5	145	8	6
Total expenditure - - -	533	13	11	872	19	10	1,198	14	10

Average of three years, 834*l.* 10*s.* 6*d.*

The works of both navigations were executed by the Commissioners of Public Works in Ireland, as part of the Lough Neagh drainage undertaking.

They were commenced on the 3rd of May 1847, and the navigations were opened for traffic on the 18th of February 1859.

Relations of the Lower Bann Navigation with other Navigations.

Name of Navigation.	Point of Junction.	Page of Report.
Upper Bann Navigation - - -	Lough Neagh - - - - -	169
The River Bann Navigation - - -	Coleraine - - - - -	*infra*

Lough Neagh is divided between the Lower and Upper Bann Navigation trusts ; the Lower Bann trustees having charge of the part of the lake in the counties of Antrim and Londonderry, and the Upper Bann trustees of that in the counties of Down, Armagh, and Tyrone.

The River Bann Navigation.

In 1683 the Coleraine Town Commissioners obtained an Act to improve the navigation of the tidal part of the River Bann from Coleraine to the sea ; but this and similar navigations are in this report considered in the nature of harbour improvements, and not connected with railway competition. The Coleraine Commissioners have entered into a contract for dredging the ford in the river.

Relations of the Upper Bann Navigation with other Navigations.

Name of Navigation.	Point of Junction.	Page of Report.
The Lagan Navigation - - -	Lough Neagh - - - - -	159
The Newry Navigation - - -	Lough Neagh - - - - -	161
The Lower Bann Navigation - - -	Lough Neagh - - - - -	167
The Tyrone Navigation - - -	Where it falls into the Blackwater - -	175
The Ulster Canal - - - -	Where it falls into the Blackwater at Moy -	177

Upper and Lower Bann Navigation (Trustees).

The Lagan Navigation.

The Lagan navigation falls into Lough Neagh within the limits of the Upper Bann trust, near the town of Lurgan.

The Newry Navigation.

This navigation extends to the entrance of the Upper Bann into Lough Neagh, but as the channel which was cut through the bar of the Upper Bann is in the Lough itself, it is in the charge of the trustees of the Upper Bann, and the duty of dredging it is cast on them by the award of the Commissioners of Public Works of the 18th of February 1859, under the Irish Drainage Acts.

The Tyrone Navigation.

This navigation originally extended to Lough Neagh, but the Blackwater River from Lough Neagh to Blackwater town was placed under the trustees of the Upper Bann.

The Ulster Canal.

This canal falls into the Blackwater below the town of Moy within the Upper Bann Navigation trust.

RAILWAY COMPANIES COMPETING WITH THE UPPER AND LOWER BANN NAVIGATIONS.

Name of Railway Company.	Page of Report.
The Ulster Railway - - - - - - -	130
The Dublin and Belfast Junction Railway - - - -	65
The Belfast and Northern Counties Railway - - - -	74

The Belfast and Northern Counties Railway competes directly with the Lower Bann Navigation, and the other railways compete with the Upper Bann Navigation, in connexion with the navigations of which it forms the connecting link.

76. THE LOUGH CORRIB NAVIGATION (TRUSTEES).

Lough Corrib Navigation (Trustees).

From Galway to Cong, with navigation channels and piers in Lough Corrib, and regulating sluices at Lough Mask and the works commenced but not completed of the Cong canal (3 miles), from Lough Corrib to Lough Mask.

Length of Navigation.

Galway Harbour to deep water in River Corrib	- ¾ of a mile.
End of canal at Galway to Cong - -	- 23 miles.
Length (including usual route across the lough)	- 23¾ "

2 locks.

Summit level, 30 feet above Ordnance datum.

				£	s.	d.
Cost of works - - - - - -				109,289	10	4
Which was provided for as follows:—						
Grant from imperial taxes - - - - -				97,406	10	4
Raised by local taxes:—	£	s.	d.			
Grand jury cess: County of the town of Galway -	2,396	2	6			
County of Galway -	7,743	12	6			
County of Mayo -	4,743	5	0			
				14,883	0	0
Total - - - - -				£109,289	10	4

The annual charges for the local taxes was levied by half-yearly instalments on particular townlands in the counties set forth in the award of the Commissioners of Public Works, June 1858, and continued during five years. Lough Corrib Navigation (Trustees).

Lough Corrib Navigation.

Income in each of three years ended the 30th of June 1867 :—

	1864-65.			1865-66.			1866-67.		
	£	s.	d.	£	s.	d.	£	s.	d.
Tolls or rates on boats - - - -	9	18	0	9	19	0	7	11	7
Wharfage and dock dues - - - -	27	6	8	23	15	7	31	15	0
Rent - - - - - -	5	13	0	8	0	0	2	0	0
Local taxation on counties - - -	240	0	0	240	0	0	240	0	0
Total income - - -	274	14	8	271	15	7	281	9	7

Average of three years, 276*l.* 19*s.* 3*d.*

Expenditure in each of three years ended the 30th of June 1867 :—

	1864-65.			1865-66.			1866-67.		
	£	s.	d.	£	s.	d.	£	s.	d.
Maintenance and repairs - - - -	45	15	0	61	10	8	44	14	5
Salaries and incidentals - - - -	224	11	4	229	18	3	223	19	1
Total expenditure - - -	270	9	1	294	8	11	268	13	4

Average of three years, 277*l.* 15*s.* 2*d.*

The works include the deepening of the channels through the following shoals in Lough Corrib :—

Cornament shoal, Annadown, Lime Island, Oalcarriel, Clydagh, and Lead Isle, and the channel to Long Pier.

A tidal basin and landing piers at Kilbeg, Oughterard, Long Keelkyle, Annaghkeen, Ballynalty, Ballykeen, and regulating sluices at Lough Mask.

The works were executed by the Commissioners of Public Works under the Irish Drainage Acts. They were commenced on the 1st of January 1848, and the navigation opened for traffic on the 30th of June 1859.

A large sum was expended upon the commencement of a canal three miles long, with three locks rising $38\frac{1}{2}$ feet, from Cong on Lough Corrib to Lough Mask, but these works were left by the Commissioners of Public Works in the incomplete state mentioned in their award under the Drainage Acts.

INLAND NAVIGATIONS UNDER COMMISSIONERS OF PUBLIC WORKS IN IRELAND.

Inland navigations were an object of the attention of the Irish Parliament so far back as 1703, and from that time proceedings and grants of public money are recorded in the journals of Parliament. The earliest Act was Stat. 2 Geo. 1. c. 12 by it Members of Parliament and Justices of the Peace of neighbouring counties were empowered to settle satisfactions to owners of land in case of inland navigations, and a company of undertakers was constituted for rendering navigable a part of the River Shannon from Limerick to Carrickdrumrusk, and power was given to constitute similar companies for other rivers. 2 Geo. I. c. 12. Irish.

In 1730 the inland navigations of Ireland were placed under public control. 3 Geo. 2. (Irish)

The Lord Lieutenant, the Lord Chancellor, the four Archbishops of Ireland, the Speaker of the Irish House of Commons, and 60 appointed Commissioners (20 for 25 Geo. 2. (Irish) each province) were constituted the Commissioners of Inland Navigation, and certain taxes placed at their disposal, for the purposes of "encouraging tillage, employing poor, "draining bogs, making canals, and making rivers navigable." The duties were hence called tillage duties. In 1752, the Commissioners were incorporated and their powers extended, and they were afterwards authorised to make over property in navigations to private undertakers with aids not exceeding one-sixth of the capital expended. In 1787, the Commissioners of Inland Navigation were dissolved and the navigations which had been constructed by the Commissioners were entrusted to parties, making certain subscriptions to complete the works.

The entire expenditure of public money on inland navigations in Ireland before 1800, was:—*

	£
Issue to the Commissioners of Inland Navigations from the produce of tillage duties from 1730 to 1790 - - - -	351,946
Grants of Parliament and King's letters from 1750 to 1800, including the local Lagan duties -	505,436
	£857,382

In 1800 five Directors-General of Inland Navigation were appointed and 500,000*l.* granted by Parliament to complete inland navigations in Ireland.

In 1831 the Directors-General were abolished, and the navigations they had charge of came under the control of the Commissioners of Public Works.

77. THE LOWER BOYNE NAVIGATION (BOARD OF WORKS).

From Carrickdexter, near Slane, to Drogheda.

(12¾ miles.)

7 locks.

Summit level, 69 feet above Ordnance datum.

	£
Cost (so far as ascertained) - - -	69,231†
Which was provided as follows:—	
Grants from general and special taxes - -	69,231

Income in each of three years ended the 31st of March 1867:—

	1864–65.			1865–66.			1866–67.		
	£	s.	d.	£	s.	d.	£	s.	d.
Rents and tolls - - - -	366	4	7	335	17	3	304	9	8
Total income - - -	366	4	7	335	17	3	304	9	8

Average of three years, 335*l.* 10*s.* 10*d.*

Expenditure in each of three years ended the 31st of March 1867:—

	1864–65.			1865–66.			1866–67.		
	£	s.	d.	£	s.	d.	£	s.	d.
Total expenditure - - - -	335	13	10	[illegible]	11	7	[illegible]	1	0

Average of three years, 262*l.* 8*s.* 9*d.*

This navigation connects the Upper Boyne navigation with Drogheda.

THE NAVIGATION.

The works were commenced in 1759 by the Inland Navigation Commissioners of Ireland, who expended on them †69,231*l.* from general or special taxation. In 1789 they were entrusted to the Boyne Navigation Company, who made the continuation to Navan.

* Report from Committee on Inland Navigation, Journals of Irish House of Commons, 22d June 1800, Vol. XIX., Pt. II., p. ccc.

† 18,000*l.* local.

In 1800 all navigations made entirely by public money were transferred by Act of Parliament to the Directors-General of Inland Navigation, who took possession of the works of the Lower Boyne.

Lower Boyne Navigation (Board of Works).

In 1831 the navigation came under the Commissioners of Public Works, on the abolition of the Directors-General of Inland Navigations.

RELATIONS OF THE LOWER BOYNE NAVIGATION WITH OTHER NAVIGATIONS.

Name of Navigation.	Point of Junction.	Page of Report.
The Upper Boyne Navigation - - -	Above Carrickdexter lock - -	155
Portion of the River Boyne under the Drogheda Harbour Commissioners.	Drogheda - - - -	*Infra.*

The navigable portion of the River Boyne, from Navan to the sea, though only 24 miles in length, is under the control of three bodies; the Upper Boyne Navigation Company, for six miles, from Navan to above Carrickdexter lock; the Public Works Commissioners, from Carrickdexter to the bridge of Drogheda, 12¾ miles, and the Drogheda Harbour Commissioners, from the bridge of Drogheda to the mouth of the Boyne, 5¼ miles.

RAILWAY COMPANIES COMPETING WITH THE LOWER BOYNE NAVIGATION FOR THE CARRIAGE OF GOODS.

Name of Railway Company.	Page of Report.
The Dublin and Drogheda Railway - - - - -	59

The Oldcastle branch of the Dublin and Drogheda Company is parallel to the Upper and Lower Boyne navigation.

---

78. THE MAIGUE NAVIGATION (BOARD OF WORKS).

Maigue Navigation (Board of Works).

From ADARE to the RIVER SHANNON.

(6 miles.)

No locks; level.

	£
Cost of construction since 1800 - - -	3,319*
Which was provided as follows:—	
Grants through the Navigation Board or from Parliament - - - - -	3,319

This navigation was originally executed by promoters, then called undertakers, constituted in 1715, under the first Act for promoting Inland Navigation in Ireland. In 1751 it was vested in the Commissioners for Inland Navigation in Ireland; in 1800 in the Directors-General of Inland Navigation; and in 1831 in the Commissioners of Public Works.

2 Geo. I. c. 12 (Irish.)

Income in each of three years ended the 31st of March 1867:—

	1864–65.			1865–66.			1866–67.		
	£	s.	d.	£	s.	d.	£	s.	d.
Rents and tolls - - - -	12	8	8	13	1	6	11	5	10
Total income - - -	12	8	8	13	1	6	11	5	10

Average of three years, 12l. 3s. 2d.

*1800 to 1851, [illegible] Irish.
1851 to 1867, [illegible]

Expenditure in each of three years ended the 31st of March 1867:—

	1864–65.	1865–66.	1866–67.
	£ s. d.	£ s. d.	£ s. d.
Total expenditure - - - -	70 3 10	34 7 0	34 1 0

Average of three years, 46*l*. 3*s*. 7*d*.

This navigation connects the town of Adare with the tidal part of the River Shannon.

THE NAVIGATION.

The works were commenced in 1715.

---

79. THE INLAND PART OF THE SHANNON NAVIGATION (BOARD OF WORKS).

LIMERICK to LOUGH ALLEN, with branches to BOYLE and STROKESTOWN.

LENGTH OF NAVIGATION.

	Miles.	Locks.
MAIN NAVIGATION.		
LIMERICK to NORTHERN END of LOUGH ALLEN - - -	143	16
BRANCH NAVIGATIONS.		
(*a*.) THE BOYLE BRANCH (from the Shannon, near Carrick-on-Shannon, to near Boyle) -	9	None.
(*b*.) THE STROKESTOWN BRANCH (from the Shannon, to near Strokestown) - -	5	None.
Total - - -	1[illegible]	16

Summit level 161 feet above Ordnance datum.

Cost since 1800 - - £683,31[illegible]

Which was provided as follows:—

	£
Grants from general taxes - - - -	410,523
Local Taxation - - - - -	272,789

SHANNON NAVIGATION.

Income in each of three years ended the 31st of March 1867:—

	1864–65.	1865–66.	1866–67.
	£ s. d.	£ s. d.	£ s. d.
Rents and tolls - - - -	2,841 18 10	[illegible] 18 9	[illegible] 14 10
Total income - - -	2,841 18 10	[illegible] 18 9	[illegible] 14 10

Average of three years, 2,491*l*. 8*s*. 1*d*.

Expenditure in each of three years ended the 31st of March 1867:—

	1864–65.	1865–66.	1866–67.
	£ s. d.	£ s. d.	£ s. d.
Total expenditure - - - -	2,733 11 0	3,217 15 1	[illegible] 11 6

Average of three years, 2,843*l*. 13*s*. 7*d*.

THE NAVIGATION.

The earliest Act of the Irish Parliament for inland navigation was as already noticed for making the Shannon Navigation from Limerick to Carrickdrumrusk.

In 1755 the works were undertaken by the Commissioners of Inland Navigation in Ireland, who expended a large sum from the taxes at their disposal upon them.

By an Act of the Irish Parliament of 1767 a company was established for completing a small portion of the navigation from Limerick to Killaloe, 12 miles. The company received a grant from public taxation to the extent of 15,323*l.** In 1806 the completion of the works was undertaken by the Directors-General of Inland Navigation in Ireland. About 1812, the company's rights were purchased.

In 1837 the Shannon Commission was constituted by statute, and works for improving the Shannon Navigation, and for drainage in connexion therewith, were carried out, the entire expenditure since 1800, being 683,312*l.*

RELATIONS OF THE SHANNON NAVIGATION WITH OTHER NAVIGATIONS.

Name of Navigation.	Point of Junction.	Page of Report.
The Grand Canal - - - -	Shannon Harbour - - -	158
The Royal Canal - - - -	Termonbarry - - -	163
The Ballinamore and Ballyconnell Navigation.	Leitrim - - -	168

The Grand Canal.

The Grand Canal crosses the Shannon at Shannon Harbour, and connects it with Dublin on the east, and with Ballinasloe on the west.

The Royal Canal.

This canal connects the upper part of the Shannon with Dublin.

The Ballinamore and Ballyconnell Navigation.

This navigation connects the Shannon with Lough Erne and the Ulster Canal.

RAILWAY COMPANIES COMPETING WITH THE SHANNON NAVIGATION FOR THE CARRIAGE OF GOODS.

Name of Railway Company.	Page of Report.
Completed Lines.	
The Great Southern and Western - - - - - - -	100
The Waterford and Limerick - - - - - - -	140
The Limerick and Castleconnell (with Killaloe Extension) - - - -	148
The Midland Great Western of Ireland - - - - - - -	119
Lines sanctioned but not completed.	
The Shannon Extension of the Limerick and Castleconnell - - - -	148
The Parsonstown and Portumna Bridge - - - - - -	63
The Midland Counties and Shannon Junction - - - - - -	69

The Limerick and Castleconnell Railway (with the Killaloe Extension and the Shannon Extension in course of construction) is directly parallel to the Shannon. The other completed lines, by establishing routes to Dublin, Killaloe, Athlone, and Carrick-on-Shannon, compete with the water communication.

* 16,000*l.*, Irish.

80. THE TYRONE NAVIGATION (BOARD OF WORKS).

From Coal Island to the River Blackwater.

(4½ miles.)

7 locks.

Summit level, 53 feet above Lough Neagh.

	£
Cost since 1800 - - - - -	31,417
Which was provided as follows :—	
Grants from general taxes - - - -	31,417

Income in each of three years ended the 31st of March 1867 :—

	1864-65.			1865-66.			1866-67.		
	£	s.	d.	£	s.	d.	£	s.	d.
Rents and tolls - - - -	321	1	4	338	16	2	304	16	8
Total income - - -	321	1	4	338	16	2	304	16	8

Average of three years, 321l. 11s. 8d.

Expenditure in each of three years ended the 31st of March 1867 :—

	1864-65.			1865-66.			1866-67.		
	£	s.	d.	£	s.	d.	£	s.	d.
Total expenditure - - - -	287	2	6	257	8	4	321	3	9

Average of three years, 288l. 11s. 11d.

This canal was projected in conjunction with the Newry Navigation with a view to supply Dublin with Irish coal. The Maghery cut from the River Blackwater to Lough Neagh and the intervening portion of the Blackwater River, was part of the undertaking, but they now form part of the Upper Bann Navigation.

THE NAVIGATION.

The works were commenced in 1739 by the Commissioners of Inland Navigations in Ireland, and continued in their charge until 1787, when the works were transferred to parties undertaking to complete and extend the canal. In 1800 the navigation came into the hands of the Directors-General of Inland Navigation in Ireland, and between 1800 and 1831 a sum of 26,240l. was expended upon the works.

In 1831, on the abolition of the Directors-General of Inland Navigation, the Tyrone Navigation was transferred to the Commissioners of Public Works, in whose charge it has since continued, and a sum of 5,177l. has been expended by them.

Connexion of the Tyrone Navigation with other Navigations.

Name of Navigation.	Place of Junction.	Page of Report.
The Upper Bann Navigation - -	At Moy on the River Blackwater -	

The Upper Bann Navigation connects the Tyrone Navigation with the Ulster Canal on the south and the Lough Neagh on the north.

Ulster Canal (Board of Works).

91. THE ULSTER CANAL (BOARD OF WORKS).

LOUGH ERNE to CHARLEMONT and MOY on the BLACKWATER.

(44 miles.)

26 locks.

Summit level above Lough Erne -	- 54 feet.
" Lough Neagh	- 157 feet.

	£
Cost - - - - -	- 294,272
Which was provided as follows:—	
Grant from general taxes - -	- 4,272
Share capital of the Canal Company	- 160,000
Public loans to the Canal Company	- 130,000
Total - -	- £294,272

ULSTER CANAL.

Income from February 1865 to the 31st of March 1867:—

	1865–1867.
	£ s. d.
Total income (the Navigation practically closed during repairs) - -	41 10 10

Expenditure from February 1865 to the 31st of March 1867:—

	1865–1867.
	£ s. d.
Maintenance and renewal of works - - - - - -	4,600 0 0
Total expenditure - - - - - -	4,600 0 0

The Ulster Canal connects the counties of Fermanagh and Monaghan and Lough Erne with the navigations which extend from Lough Neagh to Newry and Belfast.

THE NAVIGATION.

The works were commenced by the Ulster Canal Company under an Act of 1825. Loans to the extent of 130,000*l.* were made by the Commissioners of Public Works in Ireland. In 1865 the canal was transferred to the Commissioners, in discharge of the debt, more money was expended on the canal, and it is estimated that a further sum of 4,200*l.* will be required to secure an adequate supply of water. 6 G. 4. c. 193.

RELATIONS OF THE ULSTER CANAL WITH OTHER NAVIGATIONS.

The navigations in connexion with the Ulster Canal are stated in the following table:—

Name of Navigation.	Point of Junction.	Page of Report.
The Upper Boyne Navigation - -	Where it falls into the Blackwater at Moy.	143
The Ballinamore and Ballyconnell Navigation	Lough Erne - - -	168

The Ulster Canal falls into the navigable part of the River Blackwater, which is included in the Upper Bann Navigation Trust, and thus is connected with Lough Neagh and the navigations which centre in it. It leaves Lough Erne near the entrance of the Ballinamore and Ballyconnell Navigation.

RAILWAY COMPANIES COMPETING WITH THE ULSTER CANAL FOR THE CARRIAGE OF GOODS.

Name of Railway Company.	Page of Report.
The Ulster	180
The Irish North Western	109

The Irish North Western Railway connects the sea-port of Dundalk with large parts of the counties of Fermanagh and Monaghan, from which goods were formerly carried by the Ulster Canal to Newry and Belfast. The Ulster Railway connects the same district with Belfast. The traffic of the Ulster Canal was seriously affected by the competition of railways before it came into the hands of the Commissioners of Public Works.

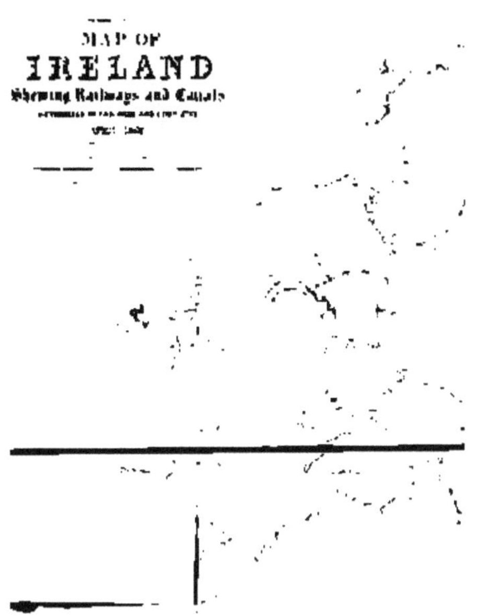
MAP OF
IRELAND
Shewing Railways and Canals

www.ingramcontent.com/pod-product-compliance
Lightning Source LLC
Chambersburg PA
CBHW021804190326
41518CB00007B/449

* 9 7 8 3 7 4 2 8 2 2 4 6 8 *